Outdoor Projects

STANLEY

Outdoor Projects

David Schiff

The Taunton Press

To Ethan Pope, a very young fellow who obviously has inherited a curiosity about how things go together

Text © 2018 The Taunton Press, Inc.
Photographs © 2018 The Taunton Press, Inc. (except where noted)
Illustrations © 2018 The Taunton Press, Inc.

The Taunton Press
Inspiration for hands-on living®

The Taunton Press, Inc., 63 South Main Street, PO Box 5506, Newtown, CT 06470-5506
Email: tp@taunton.com

Editor: Peter Chapman
Copy Editor: Diane Sinitsky
Indexer: Cathy Goddard
Cover and Interior Design: Stacy Wakefield Forte
Layout: Stacy Wakefield Forte
Photographer: David Schiff (except where noted)
Illustrator: Christopher Mills

The following names/manufacturers appearing in *Outdoor Projects* are trademarks:
EasyGate®; Eco Wood Treatment®; Homax®; Little Giant®; Quick Square®;
TallEarth.com®

Library of Congress Cataloging-in-Publication Data

Names: Schiff, David, 1955- author.
Title: Stanley outdoor projects : a homeowner's guide / David Schiff.
Other titles: Outdoor projects
Description: Newtown, CT : Taunton Press, Inc., [2018] | Includes
    bibliographical references and index.
Identifiers: LCCN 2017037054 | ISBN 9781631866746
Subjects: LCSH: Garden structures--Handbooks, manuals, etc.
Classification: LCC TH4961 .S72 2018 | DDC 643/.5--dc23
LC record available at https://lccn.loc.gov/2017037054

Printed in the United States of America
10 9 8 7 6 5 4 3 2 1

About Your Safety: Construction is inherently dangerous. Using hand or power tools improperly or ignoring safety practices can lead to permanent injury or even death. For safety, use caution, care, and good judgment when following the procedures described in this book. The publisher and Stanley cannot assume responsibility for any damage to property or injury to persons as a result of misuse of the information provided. Always follow manufacturers' instructions included with products. Don't try to perform operations you learn about here (or elsewhere) unless you're certain they are safe for you. The projects in this book vary as to level of skill required, so some may not be appropriate for all do-it-yourselfers. If something about an operation doesn't feel right, don't do it, and instead, seek professional help. Remember to consult your local building department for information on building codes, permits, and other laws that may apply to your project.

Acknowledgments

Editors, carpenters, book designers, models, illustrators, photo editors—the cast of characters it takes to create a how to book like the one in your hands is vast and varied. The opportunity to work with top-notch creative experts in so many fields is a big part of the fun and an even bigger part of the challenge of this work.

All of these people come in and out of the process at various points except for one: Taunton Executive Editor Peter Chapman was my partner throughout. From brainstorming the book's focus and projects to painstakingly reading the final draft, Peter was there to help me make this book as accurate and useful as I could possibly make it. And we had a few laughs along the way.

Another important collaborator was ace carpenter Steve Bowie, who helped me build the critter-proof fence and the garden shed projects. Steve would listen carefully as I described what I planned to do. Sometimes he would just say, "Makes sense." Other times he would say, "What if we…" and I knew the book was about to get a little better.

Then there is Dave Toht, a longtime friend, colleague, and fellow author who happened to be building a really cool chicken coop in his own backyard. Thanks, Dave, for writing and taking many of the photos for that project. Thanks also to Rebecca Toht for taking the rest of the chicken coop photos.

I'd also like to thank my ever-patient models, especially Quinn Kimball, whose flexible schedule made my life a whole lot easier.

CONTENTS

OUTDOOR PROJECTS in general are perfect for the do-it-yourselfer. Whether creating outdoor furniture in your shop or constructing a garden fence or shed, you won't be disrupting life inside your house, so who cares if a project stretches over a few weekends?

The outdoor projects in this book in particular are designed and presented specifically for those of us who spend 9 to 5 doing something other than carpentry or woodworking. If you can read a tape measure, drive a screw and a nail, and cut a straight line, you can handle any project in this book. Even if you are new to working with wood, in these pages you'll find handsome and useful projects that are perfect for getting your feet wet. Take a look at the trellis, raised bed, and garbage and recycling corral—even the barbecue cart is stone simple to build.

Some of these projects are sophisticated in their design. For example, the picnic table and benches eschew the typical lap joints and exposed bolts for sleeker hidden joinery. Calculating the part lengths and cutting angles to make the table and benches come together took some head scratching. But now with that work done for you, actually cutting the angles is a snap. The hid-

STANLEY

den joinery is easy, too, thanks to a simple-to-use biscuit joiner.

Thumbing through this book, you'll notice that some projects, most notably the garden shed, have many steps. That's because we want to offer complete guidance. You'll find that each step is easy to accomplish.

The steps are broken down into short stages. Each stage begins with a short overview that explains the logic of the steps to come.

Before you build a project, start by reading through the overviews and the step-by-step instructions. Study the drawings— they'll make it clear how the parts fit together, and each part is

labeled so you'll know exactly what "outside rail" refers to in the text.

And while you don't need pro skills to accomplish these projects, you do need time and patience. So take your time and work safely. The process will be fun and the results will both beautify and enhance the usefulness of your outdoor living space.

CHAPTER ONE

Tools &
Materials

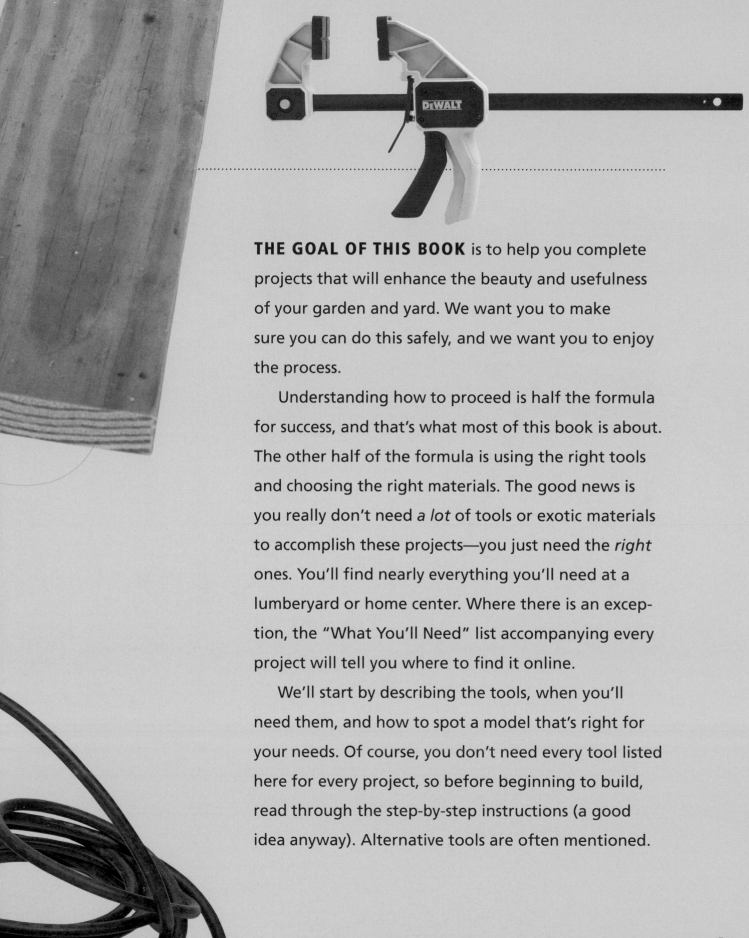

THE GOAL OF THIS BOOK is to help you complete projects that will enhance the beauty and usefulness of your garden and yard. We want you to make sure you can do this safely, and we want you to enjoy the process.

Understanding how to proceed is half the formula for success, and that's what most of this book is about. The other half of the formula is using the right tools and choosing the right materials. The good news is you really don't need *a lot* of tools or exotic materials to accomplish these projects—you just need the *right* ones. You'll find nearly everything you'll need at a lumberyard or home center. Where there is an exception, the "What You'll Need" list accompanying every project will tell you where to find it online.

We'll start by describing the tools, when you'll need them, and how to spot a model that's right for your needs. Of course, you don't need every tool listed here for every project, so before beginning to build, read through the step-by-step instructions (a good idea anyway). Alternative tools are often mentioned.

A PORTABLE CONTRACTOR'S SAW with a sliding extension table and a sturdy stand is a good compromise that will allow you to make accurate cuts up to 24 in. wide, while being able to move the tool out of the way when not in use.

Buy tools as you need them so you don't wind up with tools you never use. When you do decide to purchase a new tool, it's generally a good idea to buy the best tool you can afford. However, the best tool for your needs is not always the most expensive version. Some professional power tools are built to stand up to daily job site or shop use. There's no need to pay for super durability when a lighter-duty tool will provide a lifetime of occasional use.

Then we'll talk about how to choose materials that will withstand outdoor use. You'll learn about fasteners and adhesives. There's a lot of confusion and misinformation out there about wood and finishes. The section on "Wood and Finishes for Outdoor Projects" (p. 17) clearly and concisely provides the straight skinny you'll need to make these crucial choices.

Power Tools

Today's power tools have evolved to be lighter and easier to use than ever before thanks to rechargeable batteries that are thinner and more powerful, drills with keyless chucks, sabersaws with blades that pop in and out without a tool, and powerful, accurate tablesaws with tough, lightweight plastic bases and aluminum tables.

And then there are the tools our dads never had at all—most notably the biscuit joiner and the pocket-hole jig, two innovations that eliminate the skill once required to craft strong and attractive joinery. Following is a description of power tools used in the projects in this book. Of course, you won't need every tool here for every project, and, in fact, the projects often give alternative methods in case you don't own the preferred tool for the job.

Tablesaw

Many of the projects in this book—including the garden shed (p. 52), the garden trellis (p. 46), the raised bed (p. 92), the cold frame (p. 116), and the chicken coop (p. 126)—don't call for a tablesaw at all. And you can accomplish most of the other projects by using an inexpensive rip guide on your circular saw (see "Rip Guide," p. 64).

Still, when it comes to ripping stock accurately, safely, and conveniently, you can't beat a tablesaw. And ripping is only the most common trick in the tablesaw's bag. You can use it to make accurate crosscuts, too, and you can create rabbets, dadoes, and other joints.

Tablesaws fit into three roughly defined types: tabletop, contractor, and cabinetmaker. Tabletop models often have 8-in. blades and are handy because you can stow them away and easily lift them onto a bench when you need them. You can surely accomplish all the tablesaw tasks in this book with a tabletop model.

However, the small tables on tabletop saws aren't much good for cutting plywood and other sheet goods and they make long rips trickier. And while no hardwood is used in the projects in this book, be aware that cutting hardwood will be a strain for the small motors in most tabletop models.

Contractor saws, as the name implies, are designed for building contractors who need a rugged and accurate tool they can take on the job site. These saws usually have a 10-in. blade. They have become much lighter than older models, and their motors have all the power you'll ever need. Most have foldable stands, some with wheels. Many have sliding extension tables that let you make accurate cuts up to 24 in. wide. All of these qualities make contractor saws an excellent choice for the small shop—professional or home.

A cabinetmaker's saw is an extremely accurate tool with a 10-in. blade that will handle large pieces with ease. But it is extremely heavy and expensive. Don't expect to move one out of the way when you want to park the car in the garage.

Power miter saw

When two pieces of wood need to fit together precisely —for example, fitting the aprons to the legs of the herb planter (p. 150)—it's difficult to achieve the accuracy you

A POWER MITER SAW makes quick, accurate crosscuts. This model has a 12-in. blade that tilts and slides on two rails. As a result, it can make compound miter cuts on stock up to 12 in. wide.

need with a circular saw. You can achieve that accuracy with a hand miter saw such as the one shown on p. 14, but, of course, each cut will take longer. The speed with which a power miter saw can make accurate cuts has earned it the nickname "chopsaw."

This speed makes the chopsaw a great choice when you have multiple pieces to cut to the same length because you can use it with a stop block (see "Making and Using a Stop Block," p. 171). For some saws, like the one shown above, you can purchase a stand that includes slide-out supports on both sides with stops that flip up. With such a stand, you'll find yourself using the power miter saw to make multiple cuts even if they need not be perfectly accurate—for example, cutting studs to length for the garden shed.

Some models take 8-in. blades, others take 10-in. blades, and some take 12-in. blades. The bigger the blade diameter, the thicker and wider the stock you can cut. In some models, the blade pivots straight down only; in others, the blade slides on rails to extend the cutting-width capacity, so a sliding 8-in. blade may cut wider stock than a pivoting 12-in. blade. As a result, cutting-width capacities vary from less than 5 in. to more than 12 in.

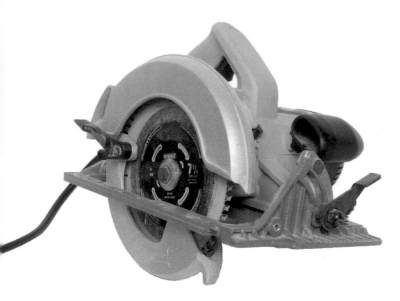

A GOOD-QUALITY CIRCULAR SAW with adjusting mechanisms that operate smoothly is one of the best investments you can make for your shop.

TIP Is there a power tool you'd really like to get your hands on for a project in this book—perhaps a power miter saw to cut the parts for the herb planter? If you can't justify buying the tool, check out your local rental center. Some home centers rent tools, as well.

Some models can cut compound miters—meaning they can cut at an angle across the face of the board while cutting a bevel on the edge—a feature you won't need for the projects in this book.

Circular saw

When it comes to bang for your tool buck, there's no better investment than a circular saw. You'll use it mostly to crosscut lumber for carpentry projects like the garden shed, but as mentioned, you can increase the tool's versatility by purchasing an inexpensive rip guide.

You don't need a heavy worm-drive saw like professional house framers use, but look for a saw with well-machined parts that operate smoothly. Try out the levers that set the height and angle to make sure they operate easily so you can make accurate settings. Avoid buying a circular saw—or any tool for that matter—that is made of stamped steel with rough edges.

Sabersaw

Some projects require you to make notches or curved cuts. You can cut notches with a handsaw and curves with a coping saw, but a sabersaw—also called a jigsaw—is the

The Right Circular-Saw Blade for the Job

There are several kinds of specialized blades you can buy for your circular saw, including blades designed just for ripping or just for crosscutting, and even abrasive blades with no teeth for cutting masonry, tile, or steel. But you can do every project in this book with just one or two blades. At far left is a fine-finish blade that will help you avoid splinters when cutting plywood and will provide a smoother cut for exposed surfaces such as the angled sides of the cold frame. There's no reason you can't use a fine-finish blade to crosscut lumber—it'll just take a little longer than if you invest in a framing blade, shown at near left. A framing blade has fewer teeth and is designed to make rougher, quicker cuts.

A SABERSAW IS USED to cut curves and notches. Use a thin blade like the one shown above for cutting curves.

TODAY'S GOOD-QUALITY CORDLESS DRILLS are powerful and come with two batteries so you can use one while the other charges. They also have keyless chucks for quick bit changes.

TIP Want justification for upgrading to a lighter, more powerful cordless drill/driver? You won't be retiring your old drill: When predrilling for screws, it's really handy to have one drill equipped with a drill bit and the other with a screwdriver bit.

A MAGNETIC DRIVE GUIDE is an inexpensive accessory for your drill/driver that will make driving screws easier and will speed bit changes.

best tool for these jobs. Use a thin fine-cutting blade for curves, and a wider blade for straight cuts such as notches.

Drill/driver

Today's cordless drill/drivers are powerful enough to handle any drilling task in this book. They come with two batteries, so you are unlikely to run out of juice. Battery technology has improved greatly over the last 10 years, so now you can purchase a lightweight compact drill driver with a 20-volt battery that's much thinner than the old 18-volt models.

Magnetic drive guide

There are several reasons you'll want to pick up this inexpensive accessory for your drill/driver. The guide accepts those short ¼-in. hex-shank bits used to power-drive screws. These bits now come in several different head configurations. You can still find the familiar Phillips-head

screws. However, Phillips-head screws are rapidly being replaced by square-drive screws, which are less likely to strip out (become mangled and unusable), and star-drive screws that are virtually impossible to strip out. There are other less common types, too, and they all come in various sizes. As a result, you'll find yourself changing screw bits often, and it's a lot quicker to pop a bit into a drive guide than to fit one directly into the drill's chuck.

And when you do pop the bit in, it becomes magnetized so the screw will stick to the bit. Drive guides have a sleeve that you can slip down over the screw and hold against the work surface for stability as you start the screw. The sleeve doesn't spin as the screw does, so you can hold onto the sleeve until the screw is fully driven, giving you more control. And finally, there are times—for example, when screwing at an angle into a corner—when the drill itself would get in the way without the added length of the guide.

A FULL INDEX OF DRILL BITS means you'll always have the right bit on hand when you need it.

A POCKET-HOLE JIG is the fastest, easiest way to make strong joints when one side of the joint will be hidden or if you don't mind looking at the pocket holes.

A BISCUIT JOINER cuts slots for football-shaped biscuits that create strong joints.

Drill bits

It makes sense to have a complete set (or "index") of drill bits, so you won't find yourself running out to get a bit you need. The one shown here has 29 bits from 1/16 in. to 1/2 in. dia. For holes wider than 1/2 in. or so, use a paddle-shaped spade bit.

Biscuit joiner

The biscuit joiner, along with the pocket-hole jig, has revolutionized the way woodworkers—pros and hobbyists alike—do joinery. Traditionally, joining the legs to the aprons on the herb planter project, for example, would involve cutting mortises and tenons to fit into them. This takes either considerable time and skill or sophisticated machinery.

Also called a plate joiner, a biscuit joiner makes it possible to make strong joints without mortises and tenons or other complicated joinery. The tool cuts crescent-shaped slots in mating parts. You glue football-shaped "biscuits"

of compressed wood into the slots. The top and bottom surfaces of the mating parts are automatically aligned while the biscuits allow side-to-side adjustment during glue-up. The biscuits come in several sizes.

Pocket-hole jig

If only one side of a joint will be visible—for example, the frames inside the storage bench on p. 168—the screws driven into pocket holes are even faster to make than biscuit joints and just as strong. Of course, you can also use pocket-hole screws where you don't care if they'll be seen—for example, this joinery is at the heart of the design for the critter-proof fence on p. 24.

The jig itself is not powered; rather, it guides a power drill/driver to make holes at the proper depth and angle. The jig shown here sets up quickly and has a built-in clamping mechanism that automatically cuts the holes at the right depth and angle. Stored on the side of the jig are two drill bits of different lengths with square heads to

A FINISH NAILER powered by an air compressor (shown here), or an electric power cord or battery, instantly inserts and sets finish nails with the pull of a trigger, eliminating the need to use a hammer and nailset. It also requires only one hand to use, leaving the other hand free to hold the work.

A HEAVY-DUTY STAPLER is required to install hex-web fencing.

A ROUTER PLAYS A KEY ROLE in modern woodworking. This router motor is shown installed in a fixed base; it also comes with a plunge base.

fit the specialized pocket-hole screws (see "Pocket-hole screws," p. 20).

Finish nailer

You can use a small hammer and a nailset for any of the finish nailing tasks in this book. But a powered finish nailer will greatly speed the work, driving and setting a nail instantly with the pull of a trigger. Some models, like the one shown here, work with an air compressor; others are electric.

Router

Routers are capable of all kinds of joinery and shaping tasks, but you can build any project in this book without one. We did pull out a router for two projects, though. Fitted with a ⅛-in. roundover bit as shown here, we used it to quickly round all the edges of the legs on the picnic table on p. 196. And we used a chamfering bit to dress up the posts on the pergola on p. 230. You can purchase

a fixed-based router or one with a plunge base. A plunge router lets you enter or exit the wood without routing all the way to the edge—for example, to make stopped dadoes. Many router motors, including the one shown here with a fixed base, are designed to fit into a fixed or plunge base. You can start out with a fixed base and buy a plunge base later if you need it or you can buy the motor and both bases as a kit.

Stapler

You'll need a heavy-duty staple gun to attach hex-web fencing for the critter-proof fence and the garden trellis. You can do the job well enough with a hand-powered gun, but the job will be much easier if you use an electric or pneumatic-powered model. The electric one shown here also shoots brads.

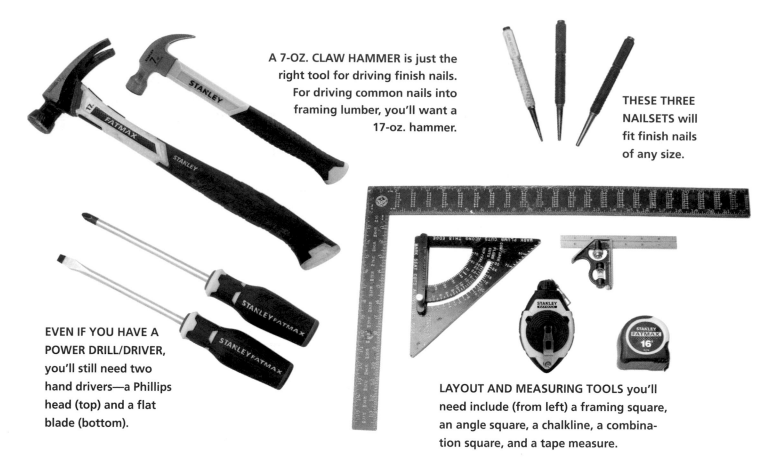

A 7-OZ. CLAW HAMMER is just the right tool for driving finish nails. For driving common nails into framing lumber, you'll want a 17-oz. hammer.

THESE THREE NAILSETS will fit finish nails of any size.

EVEN IF YOU HAVE A POWER DRILL/DRIVER, you'll still need two hand drivers—a Phillips head (top) and a flat blade (bottom).

LAYOUT AND MEASURING TOOLS you'll need include (from left) a framing square, an angle square, a chalkline, a combination square, and a tape measure.

Hand Tools

The hand tools you'll need for the projects in this book are pretty basic—you probably own most of them already. As with power tools, there's no need to purchase a new hand tool until you need it. When you do, it's always a good idea to get the best tool you can afford. Quality hand tools help you do your best work, and they last a lifetime.

Hammers and nailsets

Hammers are designed for various purposes, but the only type you need for the projects in this book is a claw hammer, which has a flat surface on one side of the head for striking nails and a claw on the other for pulling nails. Claw hammers come in a range of sizes that are described by the weight of the head. For driving finish nails, you'll want a finish hammer with a 7-oz. head. For driving common nails for framing jobs such as the garden shed, you'll want a heavier framing hammer such as the 17-oz. model shown here.

Nailsets are used to drive finish nails below the surface without marring the surface. An inexpensive set of three nailsets will ensure you have the right one for finish nails of any size.

Screwdrivers

You'll drive most screws with your drill/driver, but you'll still need a Phillips screwdriver for tasks such as installing the small hinge screws on the lid of the storage bench. Opening a can of paint or finish is about the only use you'll have for a flathead screwdriver while building projects in this book.

Layout and measuring tools

A small collection of well-made layout and measuring tools is essential for accurately marking the locations of cuts. Look for layout tools with markings that are crisp and easy to read.

You'll need a framing square for laying out wide 90° cuts, an angle square for quickly laying out shorter cuts at any angle, a chalkline for laying out long cuts, a combination square for scribing layout lines, and a tape measure. Tape measures come in various lengths—carpenters usually

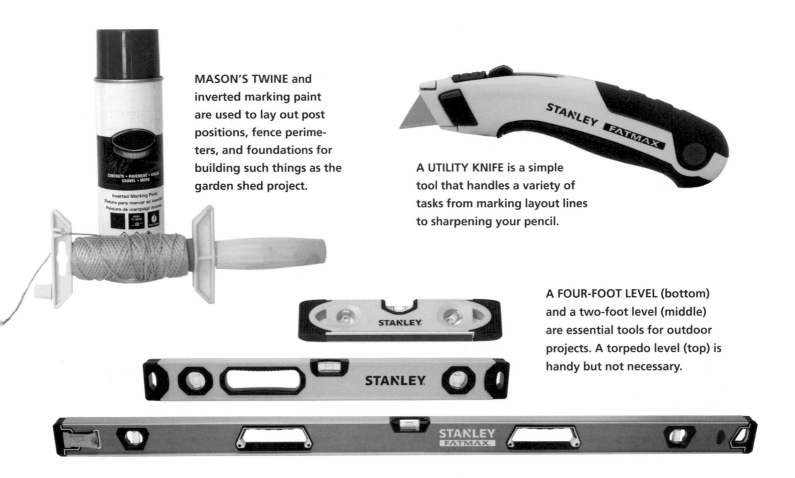

MASON'S TWINE and inverted marking paint are used to lay out post positions, fence perimeters, and foundations for building such things as the garden shed project.

A UTILITY KNIFE is a simple tool that handles a variety of tasks from marking layout lines to sharpening your pencil.

A FOUR-FOOT LEVEL (bottom) and a two-foot level (middle) are essential tools for outdoor projects. A torpedo level (top) is handy but not necessary.

carry a 25-ft. tape. However, a 16-ft. tape is convenient for all the projects in this book. A wide blade is helpful when working solo because it lets you extend the tape several feet before it collapses under its own weight.

Mason's twine and inverted marking paint

Brick masons use mason's twine to keep courses of brick straight and level. You'll use it any time you need to lay out the perimeter of a project on the ground. Other twine has strands that are simply twisted together. Mason's twine is braided so it won't come apart. It's usually yellow to make it easy to see. The twine shown here comes on a handy reel.

Once you start digging, mason's twine supported by stakes can get knocked out of place. So in most cases, you'll follow the path of the twine while spraying inverted marking paint on the ground. Then you can remove the twine and stakes. The paint comes in a can that is designed to work when inverted, unlike other spray paints. The paint itself is designed to wash away after a rainfall or two.

Levels

You'll need a level for any project that is fixed in place to make sure it is plumb and level. For most accuracy, use the longest level that will fit into the space—a 4-ft. level and a 2-ft. level will do the trick for projects in this book. A torpedo level is not essential but can come in handy in tight spots.

Utility knife

Aptly named, you'll use this essential tool for a wide variety of tasks from cutting insulation for the cold frame to sharpening your pencil. There are a few different styles of utility knives: Some close by folding, in some the blade retracts, and in others the blade folds and retracts. The most common and versatile is an inexpensive nonfolding knife that retracts the blade when you slide back a button on the top. These slip easily into an apron or tool pouch, and they have handy storage in the handle for extra blades. Make sure the retracting mechanism operates smoothly—it will get lots of use.

NO POWER TOOL can beat the handy block plane when you need to take a few licks off the edge of a board.

THIS FINE-TOOTHED HAND MITER SAW runs on guides to provide clean, accurate crosscuts at any angle.

Block plane

When you need to make something just slightly smaller—perhaps you discovered one of the garden shed doors is just a tad too big for the opening—nothing does the job faster and more accurately than a few strokes of a sharp block plane. You can also use it to save time and dust by getting square edges roughly round before refining the roundover with sandpaper.

Block planes have a knob on front for adjusting the opening for the blade (called the throat). High-quality planes like the one shown have a lever under the front knob to facilitate fine adjustments. There's another lever on top for clamping the cap to the blade and a knob at back for adjusting how far the blade extends under the base. When buying a block plane, make sure all the surfaces are smooth and flat and the mechanisms work easily and smoothly.

Hand miter saw

A hand miter saw is lighter, quieter, and makes less sawdust than a power miter saw. As a result, even if you own a power version, you'll find yourself reaching for the hand miter saw when you have just a few cuts to make. Look for a saw with a thin, sharp blade that runs smoothly on its guides. Make sure the pivot moves smoothly and stops tightly.

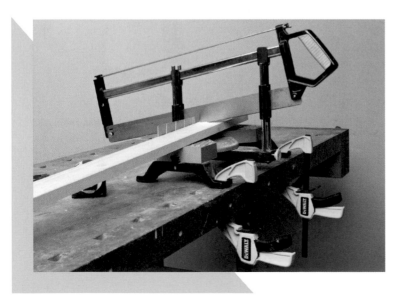

Clamp It Down

When using a hand miter box, or a power miter saw for that matter, it is important to secure the saw to your work surface. You'll work more accurately and, more important, more safely. Most saw bases have holes for screwing or bolting the tool in place, but unless you are making a permanent installation, you'll probably want to use a couple of clamps. If clamps won't fit properly, another alternative is to screw the tool to a piece of plywood and then clamp the plywood to the work surface.

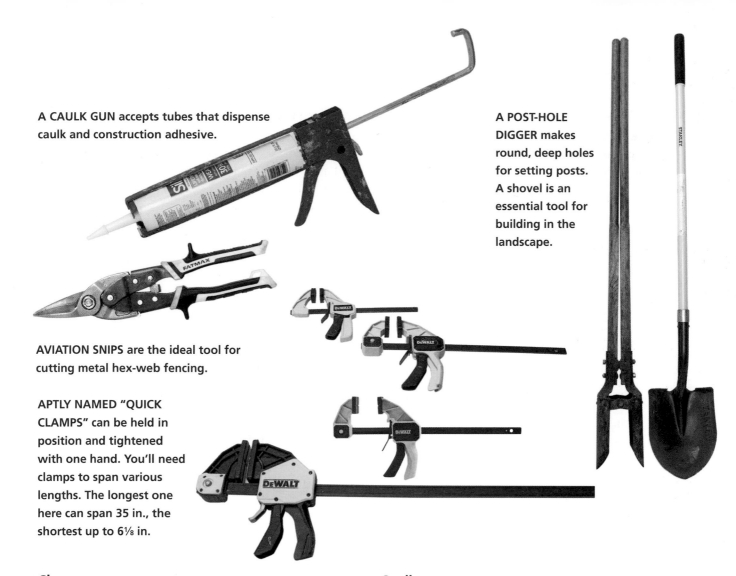

A CAULK GUN accepts tubes that dispense caulk and construction adhesive.

A POST-HOLE DIGGER makes round, deep holes for setting posts. A shovel is an essential tool for building in the landscape.

AVIATION SNIPS are the ideal tool for cutting metal hex-web fencing.

APTLY NAMED "QUICK CLAMPS" can be held in position and tightened with one hand. You'll need clamps to span various lengths. The longest one here can span 35 in., the shortest up to 6⅛ in.

Clamps

There are various types of clamps including bar clamps, pipe clamps, and C-clamps. A more recent innovation that can handle most clamping jobs is often referred to as a quick clamp. These are easiest to use because they can be held in position and tightened with one hand and because they have pads to protect the surfaces of your project.

Snips

You'll need snips to cut the metal hex-web fencing used for the critter-proof fence (p. 24) and the garden trellis (p. 46). Any type of metal-cutting snips, including tin snips, will do the job. Aviation snips, shown here, are so-named because they were developed by the aviation industry to cut metal. They are sometimes called compound snips because they have two pivot points. This helps them cut through the mesh with ease.

Caulk gun

You'll need a caulk gun to apply construction adhesive as well as caulk. The one shown here has a couple of handy features: You can stick the spout of a tube of caulk or adhesive into the hole in the handle to snip off the tip. Then you can poke the on-board tool into the spout to break the tube's inner seal.

Post-hole digger and shovel

A post-hole digger, sometimes called a clamshell digger, allows you to dig the deep, round holes you'll need to set posts for the critter-proof fence (p. 24), the pergola (p. 230), and the trash and recycling corral (p. 220). With the jaws open, you thrust the digger into the ground, then you close the jaws to pull the earth out. If your soil is rocky, you might also need a digging bar to pry rocks out, or you might decide to do the job with a power auger. You'll need a shovel to dig the trench for the critter-proof fence and to lay gravel and stone dust mix for the garden shed.

Work Safely

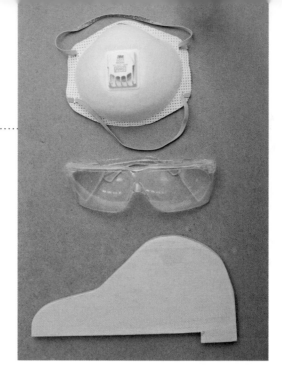

One important technique for safe, accurate, and enjoyable work isn't a step-by-step procedure at all—it's an ongoing process: Take the time as you work to keep an orderly shop or worksite. As you become immersed in the work, it's a natural tendency to just put a tool aside thinking you'll put it away later. Before you know it, your work area will be cluttered and you won't be able to quickly find what you need.

Clean up and keep organized as you go. Roll up the extension cord so you can't trip on it—it's especially important to keep the floor clear around your tablesaw. Vacuum the sawdust after making cuts. These "mindless" tasks have the bonus benefit of giving you a few minutes to think about the next procedure, sometimes preventing mistakes. You just might turn around and think, "Whoops, I was about to drill through the wrong side of that!"

THREE ESSENTIAL PIECES of safety gear are (from top) a dust mask, safety goggles, and a push stick for the tablesaw.

USE SAFETY GEAR

There are three important pieces of safety gear you want to keep within reach at all times so you will never be tempted to skip using them:

Disposable dust mask. Even if you have a state-of-the-art dust-collection system in your shop, you need to protect your lungs with a dusk mask when creating dust by sawing or sanding. It's even more crucial in the typical home shop that relies mostly on a shop vacuum. Use disposable masks with two straps and a metal strip that you pinch to fit the mask over the bridge of your nose. Replace the mask whenever you notice dust beginning to build up on the outside.

As the name implies, a dust mask is to protect your lungs from dust, not from toxic fumes. You won't need protection from toxic fumes while making the projects in this book, but if you ever do, understand that you'll need a special filtering respirator for that job.

Safety goggles. Power saws, drills, biscuit joiners, and, in fact, any power tool has the potential to send particles or splinters toward your face. Hammering nails can, too. To protect your eyes, you need a pair of safety glasses or goggles that wrap around the sides of your head. Regular prescription glasses are no substitute. If you wear prescription glasses, you can put goggles over them, or, of course, you can have a pair of prescription safety glasses made.

Push stick. Always use a push stick to keep your hand away from the blade when making rip cuts of less than about 6 in. wide on the tablesaw. You can purchase a push stick from a woodworking catalog or make one yourself, like the one shown here.

Although you'll use them less often, two other items you'll want to have are a pair of work gloves and ear plugs or protectors. Gloves will protect your hands from splinters. Ear plugs, or better, protectors that cover the ears, are a good idea if you will be using a loud power tool such as a tablesaw for a long period of time.

Wood and Finishes for Outdoor Projects

When it comes to building projects that will stand up to outdoor use, you have two lines of defense. The first is the wood you choose to build with. The second is the finish, if any, you decide to apply to the wood.

To choose your wood and finish wisely, you need a basic understanding of what happens to wood when it is left to the elements. First of all, sun and rain work together to turn all species of wood gray. The ultraviolet light of the sun breaks down the lignin in the wood's surface. Lignin is essentially the glue that holds wood fiber together. The color in the wood is contained in extractives in the wood's pores. When the sun breaks down the lignin, the rain can wash away the extractives, causing the wood to turn gray. Fortunately, however, this affects only the surface of the wood and doesn't affect the wood's structural integrity. You might, in fact, find the gray color quite pleasing and, as long as the wood can dry out quickly after a rain, almost any wood can last for decades with no finish at all.

If exposed wood doesn't dry out quickly, it will rot. Unlike graying, rot does destroy the structural integrity of the wood. That's because rot is caused by fungi and insects such as termites. Like all organisms, fungi and termites need food and water to survive. And, of course, the meal of choice for these particular organisms is wood. If water doesn't remain available long enough, wood-eating organisms won't survive. That's why you see well-weathered silvery barn siding and fences that are perfectly intact—the water can run right off vertical wood. Unfinished horizontal wood—for example, the picnic table and benches on p. 196 or the top of the storage bench— would not fare so well without finish.

Naturally rot-resistant woods

Some woods that are exposed to wet conditions have evolved extractives that are unappetizing to wood eaters. Of these naturally rot-resistant woods, cedar, redwood, and cypress are most commonly used for outdoor building projects in North America. Redwood is most readily available in the West, cypress in the South, and cedar is the typical choice in the Midwest and Northeast. Of those woods, cedar is the only one used for projects in this book simply because the projects were built in the Northeast.

CEDAR (LEFT) IS NATURALLY RESISTANT to rot. Pressure-treated southern pine is injected with chemicals that ward off rot.

It is important to note that these woods are rot-*resistant* not rot-*proof*. They will all eventually succumb to rot if conditions are right. Also be aware that the darker wood from the center of the tree, called heartwood, is more rot-resistant than the lighter-colored sapwood that comes from closer to the bark. For example, take a look at the herb planter on p. 150. Those dark legs are more rot-resistant than the lighter aprons.

Pressure-treated wood

The idea behind pressure-treated wood is simple: Take a wood that is not naturally rot-resistant—most often southern yellow pine—and use pressure to force poison into the pores so organisms won't eat it. Alkaline copper quaternary is the chemical combo of choice these days for wood used in residential construction. Pressure-treated wood

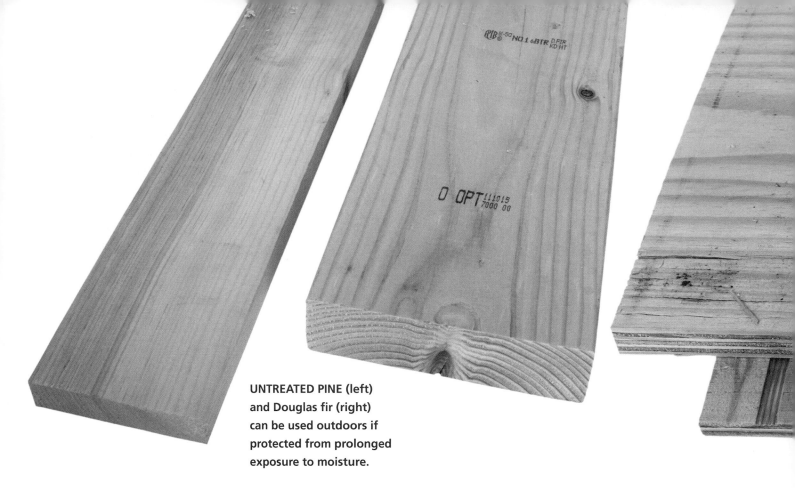

UNTREATED PINE (left) and Douglas fir (right) can be used outdoors if protected from prolonged exposure to moisture.

What Does Mildew Do?

Mildew grows on the surface of wood or even on top of a finish. It doesn't damage the wood; it's just ugly. You can remove mildew with household bleach, and some finishes include a mildewcide. Mildew is also the reason you should never use linseed oil as an outdoor finish—linseed oil is filet mignon to mildew.

is even more rot-resistant than naturally resistant woods and it's cheaper, too. But it's not nearly as attractive. Also, southern yellow pine is heavier and less porous than cedar, redwood, or cypress, so it tends to crack and twist more readily with humidity changes.

Pine and Douglas fir

The nominally 1-in.-thick boards you'll find at a home center or lumberyard are actually ¾ in. thick and most of them are pine. Meanwhile, the nominally 2-in.-thick (actual thickness 1½-in.) studs and other structural framing lumber you'll find are Douglas fir. That's because pine is better looking, but fir is a lot stronger. Neither species offers much natural resistance to rot.

In this book, untreated pine boards are used to trim the garden shed and to make the gate for the critter-proof fence. The shed boards are protected by paint, while the gate boards are stained. Because the gate boards are hung vertically with spaces between them, they'll always dry out quickly and so would probably last for decades with no finish at all. Unfinished pine boards are also used for the interior frame of the storage bench, which is never exposed to the weather.

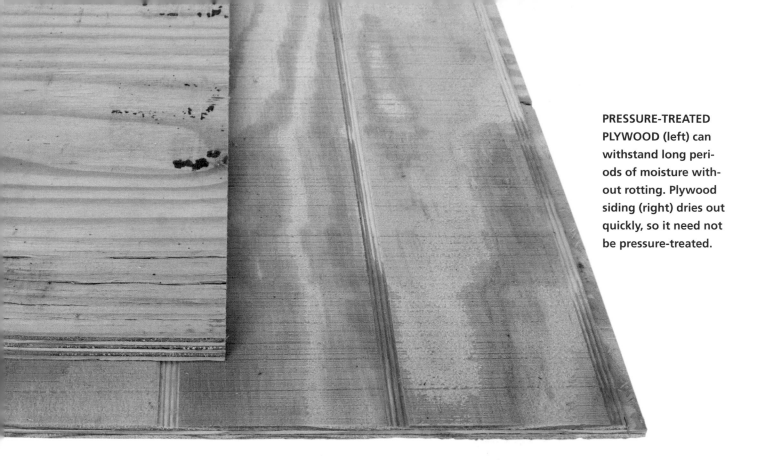

Douglas fir studs are used to frame the garden shed and the potting bench that is built into it. The picnic table and benches are made of Douglas fir that's protected by paint and the raised bed is made of Douglas fir coated with preservative as discussed in "Choosing Wood for Raised Beds" on p. 94.

Plywood

Because the planter on p. 208 will be filled with damp earth, its interior is made from pressure-treated plywood that's clad on the outside with cedar. The herb planter, on the other hand, is made solely from cedar with the interior sealed with tung oil and silicone caulk. We took this approach because we didn't want to plant edible herbs in soil surrounded by pressure-treated wood. While the herb planter should last for many years, it will likely rot before the planter.

Untreated plywood siding panels are used on the garden shed. There's no need for pressure-treated panels in that application because water quickly runs off siding. Unlike some other plywoods, the wood plies in siding panels are joined with glue designed for permanent exposure to the weather.

Paint: the ultimate protector

Scrape the paint off the siding of a well-maintained 200-year-old building and the wood below will look the same as it did the day the siding board was installed. That's because paint forms a waterproof film and its opaque pigments block ultraviolet rays. Typically, you'll apply a coat of primer and two coats of paint, although there are new formulations that combine primer into the paint.

Paint is a great choice if you are building with uninteresting-looking wood. For example, we built the picnic table and benches project from inexpensive framing lumber. We think its red paint job looks pretty snazzy. Of course, you're not going to want to slather paint on projects made from more expensive attractive wood like the cedar used for the storage bench (p. 168), the planter (p. 208), the herb planter (p. 150), or the barbecue cart (p. 184).

Clear oil finish: renewable waterproofing

Clear oil finishes, such as the pure tung oil used on most of the cedar projects in this book, penetrate into the wood and won't peel off. Oil is very easy to apply—you just brush it on, let it soak in, and wipe off the excess. That's a good thing because you'll want to add a coat or two every year or two.

TUNG OIL BRINGS OUT the beauty of woods like cedar while repelling moisture that can cause rot.

Oil does an excellent job of repelling water. Clear oils enhance the rich color of woods like cedar—but enjoy it while it lasts because oil alone offers no UV protection. Your project will turn gray just as quickly as it would with no finish. There are clear finishes—both oil and film-forming—that contain UV blockers, similar to the sunscreen you slather on at the beach. But like sunscreen, the protection breaks down over time. Also, since oil finishes soak in and don't build up, the finish may be too thin to allow the blockers to do much good.

Clear film finish: the wooden boat approach

If you want the color of the wood to come through a shiny surface, using clear film finishes on outdoor wood is a very effective but also very labor-intensive strategy. Put on a few coats and your wood will be impervious to water. If the finish has UV blocker and you add enough coats to create a thick finish, the wood will retain its color—at least for a couple of years.

Then comes the downside. When the finish turns dull, the UV blocker is no longer working. You'll need to sand off the topcoat and add more finish. If you don't do this, the UV rays will break down the surface lignin and the fin-ish will begin to flake off. If you decide to use a film finish with UV, take a tip from the nautically knowledgeable: Use marine varnish, sometimes called spar varnish. It's the most durable.

Stains: adding color, a little or a lot

Stain is essentially thinned paint—it contains varying degrees of pigment that provide varying degrees of protection from the UV rays of the sun, and it builds a thin film to keep water out. Exterior stains come in three levels of transparency and corresponding thickness. Semi-transparent has the least pigment and is the thinnest—it tints the wood while letting the grain pattern show through. Semi-solid has more pigment and partially obscures the grain. Solid color completely covers the grain and looks similar to paint, but it is thinner than paint and more of the wood's texture is revealed.

An advantage of stain over paint is that stain does not require primer. Also, you can reapply it without getting the buildup that eventually requires paint to be stripped. Solid stain soaked in very nicely on the rough-sawn surface of the plywood siding we used on the garden shed. It worked well on the pine-board gate of the critter-proof fence.

Fasteners and Adhesives

There's a wide range of screws, nails, and adhesives available today, each designed to do a specific task very well. Each project specifies exactly which fastener or adhesive to use for each purpose.

Deck screws. You'll use plenty of deck screws to assemble the projects in this book. These screws can be galvanized, but more often these days you'll find the ceramic-coated version shown on the facing page. Some, as shown, have a star-drive head that never strips out or they may have a square-drive head that works almost as well. The matching bit is usually included in the box of screws. The coarse screw threads on many of these screws stop about one-third of the way below the head. As a result, the screws drive quickly without predrilling and the top piece is drawn toward the bottom piece.

Pocket-hole screws. These screws have a square-drive head and are designed to fit the pockets made by pocket-hole jigs. The heads have flat bottoms to prevent splitting and are threaded only halfway to draw the parts

FASTENERS USED FOR PROJECTS in this book include (from left) deck screws, exterior pocket-hole screws, interior pocket-hole screws, galvanized common nails, galvanized finish nails, galvanized oval-head nails, and (bottom) finish nails for a power nailer.

THREE PRODUCTS YOU'LL NEED that are designed to withstand outdoor applications are (from left) exterior wood glue, construction adhesive, and silicone caulk.

together. You can get these screws with a coating that makes them suitable for outdoor uses such as assembling the critter-proof fence. You'll use the coarse-threaded version that is designed for softwoods, not the fine-thread version used for hardwoods.

Common nails. These nails are used for rough framing—you'll use them to frame the garden shed. They come in a "bright" finish, which means they are not coated and are designed for interior use. Or you'll find them galvanized, which can be used indoors or out. You'll use 8d, 10d, and 16d commons that are 2½ in. long, 3 in. long, and 3½ in. long, respectively.

Finish nails. These thin nails have a small head designed to be set below the surface. Lengths used in this book are 3d (1¼ in.), 4d (1½ in.), and 8d (2½ in). Finish nails that are 1 in. or shorter are called brads. You can find galvanized finish nails for outdoor use.

Power finish nails. These come in strips, and you need to buy ones that are designed to fit your specific brand of nailer. They are driven below the surface with a pull of the nailer trigger.

Oval-head nails. These galvanized nails are used when you don't want nails to be conspicuous, but you need more holding power than the small head of a finish nail can provide. They are just the ticket for installing siding or exterior trim.

Exterior wood glue. Wood glue formulated for outdoors is used in the same way as familiar yellow woodworking glue—it requires clamping pressure to work. In fact, you can use this glue for interior projects as well. In this book, exterior wood glue is used for biscuit joinery and to strengthen miter joints and, in some cases, pocket-screw joints.

Construction adhesive. Unlike wood glue, construction adhesive works without clamping pressure, although sometimes a clamp or two is handy just to hold a piece in place until the adhesive grabs. While wood glue is just for bonding wood to wood, construction adhesive will bond practically anything—in the cold frame, it's used to attach rigid insulation panels to the plywood frame. Although wood glue is stronger, construction adhesive is best when you need to bond relatively large surfaces such as attaching the cladding to the plywood on the planter.

Silicone caulk. This is the most durable caulk for outdoor projects. It comes in clear or white—paint won't adhere to it. In this book, it's used to caulk the inside of the herb planter and the window sashes used as lids on the cold frame.

PART ONE

PROJECTS FOR THE BACKYARD FARMER

STANLEY

IF YOU'VE ALWAYS WANTED to grow your own veggies and perhaps harvest your own eggs, then this part of the book will help you build everything you need to create your dream garden. All of the projects are designed to look great and work great together. Or, with the exception of the built-in potting bench, which is designed to fit inside the shed, you can build any of them as a stand-alone project.

If you build no other project, you will want to erect the critter-proof fence. Critters that want to feast on your bounty are the biggest challenge that vegetable gardeners face. It's so disappointing to plant and weed and water

and watch your crops grow only to have it all disappear. At 8 ft. high and 1 ft. deep, this fence will truly eliminate that problem. The fence we built is about 25 ft. square, which provides plenty of space to grow vegetables for a typical family without being so large that maintaining it takes over your life. Of course, the fence is in sections, so you can make it any size you like.

So browse through the projects and start planning your own garden. The first time you sink your teeth into a warm, ripe tomato right off the vine or learn what a fresh egg really tastes like, you'll know it was all worth the work.

CHAPTER TWO

Critter-Proof Fence

GROUNDHOGS, DEER, RABBITS,

and other unwelcome critters had best find another lunch spot. They won't be getting over or under this fence to help themselves to your veggies. It's 8 ft. high, goes down in the ground 1 ft., and then extends out 1 ft.

It's a simple and sturdy design. Posts are planted in the ground with concrete to support two layers of rails and cleats with a PVC-coated steel hex-web fencing sandwiched between. This fencing is designed to resist critters trying to chew through it. The PVC protects the wire from rust, while the black color makes the fencing nearly invisible.

The fence shown here encloses a garden that's 24 ft. 8 in. square. This size allows a post spacing of about 8 ft. on three sides and nicely accommodates the 8-ft.-wide garden shed you'll find on p. 52. Of course, you can make your enclosure any size you want, but for maximum sturdiness, keep the distance between posts to no more than about 8 ft.

WHAT YOU'LL NEED

FENCE

- 14 posts
  3½ in. x 3½ in. x 12 ft., pressure treated*
- 48 cleats
  ¾ in. x 1¾ in. x 86¼ in., pressure treated*
- 34 rails
  ¾ in. x 3½ in. x 95³⁄₁₆ in., pressure treated*
- 16 rails
  ¾ in. x 3½ in. x 62⅝ in., pressure treated*

GATE

- 4 rails and stiles
  1½ in. x 3½ in. x 41 in., pine
- 7 slats
  ¾ in. x 5½ in. x 72 in., pine
- 1 gate header
  1½ in. x 7¼ in. x 42 in.

HARDWARE AND SUPPLIES

- Gravel
- Quick-setting concrete
- 1 can inverted marking spray
- Mason's twine
- 1¼-in. deck screws
- 1½-in. deck screws
- 2½-in. deck screws
- 2½-in. exterior pocket-hole screws
- 1 roll hex-web fencing, 78 in. x 100 ft.**
- 1 roll hex-web fencing, 24 in. x 150 ft.**
- 1 no-sag gate kit***
- 1 gate latch and bolt
- 16d nails (if fence will be attached to shed)

* If shed will be included, replace two posts with
  two 1½-in. x 3½-in. x 95¼-in. boards and subtract
  four cleats and four rails.

** Available from DeerBusters.com

*** Available as EasyGate from Homax

The fourth side of our enclosure has four fence sections of about 5 ft. each with a 42-in.-wide gate in the middle.

The gate itself couldn't be easier to build thanks to a gate bracket kit that's available at home centers. The gate features an arced top that's echoed in the gate header. We finished the gate and the header with solid stain to match the shed (see "Wood and Finishes for Outdoor Projects," p. 17), but you can skip the finish and just let the fence weather to gray. Because the boards are vertical and have spaces between them, the gate will dry quickly after a rain and will last for many years without finish.

LAYING OUT THE FENCE

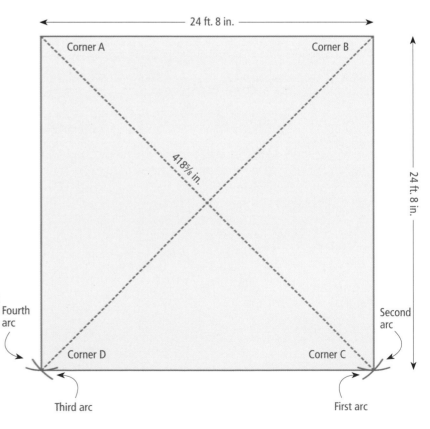

Lay Out the Garden Posts

You'll start by staking out the center points for four corners of the garden. Then you'll run strings between the stakes. You'll use the stakes as a guide to paint the perimeter with inverted marking paint—a can of spray paint designed to spray while inverted that makes lines that eventually wash away. Finally, you'll use the paint to lay out the positions of intermediary posts.

1 **LAY OUT THE FIRST SIDE. Decide where you want the first corner to be (corner A in the drawing "Laying Out the Fence") and drive in a stake at that point. Measure out the length of one side, 24 ft. 8 in. for the fence shown here, and drive in a stake at corner B. Tie a string between the two stakes and use it as a guide to spray-paint a line.**

Calculating Diagonals

An easy way to calculate the diagonal length of a square is to use the fact that for every 1 ft. of side length, the diagonal will be 16.97 in. long. The sides of the garden fence shown here are 24 ft. 8 in. long. Looking at an inches-to-decimal-foot chart (you can find one online) tells us that's 24.667 ft. Multiply 24.667 by 16.97 to get 418.6 in. or close enough to 418⅝ in.

2 **LAY OUT THE LENGTH OF THE SECOND SIDE. Measure out the distance for an adjacent side—B to C in the drawing. Have a helper hold the end of the measuring tape at stake B. You don't know exactly where corner C will be yet, so eyeball for approximately square while you hold the spray-paint can at the length mark on the tape and paint an arc that is generously in range.**

3 **LAY OUT THE FIRST DIAGONAL.** Have a helper hold the end of the tape at corner A. Hold the spray-paint can at the measurement for the length of the diagonal—418⅝ in. for this fence (see "Calculating Diagonals," p. 27)—while you draw a second arc intersecting the first. Drive in a stake at the point where the two arcs cross.

4 **COMPLETE THE LAYOUT.** Repeat the process to find the fourth corner, D in the drawing. Lay out the length for side A to D, draw an arc, then lay out the diagonal from B to D and drive the final stake at the intersecting point. Tie strings between all the stakes and use them as a guide to spray-paint all the fence sides.

Designing around Rail Lengths

When deciding on the size of your garden, make the space between posts about 95 in. so you can make the rails from 8-ft. 1x4s with about 1 in. for making square cuts. The garden shown here has a minimum of three fence sections per side. Three times 95 in. equals 285 in. Then we added in 10½ in. for the width of the two intermediary posts and half of each end post to get 295½ in. or 24 ft. 7 in. We rounded up to 24 ft. 8 in., which still leaves the boards long enough to square both ends.

5 **LAY OUT THE INTERMEDIARY POST LOCATIONS.** As shown in the drawing "Garden with Shed Layout," two sides of the garden shown here have posts located 8 ft. 2¹¹⁄₁₆ in. on center. One side has shorter distances between posts to allow for the gate. The fourth side has no posts because the fence will be supported by the sides of the shed—if you are not planning a shed, the post layout would be the same as the first two sides. Measure and mark with paint for the center of each post.

GARDEN WITH SHED LAYOUT

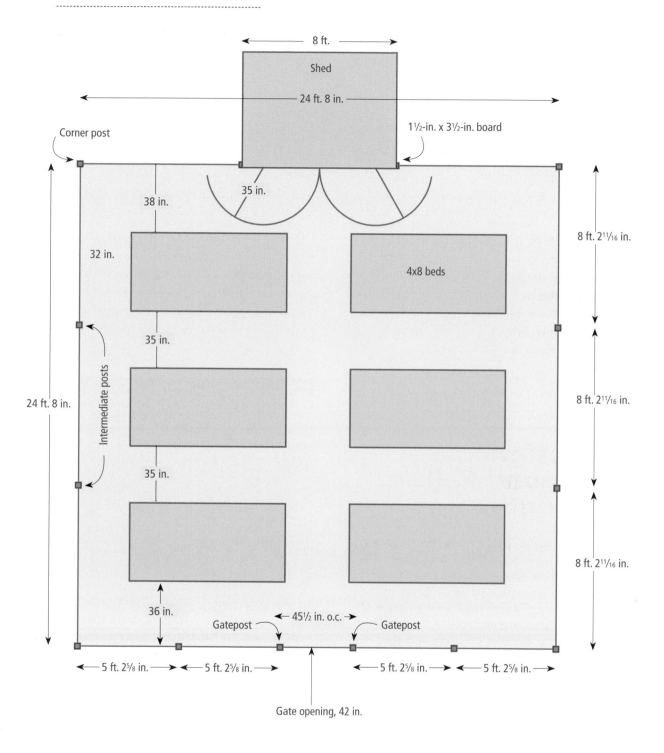

8 ft.

Shed

24 ft. 8 in.

Corner post

1½-in. x 3½-in. board

38 in.

35 in.

32 in.

4x8 beds

8 ft. 2¹¹⁄₁₆ in.

Intermediate posts

35 in.

24 ft. 8 in.

8 ft. 2¹¹⁄₁₆ in.

35 in.

36 in.

8 ft. 2¹¹⁄₁₆ in.

45½ in. o.c.

Gatepost

Gatepost

5 ft. 2⅝ in.

5 ft. 2⅝ in.

5 ft. 2⅝ in.

5 ft. 2⅝ in.

Gate opening, 42 in.

Install the Posts and Dig Trenches

You'll start by digging post holes. Then you will place a few inches of gravel in each hole and tamp it down. You'll put the posts in place, supporting them with braces to keep them plumb while you pour dry quick-setting concrete into the holes and then add water. Cutting the posts to height will be done later, after the fencing is installed.

If you are battling burrowing critters such as groundhogs, then a burrow barrier is a must. It'll keep rabbits from squeezing under your fence, too. The barrier consists of 2-ft.-wide hex-web fencing that will be attached to the lower rails of the fence. It goes down into the ground about 1 ft. and then it is bent out. Groundhogs can dig a lot deeper than 1 ft. and when they encounter a vertical barrier they may try to dig under it. However, when they encounter the buried horizontal section of the barrier, they've reached the limits of their cognitive ability and they give up. You'll dig the trench now, but you won't install the barrier until the bottom rails are in.

1 **DIG THE POST HOLES.** Dig the post holes centered on your layout marks. If your ground is soft, you can use a manual post-hole digger like the one shown here. For tougher ground, consider renting a powered post-hole auger. The depth of the post holes should be one-third the height of the posts plus about 6 in. for gravel. These posts will be 8 ft. high, so dig the holes to about 38 in. deep. Make them about 1 ft. in diameter.

2 **ADD GRAVEL AND TAMP.** Place about 6 in. of gravel in the hole, then tamp it down with a length of 4x4 or 2x4.

3 **INSTALL AND PLUMB THE CORNER POSTS.** Put a corner post in its hole and use one screw to attach a diagonal brace running from as high as you can comfortably reach to the ground. Adjust the angle of the brace until the post is plumb in the same plane as the brace. Then use another brace to plumb the post in the other direction.

4 **STAKE THE BRACES.** To make sure the posts remain plumb while the concrete sets, fix the bottom of the braces in position by screwing them to short stakes driven into the ground.

5 **SET STRINGS TO POSITION THE INTERMEDIATE POSTS.** To get the intermediate posts in the same plane as the corner posts, tie a string along the outside face of corner posts as shown.

TIP To ensure that the gateposts will be parallel, cut two pieces of 2x4 to the width of the gate opening—42 in. in this case. With the posts on the ground, toe-screw the pieces between the posts. Then raise the posts together into their holes. Plumb and brace them.

6 **INSTALL THE INTERMEDIATE POSTS.** Plumb the posts so their outside faces will be parallel to the corner posts and fix them in that plane by temporarily screwing pieces of 1x4 rail stock across the outside faces of the corner posts and the intermediate posts as shown. Then use a diagonal brace to plumb each intermediate post in the other plane.

7 FILL THE HOLES. Pour about one and a half 50-lb. bags of quick-setting concrete into each hole. Add enough water to saturate the mix—about 1½ gal. Wait at least four hours. Then fill the holes to the top with dirt and remove the braces.

8 LAY OUT AND DIG THE TRENCH. Starting at one side, put stakes in the ground 1 ft. out from each corner post. Run a string between the stakes, and use it as a guide to spray-paint a line. Then dig about 1 ft. down between the posts and out to the layout line.

Accommodating Slope

As shown in the drawing "Inside View" on p. 36, if your site slopes along the fencing, each section of fence will step down with the slope while the rails remain level. The bottom rail will be 2 in. above the highest grade between any two posts.

Likewise, the bottom of your burrow barrier trench should be approximately level. Set a board on the ground and across two posts and screw it to the post that's at the higher grade. Put a 4-ft. level on the board, raise it until it is level, and then screw it to the other post. Dig the trench to 1 ft. below the bottom of the board. Also strike lines across the posts 5½ in. above the bottom of the board. You'll use these lines later to locate the top of the bottom rails.

Prepare the Fence Frames

The edges of the hex-web fencing will be sandwiched between two pieces of 1x stock. Each fence frame rail is made of two lengths of 1x4 (actual dimensions ¾ in. x 3½ in.), while each vertical cleat is made from two lengths of ¾ in. x 1¾ in.

The cleats are made by ripping 1x4s in half, so you'll crosscut one 1x4 to length for every two cleats you need, and then you'll make the rips. The cleats will be installed on edge, so you'll predrill screw holes to prevent splitting.

The spacing between posts almost certainly varies a bit, so you'll measure and cut sets of four rail pieces to fit between each pair of posts. Then you'll drill pocket holes in the ends of each rail for pocket screws that will attach them to posts.

1 **CROSSCUT THE CLEAT STOCK. All the cleats will be 86¼ in. long to accommodate the 90-in.-wide hex-web fencing. You can cut 1x4 stock to this length with a circular saw, but the job will go quicker if you set up a stop for a power miter saw. Start by marking and cutting one 1x4 to length. Then lock the sawblade down and put the piece against the blade. Slide the stop against the workpiece and tighten it down.**

2 **RIP THE CLEATS. Usually when setting a tablesaw rip fence, you measure from the inside of the blade to the fence so that the kerf will be on the waste side of the cut. However, when ripping the cleats, you want to get two equal-width pieces from each 1x4. To do this, place the fence 1¾ in. from the center of the blade so half of the kerf will be cut from each piece.**

3 **PREDRILL THE CLEATS AND INSERT SCREWS. Place six or eight cleats on edge on your bench or sawhorses with their ends flush, and use a square to strike lines across them at 6 in. from each end and at 30 in. from each end. Predrill ⅛-in.-dia. holes at the lines. Then start 2½-in. deck screws at each hole.**

4 **CUT THE RAILS AND MAKE THE POCKET HOLES. Measure the distance between two posts. Then use a power miter saw or a circular saw (see "Making Square Cuts with a Circular Saw," p. 95) to cut four 1x4 rails to this length. Label the four pieces as "A." Work your way around the posts, measuring the distance between each pair, cutting the pieces, and labeling the sets sequentially. Drill two holes for 2½-in. pocket screws in each end of each rail piece. Make the holes about ¾ in. in from each side.**

TIP If you don't have a saw stand with built-in stops like the one shown in the top photo, you can easily make your own stop (see "Making and Using a Stop Block," p. 171).

Install the Rails, Cleats, and Hex-Web Fencing

For each section of fence, you'll start by installing the outer bottom rail. Then you'll lay in the hex-web burrow barrier and staple it in place. Next, you'll install the outer cleats followed by the outer top rails. You'll cut hex-web fencing to fit and staple it in place. Finally, you'll install the inner rail and cleat pieces.

1 **POSITION THE OUTER BOTTOM RAIL BOARD.** If the ground between a set of posts is level, strike a line on both posts 5½ in. from grade. If the ground slopes, see "Accommodating Slope" on p. 32. Put the outer piece of the bottom rail in place between posts with the top of the rail at the layout line. Use a scrap of 1x stock as a gauge to set the rail back ¾ in. from the outside of the posts.

2 **INSTALL THE OUTER BOTTOM RAIL BOARD.** Drive 2½-in. exterior pocket-hole screws into the pocket holes to attach each end of the bottom rails to a post.

3 **INSTALL THE BURROW BARRIER.** Cut lengths of 2-ft.-wide hex-web fencing to fit between posts. Position each barrier so it overlaps the inside of the bottom rail by about 1¾ in. and staple it in place. You can do this job with a manual staple gun, but a pneumatic stapler makes the job quicker and easier. Fill the trenches except for the area in front of the gate.

4 **INSTALL THE OUTER CLEATS.** Put a cleat against a post and down on a bottom rail. Use the scrap of 1x as a gauge while you drive in the screws you started in the predrilled holes.

5 **INSTALL AND MARK THE OUTER TOP RAIL BOARD.**
Put a rail board atop the cleats and install it with pocket screws as you did the bottom rail. To help position the fencing, mark the center point across the rail. Then set a combination square to ½ in. and use it to guide a pencil line ½ in. from the top of the rail as shown.

6 **CUT THE HEX-WEB FENCING.** Use snips to cut sections of hex-web fencing that are 1 in. shorter than the distance between posts. Use a piece of tape to mark the center across the top edge of each section.

7 **ATTACH THE FENCING TO THE TOP RAIL.** Align the tape on the fencing to the center mark and the horizontal line you made on the top rail. Put a staple in at that point. Then secure the fencing along the line with a staple about every 4 in.

8 **ATTACH FENCING TO THE CLEATS AND BOTTOM RAIL.**
Staple the fencing to the cleats, pulling it tight and alternating sides every few feet as you work your way down. Finally, staple the fencing to the bottom rail.

9 **ATTACH THE INNER RAILS AND CLEATS.** Attach the inner bottom rail, then the inner cleats, and finally the top rail in the same way as you did the outer frame members. Then screw through the inner rail boards and cleats into the outer boards and cleats using 1¼-in. screws about every 12 in. Stagger the screws into rails, alternating about 1 in. from top and 1 in. from bottom.

INSIDE VIEW

POST CORNER DETAIL

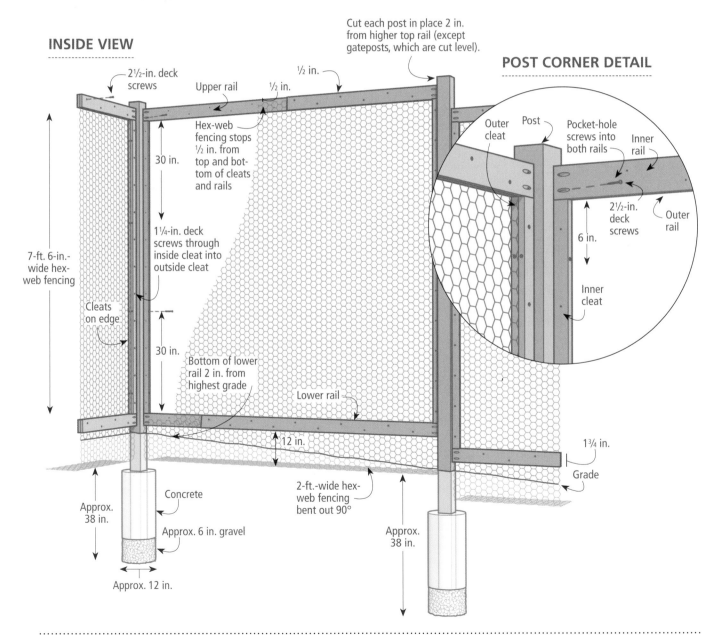

Cut each post in place 2 in. from higher top rail (except gateposts, which are cut level).

2½-in. deck screws

Upper rail

½ in.

½ in.

Hex-web fencing stops ½ in. from top and bottom of cleats and rails

30 in.

7-ft. 6-in.-wide hex-web fencing

1¼-in. deck screws through inside cleat into outside cleat

Cleats on edge

30 in.

Bottom of lower rail 2 in. from highest grade

Lower rail

12 in.

2-ft.-wide hex-web fencing bent out 90°

Concrete

Approx. 38 in.

Approx. 6 in. gravel

Approx. 12 in.

Approx. 38 in.

Grade

1¾ in.

Outer cleat

Post

Pocket-hole screws into both rails

Inner rail

2½-in. deck screws

Outer rail

6 in.

Inner cleat

Attaching the Fence to a Shed

If you're building the fence in conjunction with the garden shed project on p. 52, attaching the fence to the shed is straightforward. As described in that project, the front of the shed will be in line with the inside of the fence posts. So essentially, you'll nail pressure-treated 2x4s to the sides of the shed and assemble cleats and rails to the 2x4s exactly as you did for the posts.

BEVEL THE 2X4S AND CUT THEM TO LENGTH. Beveling the tops of the 2x4s will drain water away from the shed. You can simply make a 45-degree bevel across the face of the board, or if you have a compound miter saw, you can make a cut that also follows the pitch of the roof as shown here: Lay out the roof pitch across the face of the board using the bevel gauge as you did for the corner boards. Set the saw table to the pitch angle and tilt the blade 45 degrees to make the cuts. Then, measuring from the longest point on the bevel, square-cut the boards to 95¼ in. long.

NAIL THE 2X4S IN PLACE. Position the 2x4s flush to the front of the shed. If the shed is upslope or at the same grade as the adjoining post, position the 2x4 at 2 in. above the ground. Attach it with 16d nails staggered about 16 in. apart. If the shed is downslope, mark the adjoining post at 2 in. above grade and, using a level on a long piece of lumber, mark the same height on the shed's front corner board. Align the bottom of the 2x4 to this height when you install it.

Cut the Posts to Height

With the fencing installed, it's time to cut the posts to final height. Actually, you can do this job any time after the outer top rails are installed in case you're lucky enough to have a helper who is looking for something to do while you install the hex-web fencing.

If the site is level, you'll simply cut all the posts off at 2 in. above the top rail. If the site slopes, you'll cut each post 2 in. above the higher rail that meets it. The exception is the gateposts—you want the top of the gateposts to be level with each other, even if the ground below them slopes. You'll start each cut with a circular saw and finish it with a reciprocating saw or handsaw.

1 **MARK THE POSTS AND MAKE THE FIRST CUT.** Measure up 2 in. from the rail below and use a square to lay out cutlines across the outside face and the two faces that adjoin it. Set a circular saw to maximum cutting depth and, working from outside the fence, make a cut along the lines.

2 **FINISH THE CUT.** Put a wood-cutting blade on a reciprocating saw to finish the cut on the post. A sharp handsaw will do a fine job, too.

3 **MARK AND CUT THE GATEPOSTS.** If one gatepost is upslope from the other, mark it for a cut 2 in. above the rail, as you did in step 1. Then use a 4-ft. level to mark the other gatepost for a cut that is level to the upslope post.

Assemble the Gate Frame

The gate frame is assembled with four pieces of 2x4 joined by a hardware kit that includes four braced brackets. The hinges are incorporated into the brackets. Predrill all the screw holes with a ⅛-in.-dia. bit.

1 **CUT THE FRAME PARTS AND ARRANGE THE RAILS.** Use a power miter saw or a circular saw to cut the frame rails and stiles to 41 in. long. Two of the kit brackets have hinges. Get the parts oriented by laying the brackets and rails on the bench with the hinge barrels up and on the same side.

Which Way Should the Gate Swing?

To save space in the garden, gates usually swing out. And doors and gates hinged on the right are most natural for right-handed people to open. However, if the ground slopes up from the outside of the gate, you might have the gate swing in to clear the ground for the full arc of its swing. Likewise, if the ground slopes across the gateposts, hinge the gate on the downslope gatepost to ensure that the gate will clear the ground.

2 **ASSEMBLE THE RAILS TO THE BRACKETS.** Attach the rails to the brackets using the screws provided. Though not necessary, a clamp will help hold the bracket to the rail while you predrill and drive screws. Note that both wood screws and pan-head screws are provided. The kit includes a diagram showing which screws to use where. Also note that you need only use one of the two holes that are under the bracket's diagonal arm.

3 **ASSEMBLE THE STILES TO THE BRACKETS.** Put a stile in place against a bracket—again a clamp is handy for holding it in place. Secure the stile with two pan-head screws, then repeat the process on the other end of the stile and both ends of the other stile.

4 **INSERT SCREWS INTO THE HINGES.** Predrill and drive eight wood screws to secure the hinges to the edge of the frame.

Assemble the Gate Slats to the Frame

This gate is 41 in. wide, 1 in. less than the distance between the gateposts. The slats consist of seven nominal 1x6 pine boards (actual dimensions ¾ in. x 5½ in.). You'll start by cutting all the boards to 72 in. and then you will screw them to the frame. You'll use a simple homemade compass to scribe the arc at the top of the gate and then cut along the curved line with a sabersaw.

1 **CUT THE BOARDS TO LENGTH AND THEN MARK FOR THE CENTER SLAT.** Use a power miter saw or a circular saw to cut all the boards to 72 in. long—no need to worry about getting the cuts perfectly square since they will be cut at a curve after installation. Then lay out lines on the rails for one edge of the center slat. Locate the lines 17¾ in. from the same vertical edge.

GATE (INSIDE VIEW)

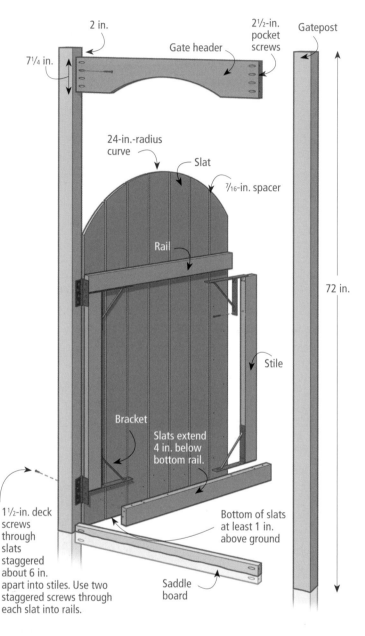

- 2 in.
- 7¼ in.
- Gate header
- 2½-in. pocket screws
- Gatepost
- 24-in.-radius curve
- Slat
- 7/16-in. spacer
- Rail
- 72 in.
- Stile
- Bracket
- Slats extend 4 in. below bottom rail.
- 1½-in. deck screws through slats staggered about 6 in. apart into stiles. Use two staggered screws through each slat into rails.
- Saddle board
- Bottom of slats at least 1 in. above ground

2 **ATTACH ONE END OF THE CENTER SLAT.** Put a square along the line you just drew on the bottom rail. Position a slat against the square with 4 in. extending past the bottom of the rail. Attach the slat with one 1½-in. deck screw.

3 **COMPLETE THE CENTER SLAT ATTACHMENT.** Make sure the other end of the center slat is along the line and square to the top rail, then attach it with two screws staggered across the width of the rail. Go back to the bottom rail and insert a second screw.

> **TIP** Most nominally ½-in.-thick plywood actually is closer to ⁷⁄₁₆ in. thick, which happens to be perfect for making spacers to gauge the spaces between slats: six spacers at ⁷⁄₁₆ in. plus seven 5½-in.-wide boards add up to 41⅛ in.—close enough to the 41-in. width of the gate.

4 **INSTALL THE REMAINING SLATS.** Make six spacers from scraps of ½-in. plywood. Lay out the slats with the spacers to one side of the center slat, remove the spacers, and use them to lay out the other side. If the end boards go past the sides of the frame, mark them in place for tablesaw rips that will make them flush. Then use a pair of spacers to position each slat as you attach it with two staggered screws across the width of both rails.

Make a Beam Compass

It will take about 10 minutes to put together a simple beam compass for laying out the arcs for the top of the gate and the bottom of the gate header. Start with a scrap of wood that's 1½ in. wide and 26½ in. long. Drive a 4d finish nail through the face of the board located about 1 in. from the end. The nail should protrude about ¾ in. through the other side. Make a mark 24 in. from the nail. Drill a hole at the mark to fit your pencil. Insert the pencil so its point protrudes about the same amount as the nail. Pin the pencil in place with another finish nail driven through the side of the board.

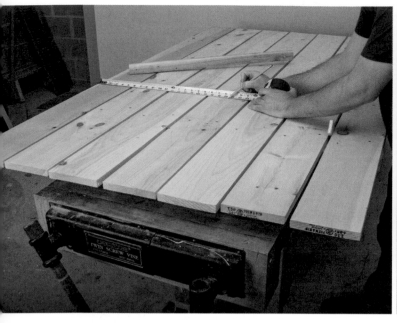

5 MARK THE PIVOT POINT. Mark the point centered across the width of the gate slats and 24 in. down from the top.

6 DRAW THE ARC. Set a compass for a 24-in. radius (see "Make a Beam Compass," p. 41) and put the compass's pivot on the pivot point. Draw an arc across the top of the gate.

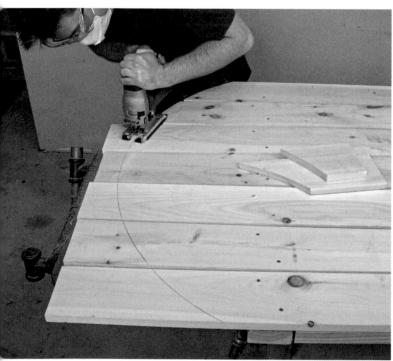

7 CUT THE ARC. Use a sabersaw to follow the arc layout, cutting off the top of all the slats.

8 SAND THE EDGES. Sand the edges of the outside slats, rounding them slightly. Pay particular attention to the arc—that's where people will be grabbing the gate to open and close it.

Make and Install the Gate Header

The 2x8 header ties the gate together visually and structurally. With the header in place, the two gateposts share the weight of the gate, instead of just the hinged post. You'll cut a piece of nominal 2x8 (actual dimensions 1½ in. x 7¼ in.) to 42 in. long to fit between the posts. Then you'll use the same beam compass to draw an arc on the bottom of the header. You'll cut an arc and install the header with pocket-hole screws.

1 **CUT THE HEADER AND MARK THE CENTER.** Cut the header to length with a power miter saw or circular saw. Clamp it across the workbench. Measure 21 in. up one edge, then use a square to strike a line across the header at that point. Make a center point mark at 3⅝ in. along the line.

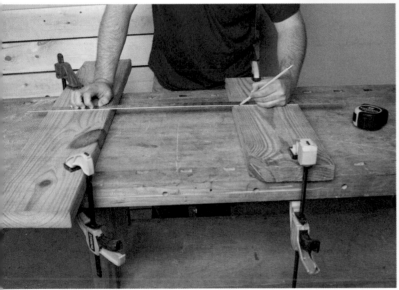

2 **SET UP A PIVOT BOARD.** When you marked the gate, the pivot point was on the gate, but for the narrow header, you need a pivot board because the pivot point falls off the header. The pivot board is the offcut from your 2x8 or any other scrap of 1½-in.-thick wood. Clamp it to the bench less than 24 in. away from the header, then use a straightedge to extend the line on the header across to the pivot board.

3 **DRAW AND CUT THE ARC.** Place the pencil of the compass on the header center point and the compass pivot on the line you drew on the pivot board. Draw the arc and make the cut with a sabersaw.

4 MARK OUT THE HEADER POSITION ON THE POSTS.
Use a square to draw horizontal lines on opposing faces of the gateposts, 2 in. from the top. Set a combination square to ¾ in., and draw vertical lines to about 8 in. down from the horizontal lines.

5 DRILL POCKET HOLES AND INSTALL THE HEADER.
Drill four evenly spaced pocket holes on each end of the header. Align the top and front of the header to the layout lines and attach it with eight 2½-in. exterior pocket-hole screws.

Install the Saddle and Gate

The gate will close against the saddle, which is a 42-in.-long piece of 2x4 that runs between the posts and is partially buried in the ground. After installing the saddle, you'll staple the burrow barrier to it and fill in the trench, completing your defense against critter attack. After installing the saddle, you will hang the gate and install its latch. The latch used here will work on either fence post.

1 LAY OUT THE SADDLE POSITION ON THE POSTS.
You want at least 1¾ in. of the saddle's width to protrude from the ground—if the ground slopes between the gateposts, it will protrude more than 1¾ in. on the downslope. So begin by using a square to mark 1¾ in. above the upslope post. Use a combination square to draw a vertical line ¾ in. from the outside of the post. Draw the vertical line on the opposing post, too.

2 **ATTACH THE SADDLE.** Drill two pocket-screw holes in each end of the saddle. Place the saddle between the posts with the front at the vertical lines on both posts and the top of one end at the horizontal line. Use a 2-ft. level to make the saddle level, then attach it with 2½-in. pocket-hole screws. Now you can staple the burrow barrier to the inside of the saddle and fill in the trench.

3 **HANG THE GATE.** Measure up 54 in. from the top of the saddle and use a square to strike a line across the post. Have a helper hold the gate in position with a level across the top rail and the top hinge aligned to the line while you drive a provided screw into the hinge. Then drive all the screws into the bottom hinge before returning to complete the screws for the top hinge.

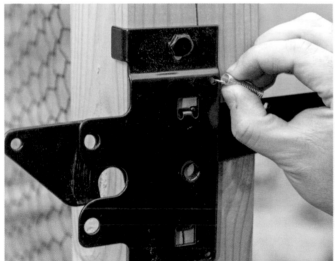

4 **INSTALL THE LATCH.** Put the latch in position on the post at the same height as the gate's top rail and mark for the two bolt holes. Predrill ¼-in. holes, then insert the bolts with a socket or box wrench. Attach the spring that makes the latch close on the bolt.

5 **INSTALL THE BOLT.** Close the gate and put the bolt in position in the latch. Mark, predrill, and install the two attachment bolts.

CHAPTER THREE

Garden Trellis

VINING VEGGIES like peas and cukes love to climb this simple trellis that you can build in just a few hours. A trellis makes much more efficient use of your garden space. It makes weeding and harvesting easier, plus your cukes will be a nice uniform green instead of white on the bottom from growing on the ground.

The A-frame trellis is hinged at the top so you can fold it up for storage at season's end. We used hex-web fencing left over from the critter-proof fence project on p. 24, but you can use any kind of chicken wire or other metal mesh.

This trellis is built from pressure-treated nominal 1x2s (actual dimensions ¾ in. x 1½ in.) and 1x4s (¾ in. x 3½ in.) available at home centers and lumberyards. If you have a tablesaw and a bunch of scrap 1x material lying around, you could easily rip it up into the dimensions you need.

- 4 legs
  ¾ in. x 1½ in. x 72 in.,
  pressure-treated lumber

- 4 cleats
  ¾ in. x 1½ in. x 53 in.,
  pressure-treated lumber

- 4 long rails
  ¾ in. x 3½ in. x 44 in.,
  pressure-treated lumber

- 4 short rails
  ¾ in. x 3½ in. x 41 in.,
  pressure-treated lumber

HARDWARE

- 1 hex-web fencing 43 in. x 59 in.
- 2 butt hinges ¾ in. x 3 in.
- 1¼-in. deck screws

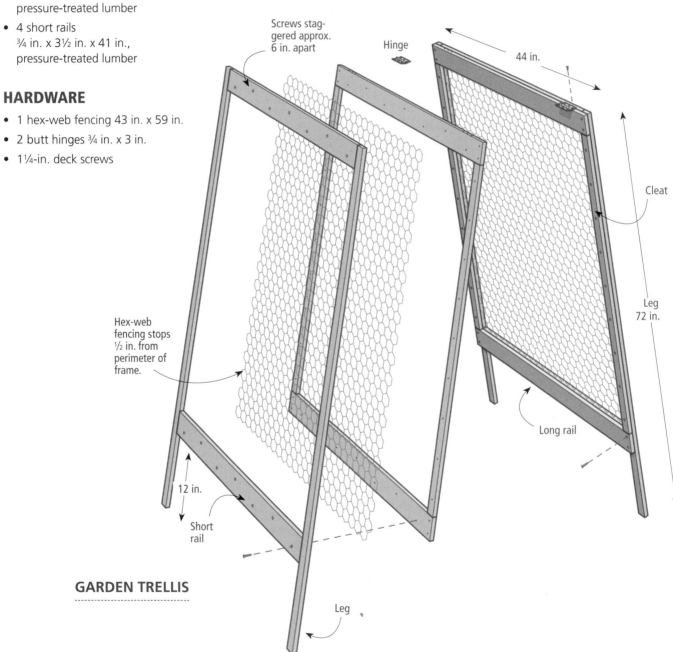

Screws staggered approx. 6 in. apart

Hinge

44 in.

Cleat

Hex-web fencing stops ½ in. from perimeter of frame.

Leg 72 in.

Long rail

12 in.

Short rail

Leg

GARDEN TRELLIS

Cut and Assemble the Pieces

The A-frame consists of two identical panels. Each panel is two layers of wood with the hex-web fencing stapled in place and sandwiched between. You'll start by cutting all the parts to length and the two pieces of fencing to size. Then you will assemble each panel individually. The last step is installing the hinges.

> **TIP** If you are using the 90-in.-wide hex-web fencing used in the critter-proof fence, cut a 59-in.-long piece and then cut the two 43-in.-wide pieces from that.

1 **CUT THE PARTS TO LENGTH AND THE FENCING TO SIZE.** Cut all of the wooden parts to the lengths listed in "What You'll Need." A power miter saw is the most convenient tool for cutting the parts to length but, as shown here, a hand miter saw will do a fine job as will a circular saw. Cut two pieces of mesh to the dimensions in "What You'll Need."

2 **LAY OUT THE MESH POSITION ON THE FIRST LEG.** Clamp one leg to your bench so it won't slide around. Make a mark 12½ in. from the bottom of each leg. Set a combination square to ½ in. and use it to make a mark ½ in. from the top of the leg and to draw a line along the outside edge down to the 12½-in. mark.

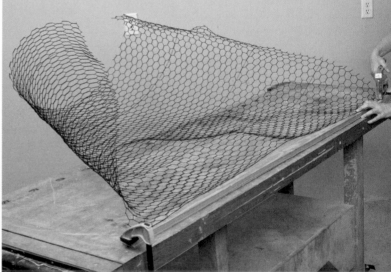

3 **STAPLE THE MESH TO THE FIRST LEG.** Align a 59-in.-long side of the mesh along the line and at the two marks. Staple both ends first and then secure the mesh to the leg with staples every few inches.

> **TIP** It's a good idea to set the staples with a hammer blow to make sure they hold the mesh securely.

4 **ATTACH THE TOP LONG RAIL.** Clamp the top long rail across the first leg. Make sure it is flush on the end and use a square to check that it is square to the leg. To prevent splitting, predrill two ⅛-in.-dia. holes, then attach the rail to the leg with two 1¼-in. deck screws.

5 **ATTACH THE FIRST CLEAT.** Clamp a cleat in place butted against the top rail and flush to the outside of the leg you already installed. Predrill holes about 6 in. apart, and screw the cleat to the leg.

6 **STAPLE THE FENCING TO THE TOP RAIL.** Flip the assembly over and staple the mesh to the top rail.

7 **ATTACH THE SECOND LEG.** Flip the assembly again. Slip the second leg in place under the top long rail. Clamp, square, predrill, and drive two screws through the rail into the leg.

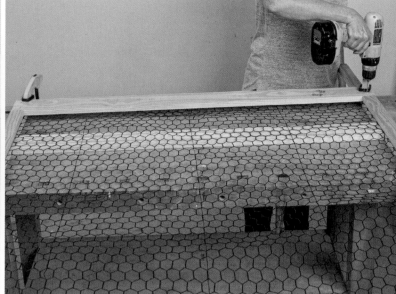

8 **STAPLE THE FENCING TO THE SECOND LEG, AND INSTALL THE SECOND CLEAT.** Put a short rail between the legs as a spacer so you don't pull the legs out of square while you staple the mesh to the second leg. Clamp, predrill, and screw the second cleat in place as you did the first.

9 **INSTALL THE BOTTOM LONG RAIL AND STAPLE FENCING TO IT.** Butt the bottom outside rail against the cleats flush to the outside, check for square, clamp, predrill, and secure with two screws at each end. Flip the assembly and staple the fencing to the bottom long rail.

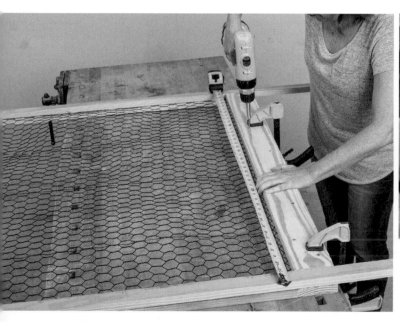

10 **INSTALL THE SHORT RAILS.** Put the top and bottom short rails in place over the long rails, and attach them with screws about every 6 in. Stagger the screws as shown. Repeat steps 1–10 for the second panel.

11 **INSTALL THE HINGES.** Stack the panels with the inside faces against each other and all edges flush. Clamp them together. Draw lines across the tops 3 in. from the outside edges. Clamp a hinge in place along the inside of the line and predrill five of the six holes. (The sixth hole will be covered by the clamp.) Insert provided screws into those holes, then remove the clamp and predrill and insert the last screw. Repeat for the other hinge.

CHAPTER FOUR

Garden Shed

THIS STURDY AND HANDSOME SHED
is 8 ft. wide and 6 ft. deep, offering plenty of storage for all your gardening tools and materials. There's even room to include a potting bench like the project on p. 100. The shed has large locking double doors for security and easy access.

There are many steps involved in building a shed, but none of them is complicated. If you have never framed a building before, this is a great project to start with. The roof is the simplest kind to build—called, appropriately enough, a shed roof, it slopes in just one direction. The walls are covered with plywood siding panels, which are also used to make the doors.

The siding and door panels received two coats of solid-color stain. Whether you choose solid, semi-solid, or transparent, stain soaks into the rough-textured surface of the siding panels, producing an excellent, durable finish. The trim boards received a coat of stain-blocking primer followed by two coats of semi-gloss exterior paint.

WHAT YOU'LL NEED

FOUNDATION AND FLOOR FRAMING

- 1 ton quarry process gravel and stone dust mix
- 3 gravel frame pieces
  ¾ in. x 3½ in. x length as needed*
- 2 foundation skids
  3½ in. x 5½ in. x 96 in., pressure treated
- 2 header joists
  1½ in. x 5½ in. x 96 in., pressure treated
- 7 joists
  1½ in. x 5½ in. x 69 in.
- 1 floor panel
  ¾ in. x 48 in. x 96 in., pressure-treated plywood
- 1 floor panel
  ¾ in. x 24 in. x 96 in., pressure-treated plywood

*For sloped site only

FRAMING

- 3 back- and front-wall plates
  1½ in. x 3½ in. x 96 in.
- 1 front-wall cap plate
  1½ in. x 3½ in. x 96 in.
- 1 back-wall cap plate
  1½ in. x 3½ in. x 89 in.
- 2 side-wall cap plates
  1½ in. x 3½ in. x 68½ in.
- 4 side-wall plates
  1½ in. x 3½ in. x 65 in.
- 2 front bottom plates
  1½ in. x 3½ in. x 14 in.
- 2 door header pieces
  1½ in. x 3½ in. x 71 in.
- 1 door header piece
  ½ in. x 3½ in. x 71 in. particleboard
- 2 window header pieces
  1½ in. x 3½ in. x 38¼ in.
- 1 window header piece
  ½ in. x 3½ in. x 38¼ in. particleboard

- 4 front-wall king studs
  1½ in. x 3½ in. x 92 in.
- 2 front-wall jack studs
  1½ in. x 3½ in. x 74 in.
- 2 back-wall jack studs
  1½ in. x 3½ in. x 61½ in. back wall
- 5 front-wall cripple studs
  1½ in. x 3½ in. x 10 in.
- 18 back- and side-wall king studs
  1½ in. x 3½ in. x 65 in.
- 1 window saddle
  1½ in. x 3½ in. x 35¼ in.
- 3 window cripple studs
  1½ in. x 3½ in. x 49¾ in.
- 7 rafters
  1½ in. x 3½ in. x 86⅜ in.
- 2 siding nailers
  1½ in. x 3½ in. x 14½ in.

ROOF

- 1 roof panel
  ½ in. x 48 in. x 96 in., oriented strand board
- 1 roof panel
  ½ in. x 38⅜ in. x 96 in., oriented strand board
- 1 roll felt roofing underlayment
- 4 pieces drip edge, cut to fit
- 2 bundles (66.6 sq. ft.) asphalt roofing shingles

SIDING

- 2 back panels
  ⅜ in. x 48 in. x 71⅞ in.
- 2 side panels
  ⅜ in. x 24 in. x 96 in.
- 2 side panels
  ⅜ in. x 48 in. x 91⅜ in.
- 2 front panels
  ⅜ in. x 38 in. x 96 in.

RAKES, SOFFITS, AND FASCIA

- 2 rake boards
  ¾ in. x 5½ in. x 96 in. rough length
- 2 soffit boards
  ¾ in. x 5½ in. rough width x 96 in.
- 2 fascia boards
  ¾ in. x 5½ in. x 96 in.

TRIM

- 4 front corner boards
  ¾ in. x 3½ in. x 96 in. rough length
- 4 back corner boards
  ¾ in. x 3½ in. x 73 in. rough length
- 1 top door casing
  ¾ in. x 3½ in. x 78 in. rough length
- 2 side door casings
  ¾ in. x 3½ in. x 80½ in.
- 2 window top and bottom casings
  ¾ in. x 3½ in. x 42 in.
- 2 window side casings
  ¾ in. x 3½ in. x 10 in.

DOORS

- 1 interior panel
  ⅜ in. x 34⅝ in. x 74½ in. siding
- 1 interior panel
  ⅜ in. x 31⅞ in. x 74½ in. siding
- 2 exterior panels
  ⅜ in. x 34⅝ in. x 78 in. siding
- 4 frame stiles
  1½ in. x 3½ in. x 74½ in.
- 3 left frame rails
  1½ in. x 3½ in. x 27⅝ in.
- 4 trim stiles
  ¾ in. x 3½ in. x 78¼ in.
- 3 right frame rails
  1½ in. x 3½ in. x 24⅞ in.
- 6 trim rails
  ¾ in. x 3½ in. x 27⅝ in.

HARDWARE AND SUPPLIES

- Inverted marking paint
- Mason's twine
- 1¼-in. deck screws*
- 6 angle connectors
  1½ in. x 2¾ in.
- 48 structural connector screws
  ¼ in. dia. x 1½ in.
- 1 tube construction adhesive
- 2-in. deck screws
- 8d common nails
- 10d common nails
- 16d common nails
- 1-in. aluminum roofing nails
- 6d oval-head siding nails and/or
  siding nails for power nailer
- 8d oval-head siding nails
- 1 window 10 in. x 35 in.**
- 1⅝-in. deck screws
- 2½-in. deck screws
- 6 T-hinges 6 in.**
- 2 barrel bolts**
- 1 locking T-handle**

* For sloped site only
** Available from shedwindowsandmore.com

Centering the Shed

To center the shed between fence posts (see the drawing on p. 29), subtract 8 ft. from the distance between posts and divide the remainder in two. For example, our posts are 24 ft. 4½ in. apart. Subtracting 8 ft. leaves 16 ft. 4½ in. Dividing by 2 tells us that the front corners of the shed will be 8 ft. 2¼ in. from the posts.

This shed will be a great addition to any yard, even if you don't have a vegetable garden. However, for the ultimate in vegetable gardening convenience, the shed shown here opens into the critter-proof garden fence project that begins on p. 24. This puts everything you need right at hand and easy to put away when your work is done.

Lay Out the Perimeter

The shed shown here is accessible from the inside of the critter-proof fence, so you'll start by aligning the front of the shed to strings run between the inside of the corner garden posts. If the shed will stand alone, just drive a stake in the ground where you want one front corner, measure out 8 ft. for the other front corner, and drive another stake in the ground. Tie string between the stakes.

Once your front wall is defined, you'll locate and drive stakes at the back corners. You'll run string between all the stakes and then use inverting marking paint to mark the shed perimeter on the ground.

1 **LAY OUT THE FRONT OF THE SHED.** Run mason's twine from the inside of one corner post to the opposing post. Measure from one post along the string and use inverted marking paint to locate one front corner of the shed. Drive a stake into the ground at that point. Hook your tape on the stake and measure 8 ft. along the line to locate the other corner. Paint a mark and drive in a stake at the other front corner.

2 **LAY OUT A PERPENDICULAR SIDE.** Hook your tape on one of the front stakes and pull it out past 6 ft. Hook another tape on the other front stake and pull it out past 10 ft. Align the 6-ft. mark on the first tape with the 10-ft. mark on the diagonal tape and drive in a stake at that point.

3 **FIND THE FOURTH CORNER.** Hook a tape measure on the back corner stake you just placed and pull it out 8 ft. Hook another tape measure on the front stake on that side and pull it out past 6 ft. Insert a stake where the 8-ft. mark on the first tape meets the 6-ft. mark on the other.

4 **MARK THE PERIMETER.** Run strings between all the stakes. Then use inverted marking paint to mark the perimeter of the shed on the ground. Remove the string but leave the stakes.

> **TIP** The 3-4-5 method is an easy way to make something square: If one side of a right triangle is 3 ft. long and another side is 4 ft. long, the diagonal hypotenuse will be 5 ft. long. Of course, you can use any multiple—6-8-10 is convenient for a 6-ft. x 8-ft. shed.

Prepare the Foundation

This shed has a "skid" foundation, which means that it sits on a pair of 8-ft.-long 4x6s. First, you will prepare a level base for the skids. The base consists of a gravel and stone dust mix called quarry process (QP). This mix drains better than stone dust alone and compacts better than gravel alone. Then, if your site is level, you just need to dig the shed area down about 3 in. If the site slopes, you'll create a three-sided gravel frame to contain the QP on the downslope side. The last step is setting and leveling the skids.

1 **FIND THE SLOPE. Dig out the upslope side to 3 in.** Place the end of a long board along one sloped side with the end of the board in the upslope corner. Put a level on the board and raise the board until it is level. Measure the distance between the bottom of the board and the ground at the downslope corner. Repeat this process on the other side. The distance in this case was 3½ in., so we used pressure-treated 1x4s for the frame. If your slope doesn't happen to correspond to a standard lumber increment, just partially bury a board to get to the right height— for example, bury 1½ in. of a 1x6 to get to 4 in.

2 **EXCAVATE THE SLOPED SIDES.** Cut a pressure-treated 1x board (in this case a 1x4) to either 6 ft. long or 8 ft. long, whichever you need to span the downslope side. Prop this board up against the perimeter stakes. Dig out swaths about 10 in. wide along both sloped sides until a long board is level when you place one end in an upslope corner and rest the other end on the frame board.

3 **INSTALL THE FRAME.** Cut two pieces of 1x long enough to contain the gravel along the sloped sides—the boards can end where the sides get about 1 in. deep. Attach the downslope frame board to these pieces with two 1¼-in. screws on each end. Then fill the perimeter excavation with gravel. Next, excavate the inside of the footprint until it is approximately level—the inside doesn't need to be perfectly level because the foundation skids will rest at the perimeter.

4 **PLACE THE FOUNDATION SKIDS.** Set the 4x6 foundation skids in place with their outside faces 6 ft. apart on both ends. Check the skids for level along their length and across both ends, adding or removing QP if necessary. If you are concerned about critters burrowing under your shed, see "Keeping Out the Groundhogs" below.

Keeping Out the Groundhogs

This shed was built in conjunction with the critter-proof garden fence (see p. 24) in an area with a groundhog problem. Groundhogs love to dig holes under structures. For this reason, we excavated the entire shed footprint and laid down hex-web fencing and then QP to prevent groundhogs from burrowing under the shed.

Later, after the joists were installed, we stapled 2-ft.-wide hex-web fencing along the three sides of the shed that will be outside the fence. The fencing is stapled near the top of the joists where it will be overlapped by the shed siding. It extends a few inches down and then it's bent out at about 90 degrees before being covered by earth.

If groundhogs are not a concern where you live, there is no need to excavate or put gravel in the middle of the shed footprint. Just make sure the 8-ft.-long sides are level and at the same height.

Build the Floor

The two header joists will be installed flush to the outside of the skids with seven joists running between them as shown in the "Floor Framing Plan" at right. You'll start by laying out the joist positions along the header joists. Next, you'll attach the header joists to the skids with angle connectors to anchor the shed to the skids. You'll nail the joists in place and then you'll install the plywood floor.

TIP Sometimes framing lumber actually is its stated length; sometimes it's a little longer. If you bought 8-footers for the header joists, check their length before you install them. They might need a trim.

FLOOR FRAMING PLAN

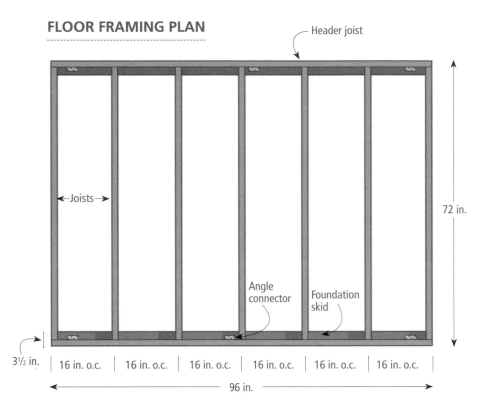

Header joist

←Joists→

72 in.

Angle connector

Foundation skid

3½ in.

16 in. o.c. | 16 in. o.c. | 16 in. o.c. | 16 in. o.c. | 16 in. o.c. | 16 in. o.c.

96 in.

1 **MARK THE HEADER JOIST.** Put the two 2x6 header joists together with ends flush and edges up. Hook a tape on one end and mark for joists spaced 16 in. on center as shown in the "Floor Framing Plan." Use a square to strike lines at the marks and draw Xs to mark the joist side of the lines (see "Marking on Center" on the facing page). Separate the header joists and use a square to extend the marks onto one face of each.

2 **ATTACH THE HEADER JOISTS TO THE SKIDS.** Place the header joists flush to the outside and ends of the skids. Attach each to its skid with three 1½-in. x 2¾-in. angle connectors using 1½-in. structural connector screws into all holes. Position the connectors about 4 in. from each end and one near the middle. Make sure you don't cover any Xs.

3 **ATTACH THE JOISTS TO THE HEADER JOIST.** Cut the seven joists to 69 in. long. Put them in place between the header joists and drive two 16d nails through the header faces into the end of each joist.

TIP The floor is made of ¾-in. pressure-treated plywood—you'll need one full 4-ft. x 8-ft. sheet and one 2-ft. x 8-ft. piece. Have the lumberyard or home center rip the narrow piece for you—they have a panel saw that quickly makes cuts that are square and straight.

4 **CHECK THAT THE FLOOR IS SQUARE.** Measure across diagonals. If the measurements differ, use a sledge to tap the skid at a corner where you got the longer measurement. When the measurements are the same, the floor is square.

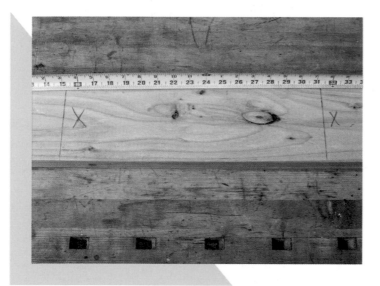

Marking on Center

When marking the header joists for joist spacing that will be 16 in. on center (o.c.), you actually want to strike lines that are ¾ in. to your left of on center and then draw an X to the right of the line. When you place a 1½-in.-thick joist along a line covering the X, it will be 16 in. o.c. Use the same method later when you mark out stud locations on the wall plates. But don't worry, there's no math to do. Tape measures indicate 16-in. intervals—on the tape shown here the numerals are in red, so you need only mark ¾ in. to the left of each red mark.

5 **APPLY CONSTRUCTION ADHESIVE.** Put a bead of construction adhesive on top of the joists and header joists. This step is not essential, but it will make the floor stronger and prevent it from squeaking.

6 **INSTALL THE FULL FLOOR SHEET.** Put the full plywood sheet across the joists, making sure it is flush at all three sides. Then attach it around its perimeter with 2-in. deck screws. Put one screw into each joist along the inside edge of the sheet and screws along the perimeter spaced about 12 in. apart.

7 **COMPLETE THE FLOOR AND SNAP LINES.** Put the half-sheet of plywood in place, making sure it is flush on the outside, and insert screws into the end joists and header joists. Then, using the nails through the header as a guide, snap lines across the two sheets along the center of each joist's width. Add screws along these lines.

Install the Bottom Plate and Lay Out the Studs

The side walls and back walls of this shed are all the same height, while the front wall is taller to create the roof slope. Each wall has three plates—a bottom plate, a top plate, and a cap plate that's attached to the top plate.

For the back wall, the bottom and top plates run the full 8 ft. of the shed length, while the cap plate stops 3½ in. short of each end. This allows the side cap plates to overlap the back top plates, helping to tie the shed together.

There is no bottom plate under the door, so the front wall has 14-in.-long bottom plates at each side, flush to the corners. Because the front wall is taller, cap plates can't overlap at the front corners. So the front top plate and front cap plate both run the full 8 ft. The side walls butt into the front walls and will be attached by nails through the studs.

You'll start by installing the bottom plates. Then you'll stack and toe-nail the top and cap plates over the bottom plates. This makes it easy to lay out the stud positions. There are three types of studs: King studs go from bottom plate to top plate; jack studs go from bottom plate to under the door header or window saddle; and cripple studs go over the door header and under the saddle. Note that there are studs every 16 in. o.c. for nailing the siding and then jacks and cripples as required by the openings.

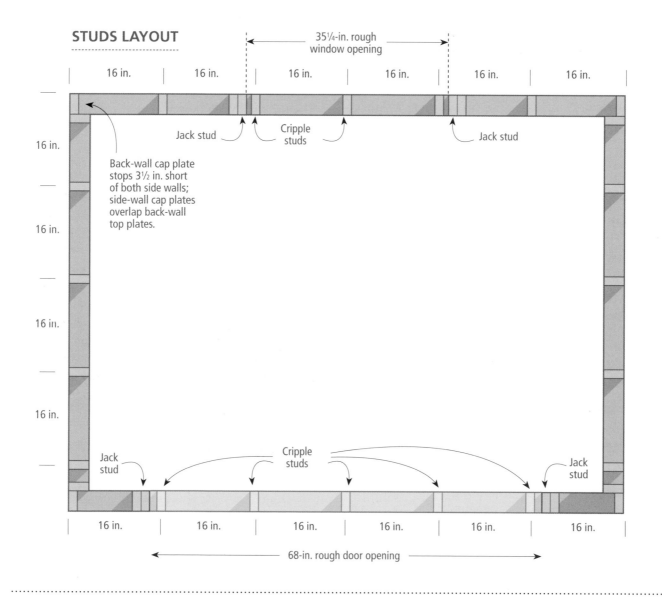

STUDS LAYOUT

35¼-in. rough window opening

16 in.   16 in.   16 in.   16 in.   16 in.   16 in.

Jack stud   Cripple studs   Jack stud

16 in.

Back-wall cap plate stops 3½ in. short of both side walls; side-wall cap plates overlap back-wall top plates.

16 in.

16 in.

16 in.

Jack stud   Cripple studs   Jack stud

16 in.   16 in.   16 in.   16 in.   16 in.   16 in.

68-in. rough door opening

1 **SNAP THE PLATE LINES.** The plate lines will help you keep the bottom plates square when you install them. Snap these chalklines 3½ in. from all four edges.

2 **CUT AND INSTALL THE BOTTOM PLATES.** Use a circular saw or power miter saw to cut all the bottom plates to the lengths listed in "What You'll Need." Install them with 16d common nails staggered with at least one nail every 16 in. Don't nail through the layout Xs, so these nails won't get in the way later when you toe-nail the studs to the bottom plates. Make sure the bottom plates are flush to the outside of the floor.

3 **STACK THE TOP AND CAP PLATES.** Put the top plates in their positions and tack them to the bottom plates with a few 8d nails toe-driven through the outside of the top plates. Drive the nails just far enough to hold the boards in place—don't drive them home. Now put the cap plates in place and attach them to the top plates with 8d nails staggered 16 in. o.c.

TIP Don't use 16d nails to install the 14-in.-long front bottom lengths—the nails will surely split the wood. Instead, install them with four 8d nails, two toe-nailed through each end of these short plates.

Name That Stud

Stud terminology: A king stud runs between a top plate and a bottom plate. A jack stud runs from a bottom plate to a header. Jacks, sometimes called trimmer studs, are nailed to a king. A cripple stud runs either between the bottom plate and a sill or between a header and a top plate.

4 **LAY OUT THE STUD LOCATIONS.** The drawing "Studs Layout" (p. 61) shows the stud locations. Use a square to strike layout lines across the cap plates, using Xs to indicate king studs and Os to indicate jacks and cripples. Then extend the lines down the outside of all three plate layers. Add X and O designations to the sides of the bottom and top plates as shown in the photo.

Build the Headers and Front Wall

With all of the stud positions laid out, you are ready to pull the tack nails to separate the top and cap plate assemblies from the bottom plate.

You'll start framing the walls by making the headers for the door and window openings. Both headers are made of ½-in.-thick particleboard or plywood spacers between two pieces of 2x4. This makes the headers 3½ in. thick to match the width of the studs.

You'll cut all the studs for the front wall and then assemble the jack studs to the king studs. You'll attach these assemblies to the top plate and then install the door header. You'll add the other king studs and then the cripple studs over the header before raising the wall and attaching it to the bottom plate. Finally, you'll temporarily brace the wall.

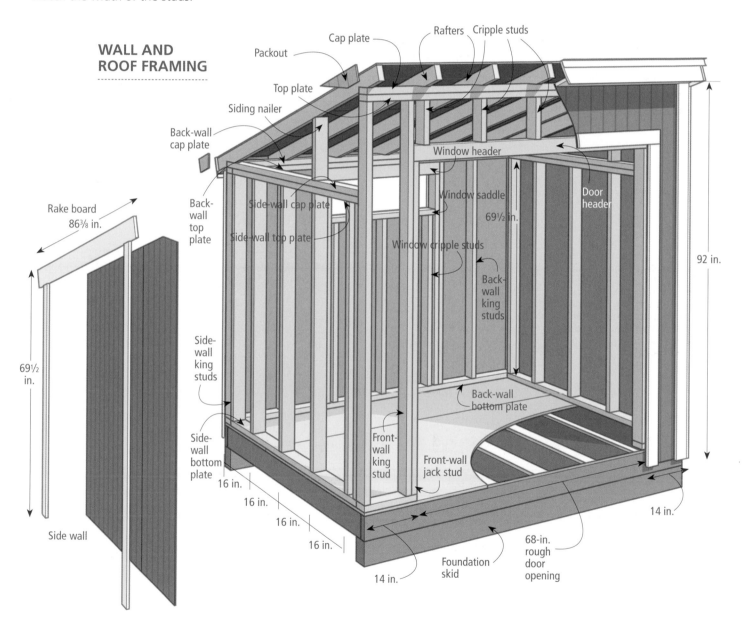

WALL AND ROOF FRAMING

Packout

Cap plate

Rafters

Cripple studs

Top plate

Siding nailer

Back-wall cap plate

Window header

Rake board 86⅜ in.

Back-wall top plate

Side-wall cap plate

Side-wall top plate

Window saddle

Door header

69½ in.

Window cripple studs

Back-wall king studs

92 in.

Side-wall king studs

69½ in.

Back-wall bottom plate

Side-wall bottom plate

Front-wall king stud

Front-wall jack stud

Side wall

16 in.

16 in.

16 in.

16 in.

14 in.

Foundation skid

68-in. rough door opening

14 in.

TIP If you purchased two 4x8 sheets of ½-in. particleboard for the roof sheathing, you can rip 3½ in. from the long edge of one panel to make the headers and still have enough to cover the roof.

1 **CUT THE HEADER PIECES.** Cut the window header and door header lumber and particleboard to the lengths listed in "What You'll Need." Use a rip fence on your circular saw to rip a 3½-in.-wide piece of particleboard, then crosscut the rip to the lengths specified.

2 **ASSEMBLE THE HEADERS.** For each header, put the particleboard spacer between the two pieces of 2x4 and make sure it is flush on all sides. Drive 8d nails spaced about 16 in. apart through one side, then flip the header over and drive nails approximately centered between the nails on the other side.

Rip Guide

A rip guide is an inexpensive accessory for your circular saw that makes it easy to cut straight, narrow rips, especially on sheet goods that are too wide to move through a tablesaw. This one has a maximum rip width of about 5 in.

3 **CUT THE PARTS AND INSTALL THE DOOR ROUGH-OPENING STUDS.** Cut the front-wall king studs and jack studs to the lengths listed in "What You'll Need." Nail each jack stud to a king stud with 8d nails staggered 16 in. apart. Make sure the studs are flush on the bottom. Toe-nail the studs to the bottom of the top plate with the jacks to the inside of the opening. Use one nail on a 1½-in.-wide face to position the stud and two into each 3½-in.-wide face.

4 **INSTALL THE DOOR HEADER.** Put the door header in place atop the jack studs. Attach it with two 16d nails through the face of each stud. Position the nails so one goes into each end of each of the header boards.

TIP Here's a quick and accurate way to use a circular saw to cut two 1½-in.-thick pieces, such as the front-wall jack studs, to exactly the same length: Clamp the two pieces together with sides and one end flush. Lay out the cut on the top piece. Set your circular saw to maximum cutting depth and make the cut. The top piece will be cut all the way through, while the bottom piece will be cut partway through. Remove the top piece, put the sawblade in the second piece's kerf, and complete the cut.

5 **ATTACH THE END STUDS AND CRIPPLE STUDS.** Toe-nail a king stud to each end of the top plate. Strike lines across the top of the header to locate the cripple studs. The cripple studs should be 10 in. long, but measure for a snug fit and then cut them to length. Toe-nail the cripple studs to the header and top plate.

6 **ATTACH THE FRONT WALL TO THE BOTTOM PLATE.** With a helper, raise the front wall into place and toe-nail all the studs to the bottom plate.

7 **BRACE THE FRONT WALL.** To hold the front wall upright until the side walls are installed, nail diagonal braces between the outside of the end studs and the side bottom plates.

Build the Back Wall and Side Walls

You'll start by cutting all the remaining king studs to length. Then you'll attach the back-wall kings to the top plate and attach the header before raising the back wall and attaching it to the bottom plate. You'll cut the jack studs to fit under the header and install them. You'll assemble the side walls without their end king studs. Then you'll nail those end kings to the front wall before raising and attaching the side walls. You'll add the back wall cripples and window saddle.

It is important for the shed walls to be plumb before you install the rafters. Buildings, especially little buildings like a shed, are not sturdy laterally until they are sheathed. So you will check the walls for plumb, shove them into position if they are not, and temporarily brace them with diagonal 2x4s.

TIP Because the back-wall and side-wall studs are all the same length, you'll save time if you cut them on a power miter saw with a stop (see "Making and Using a Stop Block," p. 171).

1 **CUT REMAINING STUDS AND ASSEMBLE THE BACK WALL.** Cut all the back-wall and side-wall king studs to the lengths listed in "What You'll Need." Toe-nail six king studs to the back-wall top plate. Butt the header under the top plate and secure it with 16d nails through the studs as you did for the door header.

2 **INSTALL THE BACK WALL AND ADD THE JACKS.** Raise the back wall and toe-nail the studs to the bottom plate. The jack studs should be 61½ in. long, but measure and cut them for a snug fit. Toe-nail the jacks up into the header with one 8d nail at each connection. Then face-nail the jacks to the studs with 16d nails as you did the door jacks.

3 **FRAME A SIDE WALL.** Toe-nail the four intermediate studs to a side-wall top plate, but don't attach the end studs.

4 **INSTALL THE END STUDS.** Remove one front wall brace. Nail side-wall end studs to a front-wall end stud using a 10d nail every 16 in. or so. Nail another side-wall end stud to the back-wall end stud in the same way.

5 **INSTALL THE SIDE WALLS.** Raise the side wall into place and toe-nail it to the bottom plate. Then drive two 16d nails through the side-wall cap plate into the back-wall top plate. Toe-nail one 8d nail through the cap plate into the front wall end stud. Toe-nail two 8d nails up through each end stud into the bottom of the top plate. Build and install the other side wall in the same way.

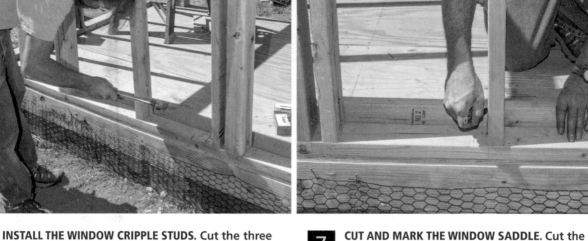

6   **INSTALL THE WINDOW CRIPPLE STUDS.** Cut the three window cripple studs to 49¾ in. long and toe-nail them to the bottom plate.

7   **CUT AND MARK THE WINDOW SADDLE.** Cut the saddle to 35¼ in. long. Place the saddle against the bottom of the cripples to scribe the cripple positions on the saddle.

8   **INSTALL THE SADDLE.** Put the saddle atop the cripples. Position the top of each cripple to its line under the saddle and then drive two 10d nails through the saddle into each cripple. Toe-nail the saddle to the jack studs.

9   **PLUMB AND BRACE THE SHED.** Check each side of each corner for plumb. If it is out of plumb, push or pull it into place. Then nail a diagonal brace to the inside of the studs.

Install the Rafters

You'll install seven rafters at 16 in. o.c. The rafters have a pitch that travels 4 in. vertically (rise) for every 12 in. horizontally (run); this is known as 4:12 pitch. That's an angle of 18.43 degrees, but you won't have to do any math to lay out the rafter cuts—you'll simply scribe the cuts in place. Then you'll cut one rafter and test its fit before using it as a template to cut the other rafters. You'll nail the rafters to the front and rear cap plates and then add a nailer to each side where the two siding panels will meet over the cap plate.

1 TACK A PATTERN RAFTER TO THE SHED. With a helper, tack-nail an 8-ft. 2x4 along the outside of the shed with the bottom of the 2x4 aligned to the top outside corner of the front cap plate and the bottom outside corner of the back-wall plate as shown in the drawing "Rafter Cut Layout" (p. 70). Make sure the overhangs on both sides are approximately equal.

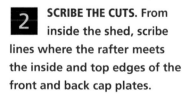

2 SCRIBE THE CUTS. From inside the shed, scribe lines where the rafter meets the inside and top edges of the front and back cap plates.

3 LAY OUT THE END CUTS. As shown in "Rafter Cut Layout," measure 5¼ in. out along the bottom of the rafter from the top of the front seat cut and the bottom of the back plumb cut. From these points, lay out square cuts across the rafter. The rafters should be 86⅜ in. long as listed in "What You'll Need," but yours may be a slightly different length.

4 MAKE THE PLUMB CUTS, SEAT CUTS, AND END CUTS. Use a circular saw to cut up to the intersection of the seat and plumb lines on both ends of the pattern rafter. Complete the cuts with a handsaw or sabersaw. Then cut the rafters to length along the end cutlines. Test-fit the pattern rafter on the shed, then use it to lay out cuts for the other six rafters. Cut all the rafters.

RAFTER CUT LAYOUT

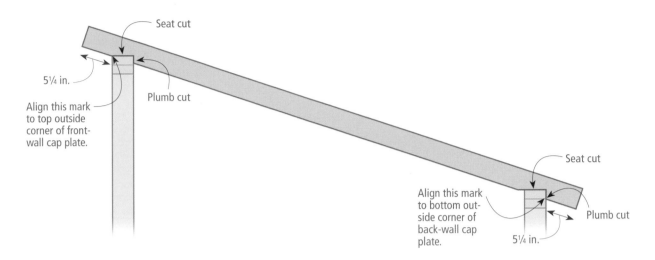

Seat cut

5¼ in.

Align this mark to top outside corner of front-wall cap plate.

Plumb cut

Seat cut

Align this mark to bottom out-side corner of back-wall cap plate.

5¼ in.

Plumb cut

5 **INSTALL THE RAFTERS.** Lay out the rafter positions 16 in. o.c. across the front and back cap plates with lines and Xs. Toe-nail the rafters to the front and back cap plates. Use one nail into each side of each end of the rafters.

6 **MEASURE FOR THE SIDING NAILERS.** The 6-ft.-wide sides of the shed will be covered with one full-width 4-ft. x 8-ft. sheet of siding and one half-width piece. So you will need something to nail the sheets to where they meet 4 ft. from the back above the cap plates. The nailer should be about 14½ in. long, but measure over the front edge of the stud at the 4-ft. position on each side so you can cut the nailers to fit.

7 **CUT AND INSTALL THE SIDING NAILERS.** Set your circular-saw blade angle to about 18½ degrees—the angle gauges on circular saws are not very accurate, but the angle need not be precise. Lay out a line across a piece of 2x4. Make the cut with the waste side to your right so that the long side of the angle will be on top. Install the nailers with four 8d nails. Toe-nail one into each side at the bottom and two on the long side of the angle into the rafter.

Sheathe the Roof and Install the Siding

The roof will be sheathed with ⅜-in. oriented strand board (OSB). You'll need one full 4-ft. x 8-ft. panel and a panel ripped to fit. Theoretically, the second panel will be 38⅜ in. long as listed in "What You'll Need." However, framing is never exact, so you'll start by installing the full sheet and then taking a measurement before cutting the second sheet.

With the roof sheathed, you're ready to install siding on the walls. When stud-built buildings are covered with nonstructural siding materials such as wood clapboards or vinyl, separate sheathing panels are used underneath to add lateral strength. The siding panels used here are designed to add lateral strength as well as stand up to weather exposure.

On this shed, the siding extends 4 in. below the floor surface. At the front, that means you'll use the full 8-ft. length of the sheets. At the back, the sheets will be 71⅞ in. long, while the side pieces will be cut to fit the slope of the roof.

You'll begin by cutting two full-width siding panels to length for the back wall. You'll install one and then cut out half of the window opening before installing the other and finishing the window-opening cut. Next, you'll cut and install the panels for the sides. You'll "pack out" the rafter overhangs with small pieces of siding plywood to make the overhangs flush with the rest of the siding on the side walls. This flush surface will be necessary because the rake boards are nailed to the siding and extend past the ends of the end rafters. Then you'll cut out the door openings from the two front panels and install those panels.

> **TIP** Sheathing panels often have lines printed on them indicating the location of framing that's 16 in. o.c. or 24 in. o.c. If lines aren't printed on your sheets, you can snap chalklines to locate the center of the rafters.

OSB or Plywood Roof Sheathing?

Plywood and oriented strand board (OSB) each have pros and cons for sheathing a roof, but when it comes to this little shed, it's a toss-up. Plywood will stand up better if repeatedly exposed to rain during construction—but you'll probably get this little roof shingled on the same day you sheathe it. OSB is cheaper than plywood—on two sheets you might save $6. OSB is also heavier, but again, you only have two sheets to lift.

1 **INSTALL THE LOWER ROOF-SHEATHING PANEL.** With a helper, put a full panel of sheathing on the roof and align it to the outside and downslope edges of the rafters. Hold it in place with one 8d nail in each corner. Then attach the sheathing with 8d nails about every 6 in. along the length of each rafter.

2 **CUT AND INSTALL THE UPPER SHEATHING PANEL.** Measure from the top edge of the lower sheathing panel to the top edge of a rafter. Snap a line at this width on the second sheathing panel and make the rip cut with a circular saw. Nail the second panel in place. (In this photo, one crew member cut and handed up the second panel while another crew member was still nailing off the first panel.)

3 **CUT THE BACK PANELS TO LENGTH.** Snap a chalkline across a siding panel at 71⅞ in. Set a circular saw for a shallow cut, make the cut, then snap a line and cut the second back panel.

Why Oval Heads?

If you happen to have a power siding nailer, of course you'll use that along with 6d nails designed for the tool to install the siding panels (although you'll still find it convenient to grab a hammer for the first few nails when you are putting up a panel).

For hand-nailing siding, 6d galvanized oval-head siding nails are an excellent choice and 8d galvanized oval-heads are great for installing trim boards. With care, you can drive most of the oval head just below the surface without marring the siding or trim, something you can't do with a flat-head nail. When you paint the siding and trim, oval heads become very inconspicuous. And while the oval head is a bit trickier to drive straight, you'll soon get the hang of it.

TIP Most siding panels are incised with vertical grooves intended to suggest vertical boards. To keep your nailing in line with studs, measure and mark 16 in. o.c. across a panel, then use the grooves as a visual clue to keep your nailing in a vertically straight line. If your siding doesn't have grooves, use a 4-ft. level to lay out plumb lines, locating the stud centers.

4 **INSTALL THE FIRST BACK PANEL.** Tuck one panel under the back of the rafters and flush to a corner. Attach it with 6d siding nails located 6 in. apart into the corner stud and the studs that are 16 in. and 32 in. o.c. from the corner. Don't nail the inside edge of the panel yet—panel edges meet at an overlap that you will nail through.

5 **CUT THE FIRST HALF OF THE WINDOW OPENING.** To keep the panel from flopping around while you cut it, secure it with one nail near the edge into the window header and one into the saddle. Then, working from inside the shed, use a reciprocating saw to cut the siding away from the rough opening.

6 **INSTALL THE SECOND BACK PANEL.** Put the second back panel in place, making sure that it's flush at the corner and aligned at the bottom with the first panel. Nail it in place through the studs at 16 in. o.c., using one row of nails through the panel overlap. Cut out the rest of the window opening.

7 **INSTALL THE WINDOW.** Put the window in the rough opening and secure it with roofing nails into every other hole in the window flange.

SIDE PANEL LAYOUTS

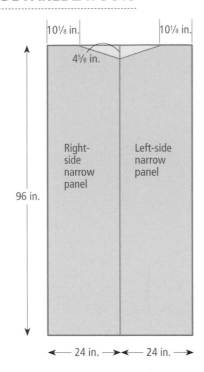

10⅛ in.   10⅛ in.

4⅝ in.

Right-side narrow panel

Left-side narrow panel

96 in.

← 24 in. → ← 24 in. →

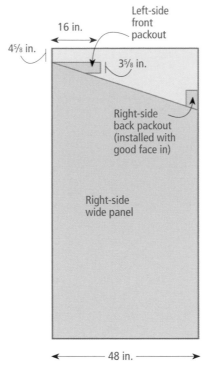

16 in.

Left-side front packout

4⅝ in.

3⅝ in.

Right-side back packout (installed with good face in)

Right-side wide panel

← 48 in. →

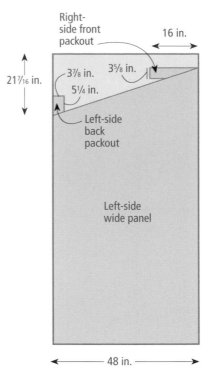

Right-side front packout

16 in.

21⁷⁄₁₆ in.

3⅞ in.   3⅝ in.

5¼ in.

Left-side back packout

Left-side wide panel

← 48 in. →

8 **CUT AND INSTALL THE NARROW SIDE PANELS.** Snap a chalkline and rip a siding panel into two 24-in.-wide panels. Lay out lines and make cuts on the outside faces of the panels between marks at 10⅛ in. and 4⅝ in., as shown in the drawing "Side Panel Layouts." Put each panel in place at the front corner of the appropriate side and nail it home.

9 **CUT AND INSTALL THE WIDE SIDE PANELS.** Lay out the cut across the outside face of a full-width siding panel as shown in "Side Panel Layouts." Make the cut for the right side panel. Then lay out the left side wide panel by reversing the slope. Install the wide panels.

10 **ADD THE RAFTER OVERHANG PACKOUTS.** The "Side Panel Layouts" drawing shows how to cut the four packouts from the side-panel offcuts. By using the angled offcuts, you need make only square cuts to make the packouts. Install each packout with one 6d nail. You'll see that you need to install the right-side back packout with the good face against the rafter.

FRONT PANEL LAYOUTS

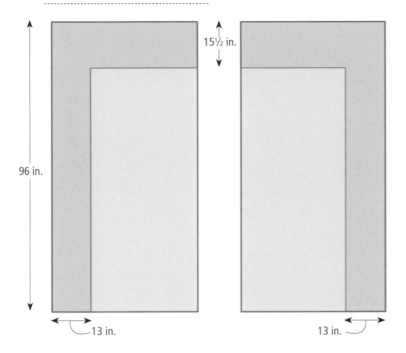

96 in.

15½ in.

13 in.   13 in.

11 **CUT THE FRONT PANELS.** The drawing "Front Panel Layouts" shows measurements for the door opening cutouts in the two front panels. Snap lines and make these cutouts with a circular saw. Cut right up to the lines—the slight overcuts in the thin panels will be covered by trim. The cutouts will be used to make the doors.

12 **INSTALL THE FRONT PANELS.** Put the front panels in place butted up under the rafters and flush to the outside corners. There will be 1 in. of rough open framing exposed all the way around. The doors will overlap this area. Nail the panels to the framing.

Trim the Rakes and Rafter Overhangs

You'll start by installing 8-ft. 1x6 boards along the rakes, letting them run long on both ends. Next, you'll install soffit boards under the rafter overhangs, and finally you'll nail fascia boards to the ends of the rafters.

MARKING SOFFITS FOR WIDTH

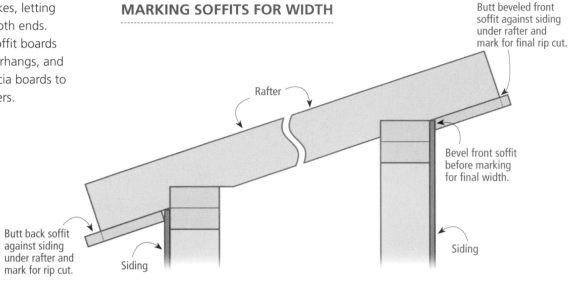

Rafter

Butt beveled front soffit against siding under rafter and mark for final rip cut.

Bevel front soffit before marking for final width.

Siding

Butt back soffit against siding under rafter and mark for rip cut.

Siding

1 **INSTALL THE RAKE BOARDS.** Position an 8-ft.-long 1x6 along one side of the shed, flush to the roof surface and with each end running past the rafter overhangs by about 5 in. Attach the rake board with a pair of 8d oval-head nails about every 16 in. Do the same on the other side.

2 CUT THE SOFFIT BOARDS. Set your circular-saw blade to an angle of 18½ degrees. Put a rip guide on the saw to remove just enough width to make the bevel, then rip the edge off an 8-ft. 1x6. Butt the board against the front siding under the rafter overhang and mark it for a final rip as shown in the drawing "Marking Soffits for Width." Mark another 8-ft. 1x6 for width for the back soffit as shown in the drawing, then rip both boards.

3 INSTALL THE SOFFIT BOARDS. Attach the soffits with two 8d oval-head nails into the overhang of each rafter.

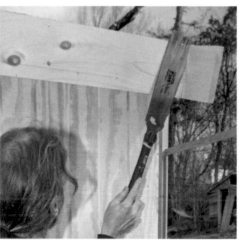

4 INSTALL THE FASCIA BOARDS. The fascia boards are 8-ft. 1x6s—cut stock to length as necessary. Position the back fascia board with its inside edge flush to the top of the roof. Position the front fascia with its outside edge in the same plane as the roof. Attach the fascia with two 8d oval-head nails into the end of each rafter. Also nail through the rakes into the ends of the fascia with two nails at each joint.

5 CUT THE RAKES. Use a handsaw to cut the rakes off flush to the fascia boards.

Install the Roofing

You'll start this mini-roofing job by covering the roof with felt underlayment. Then you'll install drip edge along the lower edge and rakes. You'll cut and install starter strips and then nail the shingles in place. Finally, you'll add drip edge to the front edge of the roof.

1 **INSTALL UNDERLAYMENT.** Use a utility knife to precut three pieces of felt underlayment to about 100 in. long. Align the first piece to the bottom edge of the roof sheathing and install it with a hammer stapler. Overlap the second piece by 2 in. and staple it in place. Align the third piece to the top edge of the sheathing, overlapping the second piece, and staple it in place.

2 **INSTALL DRIP EDGE ON THE SIDES AND BACK.** Use snips to cut a piece of aluminum drip edge to fit across the back edge of the roof, leaving a tab to fold under the rake edge (see "Cutting Downslope Drip Edge" below). Install the back drip edge with roofing nails every 12 in. to 16 in. Then cut pieces to fit the rakes and install those.

Cutting Downslope Drip Edge

Cut the drip edge about 2 in. longer than the length of the lower edge of the roof. Then, as shown at top left, snip off about 1 in. of the nailing flange and the horizontal overhang. Don't snip the vertical part (held between fingers in the photo). Measure along the flange and snip the other end so the flange and overhang will be the same length as the roof edge, but you will be left with 1-in. vertical tabs on each end. After nailing the back drip edge in place, bend the tab up the rake so it will be covered by the rake drip edge.

3 CUT THE STARTER STRIPS. Cut three starter strips from regular shingles. Do the cutting from the back of the shingle—it's easier on your utility knife blade and easier to maintain a straight line. Measure 7 in. down from the top edge of the shingles and use a framing square or other metal straightedge to guide your knife as you cut across the shingle.

4 INSTALL THE STARTER STRIPS. Align the cut edge of the first strip to the lower edge of the roof and to one rake. Install it with three roofing nails just above the shingle's tar strip. Install the second starter with four nails. Put the third strip in place and mark where it meets the other rake drip edge. Cut the third strip to length and install it.

SHINGLE LAYOUT

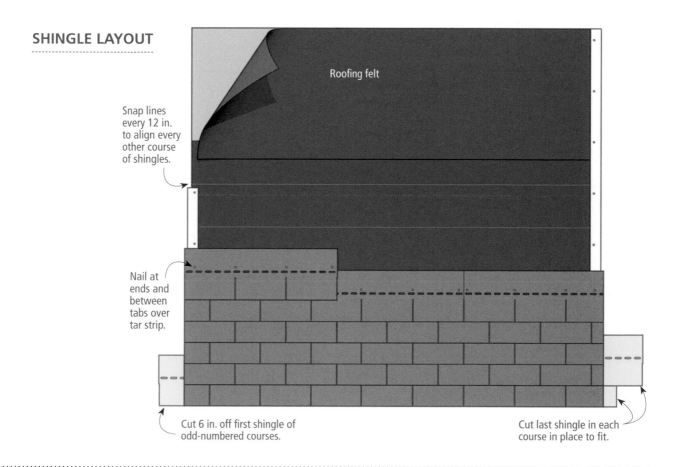

Roofing felt

Snap lines every 12 in. to align every other course of shingles.

Nail at ends and between tabs over tar strip.

Cut 6 in. off first shingle of odd-numbered courses.

Cut last shingle in each course in place to fit.

TIP You can cut and trim shingles with a regular utility knife blade, but it's easier to get smooth, straight cuts with a hook blade designed specifically for this job.

5 **INSTALL TWO COURSES.** Using a utility knife and straightedge, cut 6 in. off the ends of the first shingle as shown in the drawing "Shingle Layout" (p. 79). Install the shingle with four nails as the drawing indicates. Install the other two first-course shingles. Next, cut the last shingle flush to the rake. Install three full shingles for the second course, then cut the third flush to the rake.

6 **SNAP COURSE GUIDELINES.** To help keep the shingle courses straight, measure up both sides of the roof from the top of the second course and snap lines every 12 in.

7 **FINISH THE SHINGLES AND INSTALL THE UPSLOPE DRIP EDGE.** Install the rest of the shingles and cut the last course flush to the roof. Cut drip edge to fit with end tabs to tuck under the rake drip edge as you did for the lower drip edge. Then install the drip edge with nails about every 12 in. to 16 in.

Install Corner Trim

The corners, door opening, and window trim are all made from 1x4 pine boards. You'll start by cutting all eight corner boards to rough length. Then you'll set your miter saw to the angle necessary to miter one end of the side boards to meet the rake and to bevel one end of the front and back boards to meet the soffit. You'll reset the saw for a square cut and then scribe and cut all the corner boards to a final length that extends beyond the bottom of the siding by ¼ in. This little overhang will act as a drip edge, helping to prevent water from soaking into the bottom edge of the plywood panels.

TIP If your trim will be a different color than the siding panels, you can make the painting job easier by priming and putting one coat of paint on the panels and the trim boards before you install the trim boards. Save the second coat of paint for after installation so the paint will cover joints and nails.

1 **CAPTURE THE ROOF ANGLE.** The top edges of the front and back corner boards will be beveled to meet the soffit, while the side corner boards will be cut at the same angle across their faces to meet the rake boards. Use a sliding bevel gauge to capture this angle.

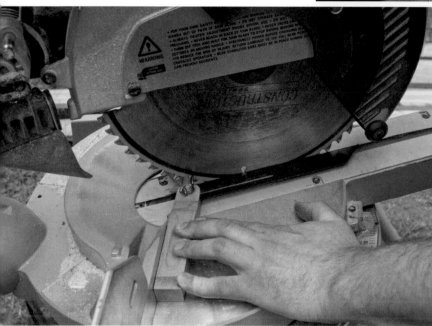

2 **CUT BOARDS TO ROUGH LENGTH AND SET THE SAW TO THE ROOF ANGLE.** First, square-cut all eight corner boards to the rough lengths listed in "What You'll Need." Then use the bevel gauge to set a miter saw to the angle you captured with the bevel gauge. Lock the miter-saw blade in the down position. Pivot the blade to the right until it's aligned with one leg of the bevel gauge while the other leg is against the fence.

3 **BEVEL THE FRONT AND BACK BOARDS.** Make these cuts with the board on edge and to the left of the blade. To bevel the edge of the two boards that will form the front soffit, place the face that will be hidden against the fence. For the two boards that will meet the back soffit, put the show side of the board against the face.

TIP Use the edge of a square to check that the front and back corner boards are flush to the side of the shed.

4 ANGLE-CUT CORNER BOARDS TO MEET THE RAKES. Make these cuts with the boards face down and to the left of the blade. For the two boards that will be on the left side of the shed as you face the door, make these cuts to the left of the blade with the hidden face down. For the boards that will be on the right side of the shed, make the cuts to the left of the blade with the show face down.

5 CUT FRONT AND BACK CORNER BOARDS TO FINAL LENGTH. Put a front corner board in place butted up under the soffit and flush to the side of the shed. Tack it in place with one nail. Use a pencil to scribe where the board meets the bottom of the siding. Mark a cutline ¼ in. below the scribe line and cut the piece to length. Do the same for the other three boards that meet the soffits and cut these boards to final length.

6 INSTALL THE FRONT AND BACK BOARDS. Install the corner boards that meet the soffits with pairs of 8d oval-head nails about every 16 in. Tuck the boards up against the soffit and butted against the inside of the rake. Make sure they are flush to the side wall. The ends of the back and front walls are framed with a 2x4 on end, so place the nails about 1 in. from the corner. Keep the nails at least 4 in. from the ends to avoid splitting the boards.

7 CUT THE SIDE CORNER BOARDS TO FINAL LENGTH AND INSTALL. Put each side corner board in place butted to the rake and flush to the face of the back or front corner board it will meet. Tack the boards in place with one nail, then scribe for a cut that's flush to the bottom of the board it will meet. Make the cut and nail the boards in place.

Install the Door Casing

The rough door opening is 68 in. wide. Like the siding, the side and top door casings will be held back 1 in. from the inside of the rough opening, so the side casings will be 70 in. apart. The 3½-in.-wide side casings will butt under the top casing, so that means the top casing should be 77 in. wide.

But lumber widths vary, and as always it's better to scribe trim in place than to rely on measurements. So you'll start by cutting the top casing to rough length and tacking it in place. Then you'll scribe and cut the side casings to length. You'll install the side casings, then scribe where they meet the outside of the top casing. Then you'll remove the top casing, cut it to final length, and nail it in place.

1 **ROUGH-CUT AND TACK THE TOP CASING.** Tack a nail into the rough door header just under the siding about halfway across the door opening. This nail will support the top casing when you tack it in place. Cut the top casing to at least 78 in. long. Put the top casing in place centered over the opening and resting on the nail. Level the casing and then tack it in place with one nail on each side.

TIP When nailing trim, it's always a good idea to start one nail near the top and one near the bottom before putting a piece in place. That way, you can align one end, drive that nail in, plumb or level the piece, and then drive in the nail at the other end.

2 **MEASURE AND CUT THE SIDE CASINGS.** On both sides of the opening, hook your tape on the bottom of the siding and measure up to the bottom of the top casing—the measurements should be the same, but it's not a problem if they differ slightly as long as you know the top casing is level. Add ¼ in. to the longest measurement and cut the side casings to length.

3 **INSTALL THE SIDE CASING.** Butt a side casing under the top casing with its inside edge flush to the edge of the siding. Use a level to make sure the casing is plumb. If the rough opening is slightly out of plumb, it won't matter. As you'll see, the doors are designed to accommodate a rough opening that is slightly out of square as long as the casing is level and plumb.

4 **SCRIBE, CUT, AND INSTALL THE TOP CASING.** Use a square and utility knife as shown to scribe cuts on both ends of the top casing. Remove the top casing, make the cuts, and nail the top casing in place, flush to the edges of the side casing.

Install the Window Casing

The window casing consists of four pieces of 1x4 that fit into flanges in the window frame. Here's a foolproof way to fit the pieces without using a tape measure.

1 **SCRIBE AND CUT THE TOP AND BOTTOM CASING.** Put a piece of 1x4 that's cut square on one end and at least 43 in. long into the window's top flange. Insert a scrap of 1x4 into one side flange and slide the square end of the top piece flush with the outside of the scrap. Put another scrap of 1x4 in the other side flange and use a utility knife to notch the top piece where it meets the outside of this piece of scrap. Remove and cut the top piece on a miter saw, then use it as a template to mark and cut the bottom piece.

2 **POSITION AND NAIL THE TOP CASING.** Put the top casing in its flange and use the 1x4 scrap to position it side to side. Nail it in place.

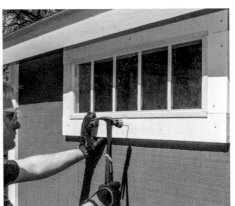

3 **SCRIBE AND CUT THE SIDE PIECES.** Cut a piece of 1x4 to about 12 in. Put it in a side flange butted up against the top casing. Next, put the bottom casing in its flange and slide it against the side casing. Use a utility knife to make a notch where the two pieces form an inside corner. Use a knife and a square to extend the notch into a layout line across the side piece. Cut the piece to this length, then use it as a template to mark and cut the other side piece.

4 **INSTALL THE SIDE AND BOTTOM PIECES.** Test-fit the side and bottom casings to make sure there are no gaps. Then nail the pieces into place.

Build the Shed Doors

The shed doors consist of frames of 2x4s laid on the flat and sandwiched between the same rough-sawn siding panels used to sheathe the shed. The doors are trimmed on the outside with 1x4s for added strength and a finished appearance.

The doors are sized to fit a rough opening that is 68 in. wide and 75½ in. tall. The exterior door panels are identical in size—they cover ¾ in. of the 1-in. reveal you left around the opening when you sheathed the front of the shed, and they overlap the floor by ¾ in. as well. They have ¼ in. between them where the doors meet in the center.

The frames are sized to allow a ½-in. gap between them, the rough opening, and the floor. For the left door, the interior and exterior panels are cut to the same width as the frame. The interior panel is installed flush to the edges of the frame while the exterior panel is shifted 1¼ in. to the left, leaving part of its center stile exposed to serve as a stop for the right door's exterior panel.

Because the right-door exterior panel laps the left-door stile, the right frame is narrower than the left frame. Like the left interior panel, the right interior panel is cut to fit flush to all sides of the right frame.

To make the doors, you'll start by cutting the rails and stiles to length and the panels to the dimensions listed in "What You'll Need." Next, for each door, you'll attach the back panel and then its front panel. You'll cut the trim boards to length and screw them in place.

> **TIP** To help keep pieces square when cutting sheet goods such as plywood sheathing, always leave factory edges where possible. For example, when ripping the cutoffs for the door panels, measure the width from the factory edge and trim the edge that was previously cut.

1 **RIP THE PANELS TO WIDTH.** As mentioned, you can make two of the door panels from the cutouts left from the two siding panels you used to sheathe the front of the shed. The remaining two panels each will be cut from full sheets. Snap lines to guide rips to the door panel widths listed in "What You'll Need." Put 8-ft. 2x4s across sawhorses to support the sheathing. Set the saw to cut about 1 in. deep so you won't cut into your sawhorses. Use four 2x4s (the ones destined to be stiles will do the trick) to support the full panels—one a couple of inches to each side of the cutline and one near each long edge.

2 **CUT THE PANELS TO LENGTH.** Because the two exterior panels are the same length and the two interior panels are, too, you can cut them in pairs. Clamp the exterior panels together atop sawhorses with the edges flush. Snap a line across them at 78 in. and make the cut with a circular saw. Cut the interior panels the same way, this time snapping the line at 74½ in.

DOOR CONSTRUCTION

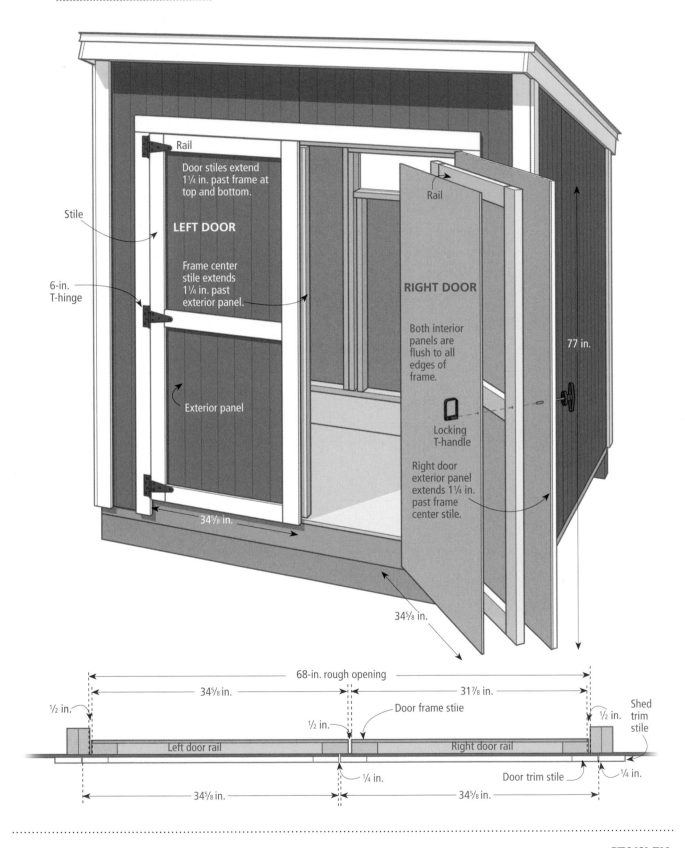

Rail

Door stiles extend 1¼ in. past frame at top and bottom.

LEFT DOOR

Frame center stile extends 1¼ in. past exterior panel.

Stile

6-in. T-hinge

Exterior panel

34⅝ in.

Rail

RIGHT DOOR

Both interior panels are flush to all edges of frame.

Locking T-handle

Right door exterior panel extends 1¼ in. past frame center stile.

77 in.

34⅝ in.

68-in. rough opening

34⅝ in.

31⅞ in.

½ in.

Door frame stile

½ in.

Shed trim stile

½ in.

Left door rail

Right door rail

¼ in.

Door trim stile

¼ in.

34⅝ in.

34⅝ in.

3 CUT THE FRAME PARTS TO LENGTH AND MARK FOR THE CENTER RAILS. Use a miter saw or circular saw to cut all the frame pieces to the lengths listed in "What You'll Need" (see "Making and Using a Stop Block," p. 171). Lay all four frame stiles on the bench with edges flush and strike a centerline across them at 37¼ in. Designate one left rail and one right rail as center rails and mark their centerlines at 1¾ in. across each end.

> **TIP** If you discover that the stiles are slightly bowed along their width, orient the bows out. Then put the interior panel in place and get it flush and screwed at the corners. Put a clamp across the panel at the middle and use it to pull the stiles tight against the center rail before you add the remaining screws.

4 LAY OUT THE LEFT FRAME. Lay two stiles on a flat surface with the three left frame rails between. Align the marks on the center rail with the marks on the stiles and align the top and bottom rails flush to the ends of the stiles.

5 ATTACH THE LEFT INTERIOR PANEL AND ASSEMBLE THE RIGHT FRAME AND INTERIOR. Place one of the wider panels over the frame. Use a framing square to draw a pencil line across the panel at 37¼ in. to locate the center rail. Make sure all the edges are flush, then attach the panel with 1⅝-in. deck screws spaced 12 in. apart. Locate the screws about ¾ in. from the edges of the panels. Next, assemble the right frame and back panel in the same way.

6 **POSITION THE LEFT EXTERIOR PANEL.** Position the left exterior panel on a frame as shown in the drawing "Door Construction" (p. 86). Have a few clamps handy to hold the panel to the frame as you measure around the perimeter and adjust the panel until you have a 1¼-in. overlap at the top, bottom, and hinge side. Make a mark 38½ in. from the top of the panel to locate the center rail and use a framing square or T-square to strike a line across the panel to locate screws.

(p. 86)

TIP If you have a tablesaw handy, here's a quicker way than measuring to position the exterior panels on the frames. Rip two 3-ft. or 4-ft. lengths of scrap to 1¼ in. wide. Clamp one scrap flush to the top edge of the panel and the other to the hinge side. Now just push the panel against the two scraps and clamp it to the frame.

7 **ATTACH THE LEFT EXTERIOR PANEL.** Use just three 1⅝-in. screws into each frame piece—later you'll put longer screws through the trim pieces that will further secure the panel to the frame.

8 **POSITION AND ATTACH THE RIGHT EXTERIOR PANEL.** Position the right exterior panel so that it overlaps its frame by 1¼ in. on the hinge side, top, and bottom. It will overlap the center stile by 1½ in. Screw the panel to the frame as you did the left exterior panel. Extend the centerline across the panel.

Trim the Doors

For each door, you'll start by cutting the trim stiles and rails to length. You'll attach one stile flush to the long edge of the door, then you'll attach the three rails and finally the other stile.

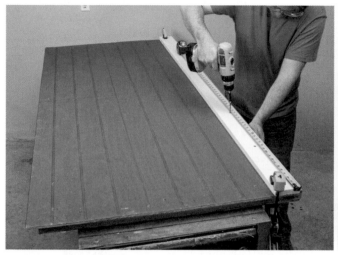

1 CUT THE TRIM PIECES AND INSTALL THE FIRST STILE. Use a miter saw with a stop block to cut the trim pieces to the lengths listed in "What You'll Need." Clamp one stile flush to a long edge of an exterior panel. Make it flush to the top of the panel so it overhangs the bottom by ¼ in. Attach the stile with 1⅝-in. deck screws spaced 12 in. apart. Locate the screws about 2 in. from the outside edges of the trim.

2 ATTACH THE TOP AND BOTTOM RAILS. Butt the top rail against the installed stile, flush to the top of the panel. Attach it with three screws. Butt the bottom rail against the stile, flush to the bottom of the stile. Check that it is square to the stile and screw it in place.

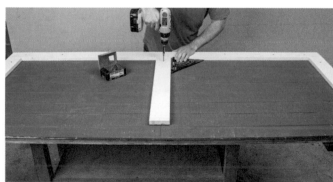

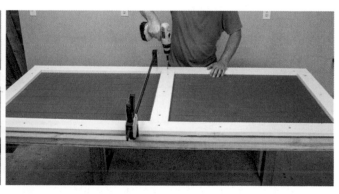

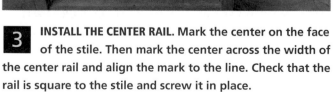

3 INSTALL THE CENTER RAIL. Mark the center on the face of the stile. Then mark the center across the width of the center rail and align the mark to the line. Check that the rail is square to the stile and screw it in place.

4 INSTALL THE OTHER STILE. Butt the second stile against the rails, make sure it is flush to the top of the door, and attach it as you did the first stile. You can use a long clamp along the rails to help make tight joints.

Install the Doors and Hardware

You'll put the doors in place, adjust the spacing, and then install the six hinges. You'll install top and bottom barrel bolts inside the left door to hold it closed. Then you'll install the locking T-handle that will hold the right door closed against the left door.

1 **PUT IN A FLOOR SPACER.** Screw a scrap of ½-in.-thick plywood or solid wood to the front of the door opening, making sure it doesn't overhang the front of the opening. You'll set the door's frame on the scrap to create the proper spacing.

2 **POSITION THE DOORS.** Lift the doors into place—remember the right door center stile will lap the left door's frame. Lean a piece of lumber against each door to keep them from falling out. Use a flatbar to adjust the door positions until you have an even gap between the door trim and shed trim and between the door center stiles. If your floor is not perfectly square to the shed stiles, you may need to shim one side of the door as shown here.

3 **INSTALL THE HINGES.** You'll install three hinges on each door using 2½-in. deck screws. Center the hinges on the center rails. But to make sure screws go into the door frame rather than poke through the areas where the panels overlap the rough opening, position the top and bottom hinges with one edge against the inside corner of the trim as shown. Drive all the screws straight in except for the two screws closest to the hinge barrel on the door side of the hinge; drive these two in at about a 45-degree angle (also to prevent those two screws from poking through the panels).

4 **INSTALL THE BARREL BOLTS.** Set a combination square to 2 in. and use it to draw a line inside the doors along the top and bottom of the center stile as shown at far left. Then hold the bolt to the inside of the line. Make sure that when the bolt is in the up position, it will clear the bottom of the door, then use a pencil as shown at near left to mark the screw-hole locations. Predrill starter holes with a ⅛-in. bit, then install the bolt with the screws provided.

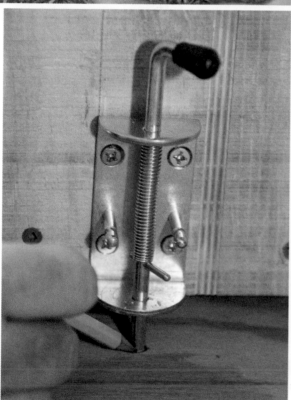

5 **DRILL THE BOLT HOLES.** After installing both bolts, close the left door and mark where the bolts will go into the floor and the rough-framing header. Then drill the holes, matching the bit to your bolt—a 5/16-in.-dia. bit worked for the bolts shown.

6 **INSTALL THE LOCKING T-HANDLE.** Drill a ⅜-in.-dia. hole through the right door at a convenient height and 2½ in. from the outside edge of the door trim stile. Slip the handle's bar through the outside of the hole, put the D-piece in place on the inside of the door, and tighten the setscrew. Finally, install the two screws provided into the exterior escutcheon.

Raised Bed

THERE ARE THREE main reasons to build raised beds. First, if your soil is rocky, clayey, or otherwise less than optimal, you can simply get above all that and fill raised beds with the soil mixture of your choice. Second, raising the beds makes planting, weeding, and harvesting easier on your back and knees. And finally, raised beds just look nice—they bring order to the garden.

This 4x8 raised bed is designed to be sturdy, inexpensive, and simple to build. It's made of two stacked 2x6 frames. Each frame is joined at the corner with lap joints, which look cooler that just butting the boards together. More importantly, it creates very strong corners because screws are installed into both sides of the corner instead of just one side as they would be in a butt joint. The two frames are held together with 12-in. spikes.

WHAT YOU'LL NEED

- 4 long boards
  1½ in. x 5½ in. x 96 in., Douglas fir
- 4 short boards
  1½ in. x 5½ in. x 47¾ in., Douglas fir
- 64 deck screws 2½ in.
- 16 galvanized spikes ⅜ in. dia. x 12 in.

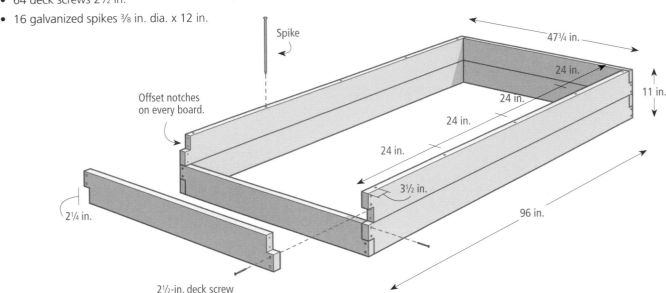

RAISED BED

Spike

Offset notches on every board.

2¼ in.

2½-in. deck screw

47¾ in.

24 in.

24 in.

24 in.

24 in.

24 in.

11 in.

3½ in.

96 in.

Choosing Wood for Raised Beds

Pressure-treated wood is the most durable wood for raised beds. And alkaline copper quaternary (ACQ)-treated wood—the kind available today—is generally considered to be safe to use in a vegetable garden. It replaced chromated copper arsenate (CCA) due to concerns that arsenic could leach into the soil and be absorbed by plants.

Still, we chose to use untreated Douglas fir lumber for our raised bed. The reason: CCA lumber was used for many years before leaching concerns arose. Is there more to be learned about ACQ? So, we decided to play it extra safe. The bed design for this project is quite easy and inexpensive to make, and we prolonged its life by coating it with Eco-Safe Wood Treatment available from TallEarth.com®. Eco Wood Treatment® from ecowoodtreatment.com is a similar product. These products turn the wood gray. We hope our raised bed will last the better part of a decade.

Another choice is to make raised beds from a naturally rot-resistant wood such as cedar or redwood. You can make these woods last even longer by coating with an ecologically safe wood treatment. While these woods surely will hold up better than Douglas fir, they cost several times more.

Cut and Notch the Boards

The longer boards are made from 8-ft. 2x6s. These often come a tad longer than 8 ft., so you may need to trim them to length. The shorter boards are 47¾ in. long to let you get two of them from an 8-ft. 2x6, allowing for the kerf and squaring the ends. After cutting the boards to length, you'll notch both ends of each board to make the lap joint. To ensure that the inside faces of the notch are square to the outside faces of the board, you'll start the notch cuts with a circular saw. You'll finish the notches with a sabersaw.

1 **CUT THE BOARDS TO LENGTH AND LAY OUT THE NOTCH DEPTH.** Use a miter saw to cut the boards to length. If you don't have a miter saw, see "Making Square Cuts with a Circular Saw" below. After cutting all the boards to length, clamp a board to the bench with one end overhanging about 6 in. Set a combination square to 1½ in.—the thickness of the boards. Use it to draw a line across the end of a board.

Making Square Cuts with a Circular Saw

Pro carpenters are good at guiding a circular saw along a cutline to produce a square cut—they should be, they do it every day. If using a circular saw isn't your daily gig, you, too, can easily produce perfectly straight and square cuts with a little help from your Quick Square®. The method shown here is also a great way to handle long offcuts, such as cutting the short raised bed boards from an 8-ft.-long 2x6.

After laying out the cutline, put the workpiece on the bench with three scraps of 2x stock underneath—one scrap near each end of the workpiece and one clamped to the bench under the cutline. Next, place the saw on the workpiece and set the cutting depth a little deeper than the stock thickness as shown in photo 1 below. Put the saw at the cutline, then slide the Quick Square up against the saw base. Hold the square firmly as you make the cut (photo 2).

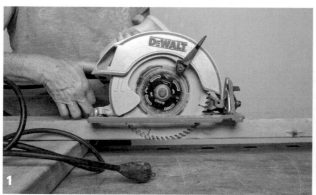

2 **LAY OUT THE NOTCH WIDTH.** Mark the halfway point on the line you just drew. It should be at 2¾ in., but measure the width of the board as it might not be exactly 5½ in. Put a square on the end of the board and use it to draw a line through the mark and extending about 4 in. past the notch-depth line. This longer line will help guide the saw when you make the cut.

3 **START THE CUTS.** Use a circular saw to cut along the notch-depth line until you reach the notch-width line. Now cut from the edge of the board along the notch-width line until you reach the notch-depth cut.

Applying Wood Preservative

If you will be coating your raised bed with wood preservative, do so before assembly so you can thoroughly treat all surfaces. Start by dipping the ends of the boards in preservative and allow the end grain to soak up the liquid for about 10 minutes. Then brush a couple of generous coats of preservative on all four sides of each board.

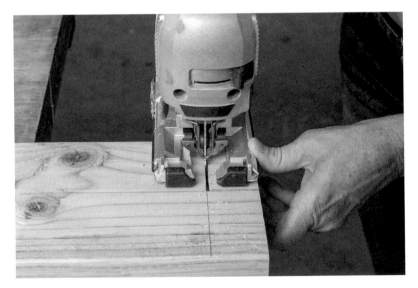

4 **FINISH THE NOTCH.** Use a sabersaw or handsaw to finish the notch. A sabersaw or handsaw blade is thinner than the blade on a circular saw, so be sure to run the sawblade along the outside of the circular-saw cuts. Now repeat the steps for each end of all the boards. Be sure that on each board, the notches are offset from each other as shown in the drawing "Raised Bed" (p. 94).

Assemble and Drill the Frames

You'll start by assembling each frame raised off the floor on scraps of 4x4. Raising the frames makes it easier to square and screw them together, and it will let you clamp the two frames together to predrill holes for the spikes that will join them. You'll assemble each of the two frames with screws. Then you'll stack and clamp them together to predrill for spikes. To make the raised bed easier to carry, you won't spike the frames together until you get them to the garden.

1 **ASSEMBLE THE FRAMES.** Assemble the four boards of one frame on the floor. Raise the frame off the floor by putting a scrap of 4x4 under each end of each board. At each corner, align the adjoining boards with a framing square. Then use a ⅛-in.-dia. bit to predrill for two 2½-in. deck screws into both sides of the corner. Insert the screws. Assemble each corner of both frames in the same way.

2 **LAY OUT THE SPIKE HOLES.** Lay out 16 spike holes. Locate them 3½ in. from each corner and then spaced at 24-in. intervals from the corners as shown in "Raised Bed." Set a combination square to ¾ in. to mark the center of each hole-layout line.

TIP When drilling the spike holes, it helps to stand directly over the drill so you can be sure it doesn't tilt in any direction as you bore down.

3 **DRILL THE SPIKE HOLES.** Place one frame atop the other. Check that all the sides are flush, then hold the frames together with clamps. Put a ⅜-in.-dia. x 12-in.-long bit in your drill. At each mark, drill straight down through both frames. Before moving the frames, mark the inside of both with an X and an arrow so you'll know which sides match and which edges are up. This is important for aligning the spike holes when you assemble the frames in the garden.

Extending the Reach of Your Drill Bit

An inch or so of your 12-in. drill bit will be inside the drill chuck, so even though the combined depth of the two frames is only 11 in., your bit may not quite make it all the way through the lower frame. If this is the case, just remove the top frame and finish the holes by drilling through the top of the lower frame.

Install the Raised Bed

Before installing the raised bed, you'll lay out the footprint and remove grass or other vegetation. Then, if necessary, you'll dig a bit more to level the area. After that, it's just a matter of putting one frame in place, the other on top, and driving in the spikes.

1 **LAY OUT THE FOOTPRINT.** If your raised bed or beds will be incorporated into a grid of 4-ft. x 8-ft. beds as shown in "Garden with Shed Layout" on p. 29, lay out the entire grid by measuring along the fence and tying strings across the fencing. Then use inverted spray marking paint to mark the bed grid. If your raised bed is not part of a grid, just put one frame down where you want it and put spikes in the ground at each outside corner. Remove the frame, tie strings between the spikes, and then paint the outline.

2 **LEVEL THE LOWER FRAME.** Use a spade to remove vegetation from the footprint. Use a 4-ft. level to check the short sides and put the level on a 2x4 to check the long sides. If the footprint slopes, remove soil from the upslope perimeter until the perimeter is level. There's no need to level the rest of the footprint area.

3 **INSTALL THE FRAMES.** Put the bottom frame in place, making sure the top side is up. Tamp it down around the perimeter with a rubber mallet. Check for level and make any adjustments by removing or adding soil around the perimeter, then tamp again. Put the second frame in place and drive the 12-in. spikes into the holes. Now, you're ready to fill and plant your new raised bed.

CHAPTER SIX

Potting Bench

TASKS LIKE TRANSPLANTING seedlings are a pleasure when you have an ample surface at the right height to work at. This compact potting bench is designed to be built into the garden shed on p. 52, so you can keep your tools and potting soil handy and out of the weather. The built-in approach makes the bench extremely sturdy and saves lumber and space, too.

The bench features a removable soil bin that hangs just below an opening in the bench surface. The opening has a lid, providing a larger continuous work surface when you're not using the soil. Just push up on the bottom of the bin to push up the lid so you can grab it when you want to remove it.

The potting bench is positioned directly under the garden shed window, so you can enjoy the view and the light while you work. Because it is protected from the weather, most of the parts are made from inexpensive untreated Douglas fir lumber. The 1-in.-thick parts are made of pressure-treated nominal 5/4 x 6 deck boards only because untreated 5/4 lumber is harder to find. If you can find untreated 5/4 stock, there's no reason not to use it.

WHAT YOU'LL NEED

BENCH

- 2 aprons
  1½ in. x 1½ in. x 41¼ in., Douglas fir
- 1 cleat
  1½ in. x 1½ in. x 41¼ in., Douglas fir
- 2 benchtop boards
  1 in. x 5½ in. x 41¼ in.,
  pressure treated
- 1 benchtop center board
  1 in. x 5½ in. x 20 in.,
  pressure treated
- 1 ledger
  1½ in. x 3½ in. x 41¼ in., pressure
  treated
- 2 bottom shelf boards
  1 in. x 5½ in. x 44¼ in.,
  pressure treated
- 1 bottom shelf board
  1 in. x 4 in. x 44¼ in.,
  pressure treated
- 2 legs
  1½ in. x 3½ in. x 33½ in., Douglas fir
- 2 feet
  1½ in. x 3½ in. x 5½ in., Douglas fir
- 4 side supports
  1½ in. x 3½ in. x 20 in., Douglas fir
- 3 crosspieces
  1½ in. x 3½ in. x 13½ in., Douglas fir
- 1 benchtop filler
  1 in. x 5½ in. x 2¾ in.,
  pressure treated
- 1 backsplash
  ½ in. x 1 in. x 41¼ in., pine

LID

- 1 center board
  1 in. x 5½ in. x 18⅜ in.,
  pressure treated
- 1 back board
  1 in. x 2⁷⁄₁₆ x 18⅜ in.,
  pressure treated
- 1 front board
  1 in. x 3¹⁵⁄₁₆ x 18⅜ in.,
  pressure treated
- 2 battens
  ¾ in. x 2½ in. x 10 in., pine

SOIL BIN

- 2 sides
  ¾ in. x 7¼ in. x 11⅞ in., pine
- 2 front and back
  ¾ in. x 7¼ in. x 15¼ in., pine
- 1 bottom piece
  ¾ in. x 7¼ in. x 16¾ in., pine
- 1 bottom piece
  ¾ in. x 4⅝ in. x 16¾ in., pine
- 2 hangers
  ¾ in. x ¾ in. x 11⅞ in., pine

TOP SHELF

- 1 cleat
  1½ in. x 1½ in. x 41¼ in., Douglas fir
- 1 shelf board
  1 in. x 5½ in. x 41¼ in.,
  pressure treated
- 2 top shelf supports
  1½ in. x 1½ in. x 9 in., Douglas fir

• HARDWARE

- 1½-in. deck screws
- 2-in. deck screws
- 2½-in. deck screws
- Construction adhesive

POTTING BENCH

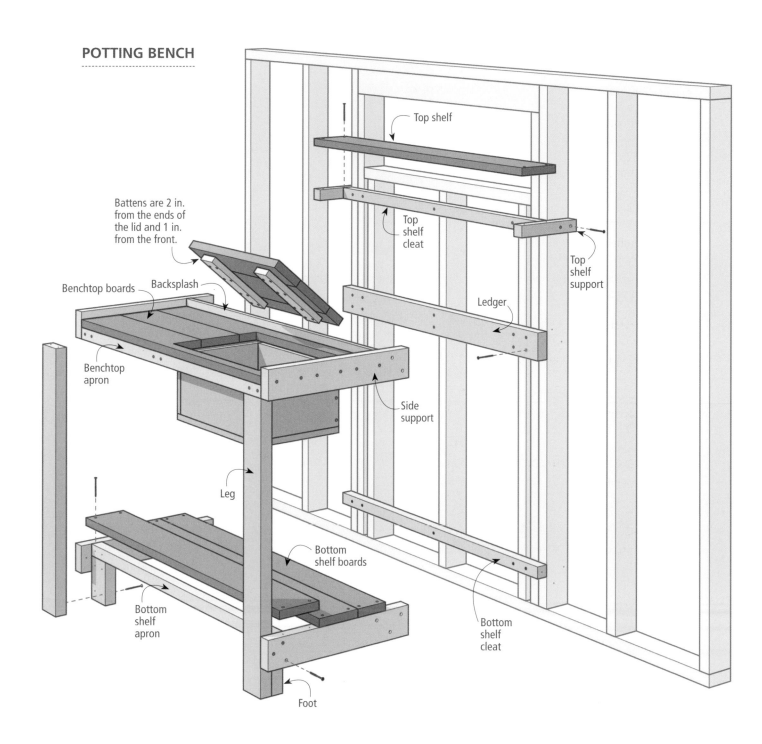

Top shelf

Top shelf cleat

Top shelf support

Battens are 2 in. from the ends of the lid and 1 in. from the front.

Ledger

Benchtop boards

Backsplash

Benchtop apron

Side support

Leg

Bottom shelf boards

Bottom shelf apron

Bottom shelf cleat

Foot

Cut the Long Parts

Because of the spacing of the studs that flank the shed window, many of the bench parts will be cut to either 41¼ in. long or 44¼ in. long. (If you're not building the garden shed, adjust the dimensions to suit your own specific framing.) All of these cuts can be made with a circular saw, but it you have a power miter saw, set it up with a stop to quickly make accurate cuts. If your saw stand doesn't have a stop, see "Making and Using a Stop Block" on p. 171.

There are two 1½-in. x 1½-in. cleats and two 1½-in. x 1½-in. aprons. You can make these parts from nominal 2x2 lumber (actual dimensions 1½ in. x 1½ in.), but it's easy enough and a little cheaper to use a tablesaw to rip the cleats from nominal 2x4s. In this case, you'll crosscut the 2x4s to finished length before ripping a cleat and an apron from each.

1 **CHECK STUD SPACING.** There are doubled studs on each side of this shed window. Before cutting any lumber, check that the distance from the outside face of one to the outside face of the other is 41¼ in. If it's not, you'll need to adjust the lengths of all the parts listed as 41¼ in. long. You'll also have to adjust the lengths of all the parts listed as 44¼ in. so that they will be 3 in. longer than your measurement.

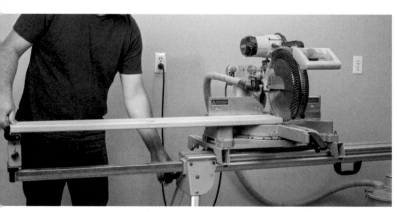

2 **CUT THE LONG PARTS TO LENGTH.** Start by using a power miter saw to cut one 5/4 x 6 to 41¼ in. long. If you have a power miter saw stand with a sliding stop like the one shown, lock the sawblade in the down position. Then place the piece you just cut against the blade and slide the stop up against the other end. Set the stop. Use the stop to cut all the parts listed as 41¼ in. long. Reset the stop to 44¼ in. and cut the three bottom shelf boards and the top shelf to length.

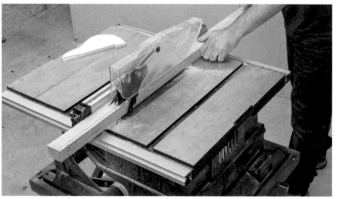

3 **RIP THE CLEATS/APRONS AND BACKSPLASH AND MAKE THE TOP SHELF SUPPORTS.** Set the tablesaw fence 1½ in. from the blade. Rip the two 41¼-in.-long pieces of 2x4 into four pieces—the bottom shelf cleat, the top shelf cleat, the bottom shelf apron, and the benchtop apron. Crosscut another piece of 2x4 to 9 in. long, then rip that into the two top shelf supports. Reset the fence to 1 in. from the blade and rip the backsplash to width.

Finish Precutting and Preassembly

It makes sense to cut all the parts to size before you attach the bench to the shed. The exception is one bottom shelf board that you'll cut to length in advance but rip to width to fit. Likewise, some assembly steps are easier to do before attaching the bench, while others are better done after.

To this end, you'll preassemble the feet, the bottom shelf apron, and the benchtop apron to the legs. You'll notch benchtop boards to make the bin opening. Next, you will rabbet two of the crosspieces to accept bin hangers. Then you will screw the crosspieces to the bottom of the benchtop boards.

1 **CUT THE SIDE SUPPORTS AND LEG PIECES AND ATTACH THE FEET. Use a** miter saw or the miter gauge on a tablesaw to cut the side supports, legs, and feet to the lengths listed in "What You'll Need." Predrill ⅛-in.-dia. holes, then attach each foot flush to the bottom of a leg with four 2½-in. deck screws.

2 **ASSEMBLE THE LEG PIECES TO THE BOTTOM APRON. Place** the bottom apron across the legs against the feet and flush to the outside of the legs. Predrill for two screws at each connection using a Quick Square to help keep the apron in position as you drill. Attach the apron to the leg with 2½-in. screws.

3 **ATTACH THE TOP APRON. Place** the top apron across the top of the legs flush to the ends. Predrill and attach the apron with two 2½-in. screws into each leg.

4 **LAY OUT THE BENCHTOP BOARDS.** As shown in the drawing "Benchtop Assembly" (p. 108), the two outer benchtop pieces get 18½-in.-long notches beginning 2¾ in. from the right side. The notch in the back board is 2½ in. deep, while the front-board notch is 4 in. deep. Use a square to lay out the notch widths across the boards, then set a combination square to guide a pencil as you lay out the notch depths.

5 NOTCH THE OUTER BENCHTOP PIECES. Clamp the back and front benchtop pieces to the work surface so they can't slide around, then make the cuts with a sabersaw.

6 CUT THE REMAINING BENCHTOP PIECES AND CROSSPIECES TO LENGTH. Use a miter saw or circular saw to cut the benchtop center board, the benchtop filler, and the three crosspieces to the lengths listed in "What You'll Need." To keep your hand at a safe distance from the blade, hold the longer part of the board and let the filler fall off as an offcut.

Cutting Corners

Wider sabersaw blades are better for making long straight cuts such as the benchtop notches. However, you can't make tight turns at the corners with a wide blade. So start by cutting along one of the side-cut layout lines until you reach the corner. Then make another cut through the waste that gradually sweeps toward the corner to meet the first cut. Now you can put the blade against the cutline for the back of the notch and continue to the other corner. Finally, cut along the other side cutline to complete the notch.

7 SET THE TABLESAW FOR RABBET CUTS. As shown in "Benchtop Assembly" (p. 108), two of the crosspieces get a ¾-in. x ¾-in. rabbet along one edge (to accommodate the soil bin; see p. 109). Set a combination square to ¾ in. and use it to set the tablesaw blade to ¾ in. high. Then set the fence ¾ in. from the blade.

8 CUT THE RABBETS. With a 3½-in. face down on the saw table (top), run the two crosspieces over the blade. Then run the pieces through again with a 1½-in. face down to complete the rabbets (above).

Tablesaw Safety

The safety guard on your tablesaw protects you in two ways: It has a splitter to prevent binding that causes dangerous kickback and to prevent your fingers from coming in contact with the blade. You'll need to remove the safety guard from your saw to rabbet the crosspieces. This can be safely done because you will not be cutting all the way through the workpiece, eliminating the kickback problem. Also, your hands will not be exposed to the blade through most of the cut; just be sure to keep your hand away from the blade as it emerges from the back of the cut. And, of course, be sure to replace the tablesaw guard when the rabbet cuts are completed.

9 PREDRILL ANGLED HOLES. Each crosspiece gets a pair of angled holes on one end for screws that will attach them to the ledger. Draw guidelines across the pieces 1 in. from the ends. Start the holes on the lines and drill at a 45-degree angle.

TIP When drilling at a 45-degree angle, you may find that the bit skips across the surface instead of engaging the wood. To solve this, just drill straight down for ⅛ in. or so and then angle the drill to finish the hole.

10 **ASSEMBLE THE BENCHTOP.** Clamp the three benchtop boards together upside down on your work surface. Then clamp a 1½-in.-wide board flush to the front edge to act as a spacer for the crosspieces. Place the three crosspieces, making sure the rabbets are flush to the opening and the benchtop pieces are flush as shown in "Benchtop Assembly." Predrill holes for two 2½-in. deck screws in a staggered pattern into each benchtop piece. Put four holes in the filler. Install the screws.

11 **ATTACH THE BACKSPLASH.** Apply glue to a ½-in.-wide face of the backsplash and clamp it along the back of the benchtop.

TIP To keep the crosspieces from shifting while you are drilling holes, start by drilling a hole in one end and inserting the screw. Do the same on the other end. Now predrill the rest of its holes and insert the remaining screws.

BENCHTOP ASSEMBLY

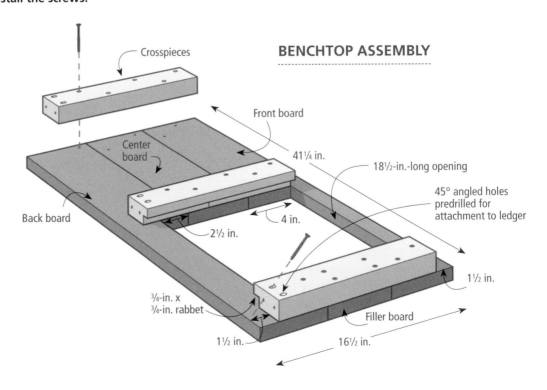

- Crosspieces
- Front board
- 41¼ in.
- 18½-in.-long opening
- Center board
- 45° angled holes predrilled for attachment to ledger
- Back board
- 4 in.
- 2½ in.
- 1½ in.
- ¾-in. x ¾-in. rabbet
- Filler board
- 1½ in.
- 16½ in.

Make the Lid and Bin

The lid is made from three pieces of 5/4 x 6. The center board is left at the full 5½-in. width of the stock, while the two outer boards are ripped to widths that will make the lid joints line up with the benchtop joints. You'll cut the lid boards to length and width. Then you'll rip the two battens to width, cut them to length, and screw them to the lid boards.

The bin is a simple box made from a piece of 1x8 pine. You'll cut the parts to length and assemble them with glue and screws. Then you'll cut two hangers and glue them to the bin. When you drop the bin in the opening, the hangers will sit in the rabbets, supporting the bin. The drawing "Soil Bin Elevation" shows how the lid and bin fit in the bench.

SOIL BIN ELEVATION

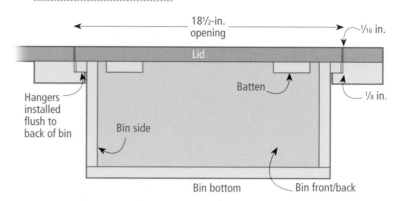

18½-in. opening — ¹⁄₁₆ in.

Lid

Batten — ⅛ in.

Hangers installed flush to back of bin

Bin side

Bin bottom — Bin front/back

1 **CUT THE LID PARTS.** As listed in "What You'll Need," the lid boards are sized to make the lid ⅛ in. shorter and narrower than the benchtop opening. Measure the size of your opening in case you need to make an adjustment. Then cut the boards to length. Rip the two outer boards to the widths listed in "What You'll Need." Cut and rip the battens to the length and width listed.

2 **LAY OUT THE BATTEN POSITIONS.** Use a combination square to lay out the batten positions on the lid boards. The battens should be 1 in. from the front of the lid and 2 in. from each side.

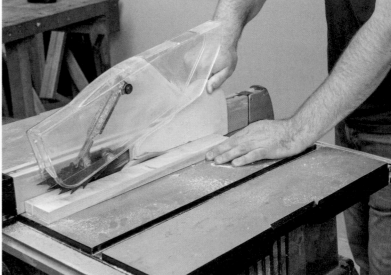

3 **ASSEMBLE THE LID.** Clamp the lid boards together, flush on the ends, and attach the battens with two staggered 1½-in. deck screws into each board.

TIP Boards as wide as 1x8s often have a bit of bow in them. No problem. When assembling the bin, just make sure the bow is out. The clamps and screws will pull the boards flat.

4 **CUT THE BIN SIDES, FRONT, AND BACK AND HANGERS.** Cut the sides, front, and back to the dimensions listed in "What You'll Need." To make the hangers, first cut a length of 1x material to 11⅞ in. long. Then set the tablesaw fence ¾ in. from the blade and rip the two hangers.

5 **PREDRILL FOR SCREWS.** Clamp the bin front and back between the sides. Make sure the pieces are flush at top and bottom and along their length, then predrill ⅛-in.-dia. screw holes. You'll drill four evenly spaced holes through each side, but the clamps will be in the way, so at each joint, drill for top and bottom screws, insert 2-in. deck screws in those holes, then remove the clamps and drill the remaining holes.

6 **ASSEMBLE THE SIDES TO THE FRONT AND BACK.** Remove the screws, but before you do, mark both sides of inside corners with corresponding letters—A, A, B, B, etc. You want to mate the same corners so the screw holes will line up. Assemble each joint individually. Put glue on the end of a front or back piece, put a side piece in place, and drive in 2-in. deck screws.

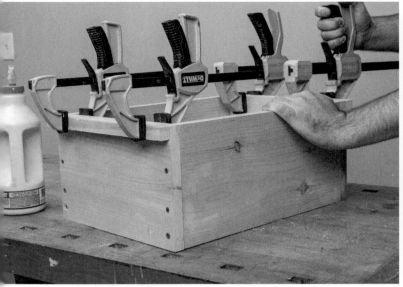

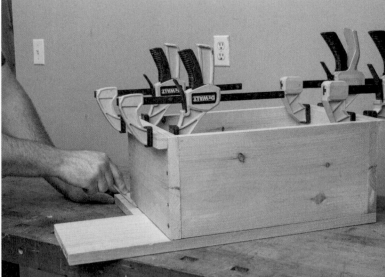

7 **ATTACH THE HANGERS.** Apply glue to the hangers and clamp them along the top of the bin sides.

8 **SCRIBE AND CUT THE BOTTOM PIECES TO LENGTH.** The bottom will be glued up from two pieces—a full-width 1x8 (actual width 7¼ in.) and a piece of 1x stock ripped down to 4⅝ in. Start by aligning two pieces of 1x8 under the bin and scribe the length of the bottom on the boards. Cut the boards to length, then rip one to 4⅝ in.

9 **GLUE UP THE BOTTOM.** Put glue along the mating edges and join the bottom pieces with three clamps.

10 **INSTALL THE BOTTOM.** Put the bottom in place on the bin. Predrill two screw holes at opposing corners, and insert 2-in. screws to hold the bottom in place while you drill three holes into each side, the top, and the bottom. You can use a combination square set to ⅜ in. as a guide to center the screws across the thickness of the boards below. Mark one side of the bin and bottom as shown so you can easily replace the bottom in the same orientation. Put glue on the bin and screw the bottom into place.

Install the Bench

Now it's time to assemble the bench to the shed studs. You'll start by installing the ledger and bottom cleat. You'll add the benchtop front leg assembly and crosspieces before installing the bottom shelf boards. Finally, you'll add the bottom and top side supports.

TIP It's easier to drive screws and hold the ledger or cleat against the layout line if you start a row of screws into the piece before you put it in place. Lay the ledger or cleat on the floor next to the studs so you can see where to place them.

1 **SCRIBE THE LEDGER AND BOTTOM CLEAT POSITIONS.** The ledger will be at the same height as the benchtop apron, and the bottom cleat will be at the same height as the bottom shelf apron. Hold the leg assembly against the wall and use it to scribe the height of the ledger on the studs. Now flip the leg assembly around so the bottom apron is against the studs. Scribe along the apron to mark the bottom cleat's height.

2 **ATTACH THE LEDGER AND BOTTOM CLEAT.** Place the top of the ledger along the line and install it with two 2½-in. deck screws into each stud except the studs closest to each end—you have plenty of attachment, so there's no need to risk splitting by putting screws too close to the ends of the ledger. Install the bottom cleat with one screw into each stud except the end studs. Predrill the screw holes into the narrow cleat so you don't split it.

3 **POSITION THE BENCHTOP AND ATTACH THE FRONT LEGS.** Set the back of the benchtop on the ledger and put the leg assembly in place at the front. Clamp the top to the apron. Predrill and drive two 2½-in. screws through the benchtop apron into each benchtop crosspiece. Be careful not to drill into the rabbet spaces.

4 **ATTACH THE CROSSPIECES TO THE LEDGER.** Secure the crosspieces to the ledger by driving 2½-in. screws through the angled holes you drilled earlier.

5 ATTACH THE LOWER SIDE SUPPORTS. Clamp a lower side support in place butted against the sheathing and flush to the top of the apron and back cleat. Drive a 2½-in. screw into the stud and another into the leg, then remove the clamps to get them out of the way. Drive screws into the end of the cleat and apron, into the side of the foot, and another into the stud. Install the other lower side support in the same way.

6 ATTACH THE UPPER SIDE SUPPORTS. Butt an upper support against the sheathing and make sure its bottom edge is flush with the bottom of the benchtop crosspiece and the top of the backsplash. Clamp the support in place and attach it with two screws into each stud and two screws into each end of each benchtop board.

TIP You want the upper support screws to go into the middle of the benchtop's edges. To ensure this, set a combination square to 1½ in. Run the square along the top of the support as you draw a pencil line along its length. Drive the screws at the pencil line.

7 INSTALL TWO BOTTOM SHELF BOARDS. Put the front-most bottom shelf board in place on the lower supports and lower apron. Butt the board against the inside of the leg. Screw it in place with two 2-in. deck screws into each end of each support and three evenly spaced screws into the apron. Screw the second board in place butted against the first, using two screws on each end.

8 MEASURE, RIP, AND INSTALL THE THIRD BOTTOM SHELF BOARD. This board should be 4 in. wide, but measure between the second board and the studs to make sure and then rip it for a nice snug fit. Predrill and install the board with two screws on each end.

Install the Top Shelf

The top shelf is positioned just below the window so the sill framing can act as a backsplash. To complete the project, you'll position and attach the top shelf cleat and top supports. Then you'll attach the top shelf.

1 **MARK FOR THE SHELF CLEAT.** Measure down 2½ in. from the top of the windowsill and make a mark on the center stud. Place a 4-ft. level on the mark and draw a level line across the studs.

2 **INSTALL THE CLEAT.** Put the cleat in place and mark it where it crosses all the studs (except the outermost ones). Predrill screw holes at each mark. Place the top of the cleat along the layout line and drive a 2½-in. deck screw into the center stud. Level the cleat, then drive in the other screws.

3 **MARK FOR THE TOP SHELF SIDE SUPPORTS.** Use a combination square to lay out lines on the sides of the outer studs. Make the lines at the same height as the top of the cleat.

TIP After the potting bench is installed, use #80 grit sandpaper to smooth areas that hands will contact, such as the top of the upper side supports and the outside face and edge of the top apron. Also, use the sandpaper to round over corners you might bump into, including the ends of the upper side supports and shelf supports.

4 **INSTALL THE SHELF SIDE SUPPORTS. Predrill two holes** in each side support. Position each side support along its line and drive 2½-in. deck screws through the holes into the studs.

5 **ATTACH THE SHELF. Put the shelf in place and secure** with two 2-in. deck screws into each support and three more evenly spaced into the cleat. Put the bin and lid in place and get to work; those seedlings are waiting!

Cold Frame

JUST BECAUSE AUTUMN rolls around doesn't mean you'll stop craving those fresh salad greens and other veggies like radishes, carrots, and leeks. The simple solution is a cold frame. It'll also let you get your seedlings started earlier in the spring, and once they sprout, you can harden them off by opening and closing the frame instead of bringing them in and out of the house.

Every cold frame, of course, needs a lid or lids that will allow sunlight through. Various types of plastic are often used, but perhaps the most common and easiest approach is to find an old window sash or two. You'll often find window sashes in pairs that were used in a double-hung window, and that's the basis of the two-lid design presented here.

This cold frame is easy to build in an afternoon. It's constructed of rot-resistant ¾-in.-thick cedar tongue-and-groove boards lined on the inside with 1-in.-thick foil-faced rigid insulation. The insulation stiffens the boards and reflects sunlight into the frame. Blocks of 2x4 join the corners. The result is an especially lightweight frame that's easy to move if you want to use the garden space uncovered during the warmer months or if you just want to try a new spot for the frame.

WHAT YOU'LL NEED

- 3 long boards
  ¾ in. x 5 in. x 66 in.,
  cedar tongue and groove
- 1 long board
  ¾ in. x 2½ in. x 66 in.,
  cedar tongue and groove
- 4 short boards
  ¾ in. x 5½ in. x 31¼ in.,
  cedar tongue and groove
- 2 corner blocks
  1½ in. x 3½ in. x 9¾ in,
  framing lumber

- 2 corner blocks
  1½ in. x 3½ in. x 7¼ in.,
  framing lumber
- 1 interior panel
  1 in. x 9¾ in. x 59 in.,
  foil-faced rigid foam insulation
- 1 interior panel
  1 in. x 7¼ in. x 59 in.,
  foil-faced rigid foam insulation
- 2 interior panels
  1 in. x 9¾ in. x 26¾ in.,
  foil-faced rigid foam insulation

- 2 window sashes
  1½ in. x 31¾ in. x 34 in.
- 24 pavers
  2½ in. x 4 in. x 8 in.

HARDWARE AND SUPPLIES

- 1½-in. deck screws
- 1⅝-in. deck screws
- Construction adhesive
- 4 galvanized T-hinges, 4 in.
- 2 handles

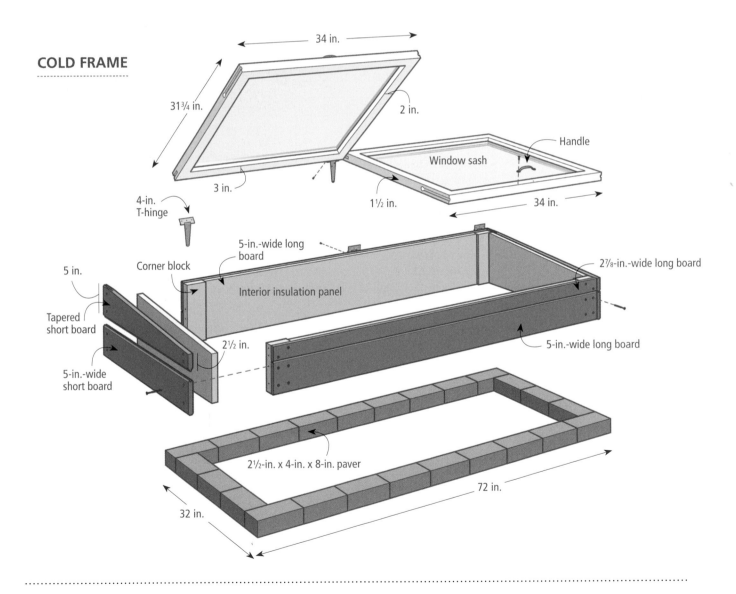

COLD FRAME

34 in.

31¾ in.

2 in.

Handle

Window sash

3 in.

1½ in.

34 in.

4-in.
T-hinge

5-in.-wide long board

2⅞-in.-wide long board

5 in.

Corner block

Interior insulation panel

Tapered short board

5-in.-wide short board

2½ in.

5-in.-wide long board

2½-in. x 4-in. x 8-in. paver

72 in.

32 in.

The frame sits on a perimeter of pavers that will take just a few minutes to lay down or take up should you decide to move the frame. The pavers keep the bottom of the frame off the ground to further ward off rot.

Cold frames can be any size, and you'll need to adapt the dimensions given here to the window sashes or sash you find. Fortunately, that's really easy to do (as explained in "Design Considerations" on p. 121).

Our frame is only 12½ in. tall at the back, including the thickness of the pavers. That's high enough to grow salad greens or carrots and to start seedlings. If you want to grow taller plants, you can simply add another course of tongue-and-groove boards to make your frame 17½ in. tall.

If possible, you'll want your cold frame to face south so it can gather the most sunlight. It's also a good idea to place it next to your house or other structure to protect it from cold winds. Our cold frame lives next to the south side of the garden shed project on p. 52.

Your cedar cold frame will hold up fine with no finish at all. We colored ours with the same solid stain we used for the shed, and we painted the window sashes white to match our shed trim.

Four Steps to Accurate Crosscuts

Here's a foolproof technique for laying out and making accurate crosscuts.

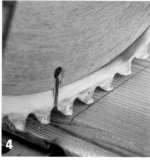

- **Make a tick mark.** Measure out the distance you need with a tape measure and then place the point of a sharp pencil at the mark. From that point, draw your pencil out to make a tick mark—this is simply to make it easier to find the point.

- **Set the pencil.** This is the secret to an accurate layout line. Intuition says to put the square at the point. Instead, put the pencil at the point.

- **Draw the line.** With the pencil still on the point, push the square up to the pencil and draw the layout line.

- **Align to the saw tooth.** The teeth on all sawblades have alternating offsets—one tooth is offset to the right, the next to the left, and so on. The offset is slight on a fine-toothed hand miter saw; it's more obvious on a circular-saw blade. If your waste is to your right, you want to position the workpiece so that a left-offset tooth just covers the layout line. If the waste is to your left, do the same with a right-offset tooth. Now, make your perfectly accurate cut.

Cut the Boards

As shown in the drawing on p. 118, each side of the cold frame consists of two courses of tongue-and-groove-boards held together by corner blocks. You'll start by cutting all these pieces to size. Because the front of the frame is shorter than the back, you'll rip down the top front board. The tongues on cedar boards tend to be brittle when not contained in grooves, so you'll rip the tongue off all the bottom boards. Then you'll taper the top side boards.

1 **CUT BOARDS TO LENGTH.** Cut all the cedar boards to the lengths listed in "What You'll Need." For guaranteed square cuts, do this with a hand or power miter saw. Carefully following layout lines with a circular saw will do fine, too.

2 **CUT THE BLOCKS TO LENGTH.** Perfectly square cuts aren't crucial for the corner blocks because the ends won't join anything. Use a power miter saw for convenience if you have one. Otherwise, clamp the 2x4s to a workbench or sawhorses and make the cuts with a circular saw.

How Wide Are These Boards Anyway?

When you go to the lumberyard or home center, you'll ask for "1x6 cedar tongue-and-groove boards." What you'll get actually will measure ¾ in. by about 5⅜ in. However, that width includes the ⅜-in.-wide tongue that will fit into the adjoining board's groove, so the *coverage* of each board is 5 in. That's two full-width boards to make the 10-in.-tall back of the frame.

3 **RIP A LONG BOARD.** The top front long board needs to be ripped to 2⅞ in. wide, including the tongue. (Once the tongue is in the groove, the board will add 2½ in. to the height of the front.) Make the rip on a tablesaw if you have one. Otherwise, as shown here, clamp the workpiece to your bench and make the cut with a rip guide on the circular saw.

4 REMOVE THE TONGUE FROM THE BOTTOM BOARDS. The tongues are fragile when they are not contained in the grooves, so it's best to rip them from the bottom boards. Again, do this with a tablesaw or with a rip guide on the circular saw. If you use the circular saw, use a scrap of tongue-and-groove board as shown here to set the guide.

5 LAY OUT THE SHORT BOARD TAPERS. The two top short boards need to be tapered along their length from their full width of 5 in. (not counting the tongue) to 2½ in. at front. Place the boards on the bench so that the tongues face each other as shown. At one end of each board, make a mark 2½ in. in from the edge of the board, not counting the tongue. Extend a straight edge from the mark to the opposing corner of each board and draw a line.

Design Considerations

Here are two things to keep in mind when designing a cold frame around the size of salvaged window sashes:

• You want the sashes to overhang the front of the frame by about ½ in. and the sides of the frame by about ¼ in. These overlaps will act as drip edges so water doesn't run down the sides of the frame, and they also give you a little leeway in case your frame size varies a bit. The sashes will be hinged flush to the back of the frame.

• As a rule of thumb, you want the lid of your cold frame to be sloped roughly 1 in. per foot. The sloped sides of our frame, for example, are 31¼ in. long. That's roughly 2½ ft., so the front of our frame should be about 2½ in. shorter than the back. That's why we made the mark at 2½ in. in step 5.

TIP When you stop a cut and remove the blade as you will in step 6, tension in the wood may cause the sawkerf to close. To make it easier to replace the blade, use a shim to open the kerf.

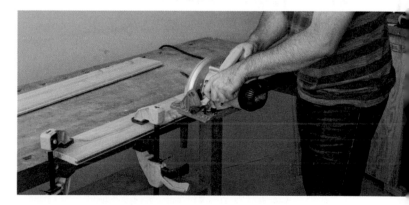

6 TAPER THE SHORT BOARDS. Clamp the boards to a work surface and cut the tapers with a circular saw. You'll need to stop the cut when you reach a clamp so you can move the clamp and continue cutting.

Cut the Panels and Assemble the Frame

You'll start by assembling the front and back panels to the corner blocks. To protect them from damage when closing the lids, the rigid insulation panels are ¼ in. shorter than the sides. You'll cut all the panels to height, but you won't taper the side panels yet. Then you'll scribe and cut the front and back panels to fit between the corner blocks and attach them with construction adhesive.

Next, you will screw the sides to the front corner blocks and then the back corner blocks, completing the frame. You'll scribe and cut the side insulation panels to fit between the corner blocks. Then you'll lay out a line inside both short sides. The line will be located ¼ in. from the bottom. You'll dry-fit the still-rectangular side panels between the corner blocks and along the lines. This way, you can just run your utility knife along the top edges of the sides to score the panels along the slope. Remove the panels, deepen the cuts, and snap off the waste. Then glue the side panels in place flush to the bottom of the frame and you'll have your ¼-in. offset along the top.

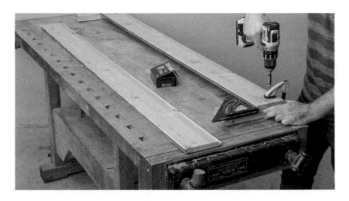

1 **ASSEMBLE THE BACK BOARDS TO THE LONGER BLOCKS. Put the longer blocks on your workbench, wide face down. Put the bottom back board in place aligned flush to the bottom and outside edges of the blocks. Check one end for square and clamp the board and block to your bench so they won't shift as you use a ⅛-in. bit to predrill holes for four 1⅝-in. deck screws. Drive in the screws and then attach the block on the other end in the same way. Put the top back boards in place, predrill for four screws on each end, and insert the screws.**

2 **ASSEMBLE THE FRONT BOARDS TO THE SHORTER BLOCKS. The process for attaching the front boards to the shorter blocks is the same as for the back boards except you'll use only two screws into the narrower top board. Stagger those screws as shown.**

3 **CUT THE INSULATION TO ROUGH LENGTH. Crosscut the rigid insulation to about 60 in. long. To do this, measure down 60 in. on both sides of the piece and make notches with a utility knife. Place a framing square or other metal straightedge across the notches and cut into the insulation with the utility knife—the knife need not go all the way through. Then fold the insulation back until it snaps apart along the cut. Separate the two pieces by cutting through the foil facing on the back of the piece.**

4 **CUT THE INSULATION TO WIDTH. Using a utility knife, make notches at 9¾ in. in from both ends. Snap a chalkline between the notches. Hold a straightedge along the line as you score with the utility knife, then fold, snap, and separate the pieces. Cut another 60-in. piece to 7¼ in. wide.**

TIP If the boards prove to be bowed a little, attach them to one corner block first, then use a clamp to pull the tongue of one board into the groove of its mate.

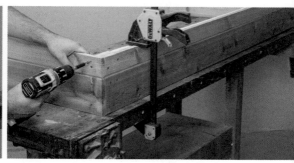

5 **SCRIBE AND CUT THE FRONT AND BACK PANELS TO FINAL LENGTH.** Put the wider panel against one of the back corner blocks and use a utility knife to notch where it meets the other back corner block. Cut the panel to length, then do the same for the narrower front panel.

6 **INSTALL THE FRONT AND BACK PANELS.** You'll notice that the foil on one side of the panel is shiny, whereas the other side is dull. Of course, the shiny side will reflect more sunlight, so you always want to install the dull side against the inside of the frame. Test-fit the front and back panels. Then put construction adhesive on the inside of the front and back boards and press the panels into place, making sure they are flush to the bottom.

7 **INSTALL THE SIDE BOARDS.** Stand the front up and put a bottom side board in place, groove up. Predrill and secure it with two screws into the corner block. Put a tapered side board in place and secure it to the corner blocks with two screws. Install the side boards on the other side in the same way. Finally, put the back in place and attach the sides to it in the same way as you attached the sides to the front.

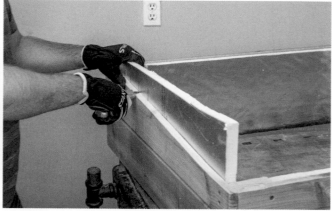

8 **CUT AND FIT THE SIDE PANELS.** Start with two pieces of insulation that are at least 11 in. wide and at least 28 in. long. Scribe them to fit between the back corner blocks and the front corner blocks and then cut them to length. Now set a combination square to ¼ in. and use it to guide a pencil line along the bottom on the inside of each side.

9 **TRIM AND ATTACH THE SIDE PANELS.** Test-fit the side panels with their bottom edges along the ¼-in. line. Then run your utility knife flat along the top of each side, scribing a line along the top of the insulation. Remove the insulation and run your knife in the score to deepen it. Snap off the waste. Then put construction adhesive on the sides and install the side panels flush to the bottom of the frame.

Install the Hardware

All that's left to do is to install the T-hinges and handles. It's easiest to do these steps while the cold frame is still on your workbench and then detach the window sashes from the hinges to make it easy to carry the frame to its site. Once on site, you'll just zip the hinge screws back into the sashes.

> **TIP** If you plan to paint your cold frame, it's easiest to do so before you install the hinges.

1 **INSTALL THE OUTSIDE HINGES. Put the two window sashes in place against each other with equal overhangs on each side. For each outside hinge, align a square to the end of the back boards and extend a line up each sash. Put the hinge along the line as shown and attach it to the frame and the sash.**

Critter-Proof Your Cold Frame

Do you reluctantly share your yard with groundhogs or other burrowing critters that might just tunnel under the brick perimeter to pilfer your tender greens? To keep them out, dig out the soil inside your frame to a depth of about 1 ft. and line the hole with chicken wire or hardware cloth. We used hex-web fencing left over from the critter-proof fence project on p. 24. Do the digging after you put the bricks in place but before placing the frame.

You'll want to staple the wire mesh to the bottom of the frame. Staples won't hold in the insulation panels, so you'll need to cut scraps about 2 in. wide to fit between corner blocks on all four sides. We ripped scraps of the 3/8-in.-thick plywood siding that covers the shed project on p. 52, but you can use any plywood or solid-wood scraps that are no more than 3/4 in. thick. You can attach the strips with screws that are long enough to go through the insulation plus 1/2 in. into the cedar. Or, if you don't have screws of the right length handy, you can attach the strips with construction adhesive. Once the mesh is stapled in place, check again that the frame is square; you won't be able to push it into square after you replace the dirt in the cold frame.

Double-hung window sashes have a parting rail. The parting rail of one sash meets the parting rail of the other when the window is closed. The parting rail is usually thinner than the other rail, so you don't want to hinge to it.

On these sashes, the glass was fitted into a slot in the parting rail and the other three sides were secured into rabbets with glazier's points and glazier's putty. Because the parting rail will be on the downslope side, water will run down the glass and could seep into the slot, causing rot. For that reason, it's a good idea to seal up the slot with a bead of silicone caulk. The caulk comes clear or white—it doesn't hold paint. After applying the caulk with a caulk gun, smooth it with your finger as shown.

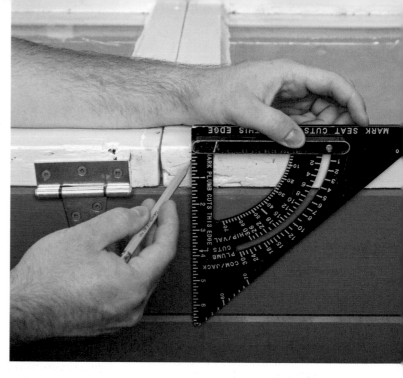

2 **INSTALL THE INSIDE HINGES.** Strike lines 1 in. in from the inside edge of each sash as shown and install the inside hinges.

3 **INSTALL THE HANDLES.** Make a mark halfway across the width of each sash. Use the mark to eyeball as you center the handles and screw them in place.

TIP The pavers' perimeter need not be perfectly level—it's okay if the cold frame slopes in either direction. However, the pavers should all be in the same plane so there are no gaps under the frame. You might have to add or subtract some soil from under some of the pavers to achieve this. If necessary, use a string between stakes as shown in the photo at right to gauge the plane.

4 **LAY OUT THE PAVERS.** As shown in the drawing on p. 118, the cold frame sits on a rectangle consisting of two rows of nine pavers and two rows of three pavers. Simply lay the pavers out where you want the cold frame to be. Before setting the frame, use a framing square to check the corners in case you wracked the frame a bit out of square when transporting it. When it is square, you are ready to set your cold frame on the pavers and reinstall the sashes.

Chicken Coop

STYLED WITH TRENDY mid-century modern architecture in mind (no jokes about "Mad Men" meets "Mad Hen," please), this chicken house was designed with the needs of both chickens and humans in mind. For the hens, there is 32 sq. ft. of outdoor space for scratching around. That's ample room for up to eight layers. Roosts indoors and out let the girls enjoy a good perch whatever the weather. The reflective roof keeps the summer sun at bay; the ½-in. mesh does the same for predators. The enclosed coop has four nesting boxes and plenty of ventilation. Windbreak walls under the coop let the hens enjoy the outdoors even in rough weather.

For humans, the raised coop means there is no crawling around

WHAT YOU'LL NEED

COOP SIDES

- 1 vent and nesting box hatch side
  ½ in. x 42 in. x 66 in.,
  exterior-grade plywood

- 1 cleanout door side
  ½ in. x 36 in. x 66 in.,
  exterior-grade plywood

- 1 hen access side
  ½ in. x 42 in. x 42 in.,
  exterior-grade plywood

- 1 fixed wall side
  ½ in. x 36 in. x 42 in.,
  exterior-grade plywood

OTHER COOP PARTS

- 2 long coop floor cleats
  1½ in. x 1½ in. x 41 in.,
  pressured-treated pine

- 2 short coop floor cleats
  1½ in. x 1½ in. x 33 in.,
  pressured-treated pine

- 2 coop floor and top
  ½ in. x 35 in. x 41 in.,
  exterior-grade plywood

- 1 cleanout door stop
  ½ in. x 4 in. x 38½ in.,
  exterior-grade plywood

- 1 vent hatch stop
  ½ in. x 4 in. x 40 in.,
  exterior-grade plywood

- 1 nesting box hatch stop
  ½ in. x 4 in. x 40 in.,
  exterior-grade plywood

- 2 skids
  1½ in. x 5½ in. x 120 in.,
  pressured-treated pine

- 2 #1 uprights
  1½ in. x 3½ in. x 77½ in.,
  pressured-treated pine

- 2 #2 uprights
  1½ in. x 3½ in. x 72½ in.,
  pressured-treated pine

- 2 #3 uprights
  1½ in. x 3½ in. x 66½ in.,
  pressured-treated pine

- 2 #4 uprights
  1½ in. x 3½ in. x 61 in.,
  pressured-treated pine

- 2 rake boards
  ¾ in. x 3½ in. x 10 ft.,
  pressured-treated pine

- 4 roof crosspieces
  1½ in. x 3½ in. x 45½ in.,
  pressured-treated pine

- 2 bottom crosspieces
  1½ in. x 3½ in. x 39½ in.,
  pressured-treated pine

- 1 midway crosspiece
  1½ in. x 3½ in. x 42½ in.,
  pressured-treated pine

- 2 door rails
  1½ in. x 3½ in. x 29¾ in.,
  pressured-treated pine

- 2 door stiles
  1½ in. x 1½ in. x 61 in.,
  pressured-treated pine

- 1 door brace
  ½ in. x 6 in. x 33 in.,
  exterior-grade plywood

- 1 door stop
  1½ in. x 3½ in. x 38 in.,
  pressured-treated pine

- 1 nesting box top
  ½ in. x 12 in. x 38 in.,
  exterior-grade plywood

- 1 nesting box bottom
  ½ in. x 12 in. x 3 in.,
  exterior-grade plywood

- 5 nesting box partitions
  ½ in. x 12 in. x 12 in.,
  exterior-grade plywood

- 2 nesting box lips
  ¾ in. x 3½ in. x 38½ in.,
  exterior-grade plywood

- 1 ramp
  1 in. x 5½ in. x 74 in.,
  cedar deck plank

- 5 decorative bars
  ¾ in. x 1½ in. x 71 in.,
  #2 pine

- 6 handle blocks
  ¾ in. x 1½ in. x 1½ in.

- 3 handles
  ¾ in. x 1½ in. x 8 in.

HARDWARE AND SUPPLIES

- 6 barrel bolts, 2 in.

- 6 hinges, 2 in., for coop hatches

- 2 hinges, 3 in., for door

- 2 windowpanes, ⅛ in. x 14 in.
  x 14 in., clear acrylic sheet

- 2 rolls, 3 ft. x 30 ft., of ½-in. x ½-in.
  plastic screening

- 2 sheets of 26-in. x 10-ft. corrugated
  plastic or aluminum roofing

- 2 acrylic sheets, 12 in. x 12 in.

- 2 pieces of tree limb for roosts

- 1 rigid conduit, ½ in. x 8 ft.
  (cut to 84 in.)

- 14 ft. ³⁄₁₆-in. wire rope

- 4 flush-type wire rope clamps

- 2 cheap carabiners for supporting
  the feeder and waterer

- 2 hooks and eyes, 4 in.

- 4d galvanized nails

- 1⅝-in. deck screws

- 2½-in. deck screws

- 1¼-in. deck screws

- 16 pan-head screws, #10 x ¾ in.

- 100 #9 x 1-in. roofing screws

- 1-in. roofing nails

- 8 pan-head screws, ¾ in.

- Exterior wood glue

on your hands and knees to feed, clean, and gather eggs. Two large hatches make it easy to get at the coop interior. A good-size door gives access to the run area, so you can refresh the water and harvest chicken manure for the compost pile.

This chicken house is easy to build. If you are comfortable making accurate measurements, using a drill/driver, and cutting with a circular saw, you'll have no trouble constructing it. As a bonus, the result not only will be a chicken coop that suits the hens and their keeper, but it will also be easy on the eyes for your neighbors—an advantage if they are uneasy about your back-to-the-land impulses.

CHICKEN COOP

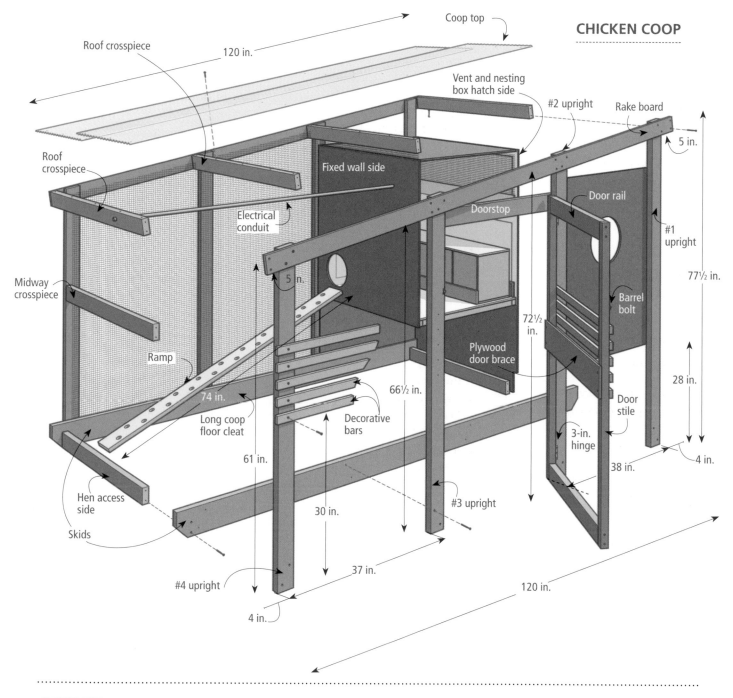

Coop top

Roof crosspiece

120 in.

Roof crosspiece

Vent and nesting box hatch side

#2 upright

Rake board

5 in.

Fixed wall side

Electrical conduit

Doorstop

Door rail

#1 upright

77½ in.

Midway crosspiece

5 in.

Barrel bolt

72½ in.

28 in.

Ramp

Plywood door brace

Door stile

74 in.

Long coop floor cleat

Decorative bars

66½ in.

3-in. hinge

38 in.

4 in.

61 in.

Hen access side

30 in.

#3 upright

Skids

37 in.

120 in.

#4 upright

4 in.

Cut the Coop Sides and Openings

The boxlike coop where the chickens sleep and lay their eggs is the heart of this structure. It is also the most demanding section to build. Made of ½-in. pressure-treated plywood, it shelters the chickens from rough weather and gives them the privacy they demand to get down to the job of producing eggs. To build it, you'll need to make some long, straight cuts.

You'll start by cutting the four sides of the coop to size: These are the vent and nesting box hatch side, the clean-out door side, the hen access side, and the fixed wall side. Actually, the long back side that will include the cleanout door will later be cut back another 5½ in. to make room for a bottom skid. Leaving it the same length as the other long side for now will make some assembly steps much easier because you'll be able to stand the coop up while you do them.

As shown in the drawing "Opening Layouts" on p. 133, both of the long sides will have openings cut into them. However, before you cut these openings, you'll install the hinges and latches to locate all the attachment holes. Then, as you make the cutouts, you'll reinstall the hardware. This will keep the cutout from binding during cutting and it will all but guarantee that your hatches and door will open and close easily.

With the square openings cut, you'll cut the round holes in the hen access side, the fixed wall side, and the cleanout door.

> **TIP** Two adjacent sides of the coop (the vent and nesting box hatch side and the cleanout door side) run all the way to the ground to make a windbreak so the hens can enjoy the outdoors even in rough weather. They also act as bracing to keep the structure from racking. Think ahead to orient these long sides into the wind where they'll do the most good.

1 **BEGIN CUTTING THE LONG SIDES. Start by cutting the vent and nesting box hatch side and the cleanout door side. Support the plywood with two pieces of 2x set perpendicular to the cutline. To set up your saw to make a long, accurate cut, begin by using a Quick Square to position the sawblade on the cutline as shown in the photo. Then clamp the square in place and make enough of the cut so that the heel of the saw base is all the way on the plywood.**

2 **COMPLETE THE CUT. Stop the saw and carefully set a drywall T-square next to the saw base. Clamp both ends of the T-square and complete the cut.**

PLYWOOD CUTTING SCHEME

You can get all the plywood parts for this project from four ½-in. sheets of 4x8 exterior-grade plywood.

TIP Before cutting with a circular saw, unplug it and set the blade so it extends about ¼ in. below the material you are working with.

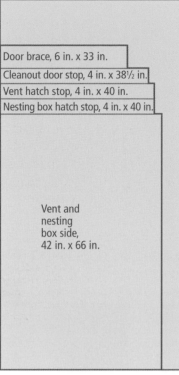

Door brace, 6 in. x 33 in.

Cleanout door stop, 4 in. x 38½ in.

Vent hatch stop, 4 in. x 40 in.

Nesting box hatch stop, 4 in. x 40 in.

Vent and nesting box side, 42 in. x 66 in.

SHEET 1

Cleanout door side, 36 in. x 66 in.

SHEET 2

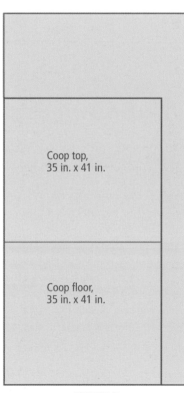

Coop top, 35 in. x 41 in.

Coop floor, 35 in. x 41 in.

SHEET 3

Fixed wall side, 36 in. x 42 in.

Hen access side, 42 in. x 42 in.

SHEET 4

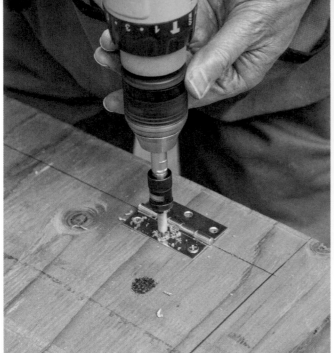

3 **ATTACH THE HINGES AND BARREL BOLTS.** Measure and mark the openings for your hatches and doors as shown in the drawing "Opening Layouts." *Before cutting each opening,* position the 2-in. hinges and barrel bolts in their intended location. Install just two screws to hold the hardware, then drill all the holes.

TIP A self-centering punch makes it easy to start your drill in the exact center of each screw hole. Simply set it in place and give it a tap.

4 **COMPLETELY INSTALL THE HARDWARE.** Add all the fasteners, completely installing each hinge and barrel bolt. Then do the counterintuitive—remove each piece of hardware, carefully saving the screws. This will clear the way for you to make a plunge cut with a circular saw. When you reinstall the hardware, the door or hatch will have consistent clearance all around its edge.

What Chickens Need

For their health and happiness, your laying hens need the following in return for their eggs. This chicken house provides all this and more:

- Comfortable nesting boxes
- At least 8 in. of perch per bird
- 4 in. of feed trough per bird
- 4 sq. ft. of indoor/outdoor space per chicken
- A rainproof and windproof coop
- Ventilation for cooling the coop in hot weather and, just as important, venting moisture in winter
- Clean water and feed in suspended containers
- Open-air foraging space

OPENING LAYOUTS

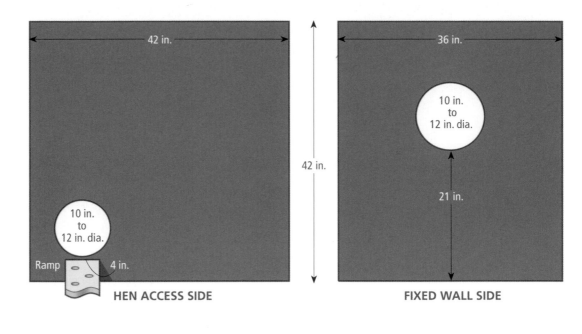

42 in.

42 in.

10 in.
to
12 in. dia.

Ramp   4 in.

HEN ACCESS SIDE

36 in.

10 in.
to
12 in. dia.

21 in.

FIXED WALL SIDE

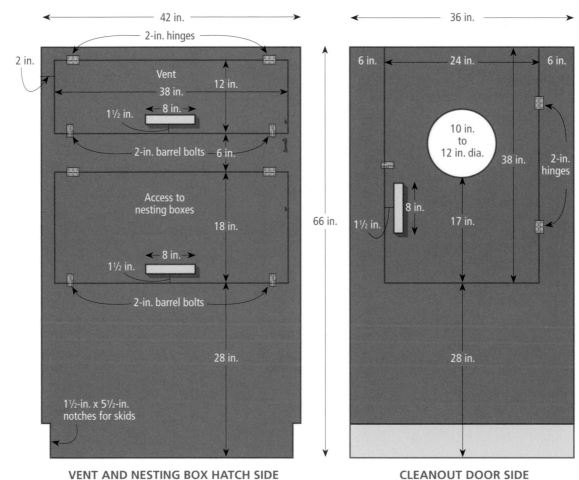

42 in.

2-in. hinges

2 in.

Vent

12 in.

38 in.

1½ in.   8 in.

2-in. barrel bolts   6 in.

Access to
nesting boxes

18 in.

8 in.

1½ in.

2-in. barrel bolts

28 in.

1½-in. x 5½-in.
notches for skids

VENT AND NESTING BOX HATCH SIDE

66 in.

36 in.

6 in.   24 in.   6 in.

10 in.
to
12 in. dia.

38 in.

2-in.
hinges

8 in.

1½ in.   17 in.

28 in.

CLEANOUT DOOR SIDE

5 CUT THE RECTANGULAR OPENINGS. Set the plywood high enough above the sawhorses or work surface so the sawblade has clearance. Make a plunge cut by setting the toe of the saw on the plywood and lining up the blade with the cutline. Start the saw and, tipping from the toe, carefully lower the blade into the cutline. (Practice this technique on scrap plywood if you've never done it before.) Cut the length of line, stopping at the corner. Saw all four sides of each opening.

6 COMPLETE THE CUTS. A circular-saw blade won't quite complete the cut, so you'll need to use a sabersaw to cut all the way into each corner. So the hatch doesn't bind or fall through as you finish cutting, reinstall the hardware as you complete a cutline to hold the hatch in place. That way, once installed, the bolts and hinges will hold things together as you complete the cuts. The result: a perfectly centered hatch!

7 LAY OUT THE PORTHOLE WINDOWS AND HEN ACCESS HOLE. Cut out the hen access and fixed wall sides. "Opening Layouts" on p. 133 shows the positions of the three round openings on the coop sides. Trace around a 10- to 12-in.-dia. bowl to mark a cutline for each opening.

8 CUT THE PORTHOLE WINDOWS. Bore a couple of ½-in. access holes before using a sabersaw to cut out the windows. You'll install the acrylic windowpanes after painting the coop.

Assemble the Coop

Assembling the boxlike coop is the most challenging stage of this project because you'll be nailing large pieces together with little margin for error. You'll start by cutting the 2x2 floor cleats to length. Then you'll cut the plywood floor and top.

You'll attach a cleat to one coop side and then attach the floor to that cleat. Next, for each of the other sides, you'll attach a cleat and then fasten the cleat to the floor. As you go, you'll secure the edges of the coop sides with glue and finish nails.

Next, you'll add the coop's plywood top. The space between the top and the corrugated roofing helps cut the effects of the summer sun and seals in warmth during the winter. As a bonus, the space offers a handy storage area for gloves and other bits and pieces. For a clean appearance, the top is set into the four sides rather than sitting on top of them. You'll temporarily screw a couple of scraps to the top. The scraps will extend over the coop sides, so the top will automatically be flush to the top of the sides when you drop it in place.

Because the uprights are attached directly to the outside of the coop, the side that contains the vent and next box hatches needs to be notched for the skids to pass through. And now is the time that you will trim 5½ in. off the cleanout-door side to allow a skid to pass underneath.

1 **INSTALL THE FIRST FLOOR CLEAT.** Cut the four floor cleats to the dimensions given in "What You'll Need." Attach a long cleat to one of the 66-in.-long plywood coop sides. Measure 28 in. up from the bottom edge of the plywood and use a framing square or drywall T-square to mark a guide line across the width. Using a scrap of ½-in. plywood as a spacer as shown, align the top of the long cleat along the line and clamp it in place. Flip the panel over and use 1⅝-in. deck screws to fasten the cleat.

2 **CUT AND INSTALL THE COOP FLOOR.** Cut the plywood floor and the plywood coop top to the dimensions listed in "What You'll Need." Clamp the floor to the top of the cleat and then fasten it to the cleat using 1⅝-in. deck screws about every 6 in.

3 ADD THE OTHER SIDES. Measure 28 in. up from the bottom edge of the other long plywood side and strike a perpendicular line. Using a scrap of 2x2 as a spacer, attach a short coop floor cleat so it is 1½ in. from each side. Line up the side and attach the floor to the cleat using 1⅝-in. screws. Fasten the side edges with exterior wood glue and 4d galvanized nails. Drill ⅛-in. pilot holes to keep the nails from splitting the plywood. Roll the structure a quarter turn as you add the other sides, fastening in the same way.

4 INSTALL THE TOP. Clamp a strip of plywood or a plank to the coop to hold up the short sides while you work. Temporarily screw scraps of wood to the top piece to hold it in place. Make the scraps longer than the top as shown so that when you set the top into the coop it will be flush with the top edges of the sides. Apply exterior wood glue to the edges of the top, drop it in place, and fasten with 4d-galvanized nails.

5 CUT SIDES TO ACCOMMODATE THE SKIDS AND ATTACH PLYWOOD STOPS. Use a scrap of 2x6 to lay out the two notches at the bottom of the side that contains the vent and nesting box hatch. These notches are shown in "Opening Layouts" (p. 133). Cut the notches with a sabersaw. Now lay a line across the cleanout-door side 5½ in. from the bottom. Make this cut with a circular saw, as shown. Cut the plywood stops for the cleanout door, vent hatch, and nesting box hatch to the dimensions listed in "What You'll Need." Attach them to the bottom inside edge of each opening so 1 in. of the stop is exposed to catch the door or hatch.

Make the Front and Back Frames

The open-air run gives your hens plenty of sheltered space for scratching. For ease of cleaning and replenishing feed and water, it has a nice, wide access door. The coop and run are tied together by 2x6 skids that eliminate the need for any sort of foundation and make it possible to drag the house to a new location when needed.

Mirror-image frames for the front and back of the run attach to the coop to tie everything together. The result is a light yet solid structure to house and protect your hens.

You'll start by cutting angles on the ends of the skids to make the coop easier to drag should you ever need to move it. Then you will attach uprights to the skids, leaving them long. You'll scribe a line along the uprights to cut them to follow the roof slope. After cutting the uprights, you'll add rake boards along the slopes and then crosspieces to tie the top of the frames together.

1 **ANGLE-CUT THE SKIDS.** The skids are made from 10-ft.-long 2x6s. At both ends of both skids, measure in 2 in. and make a 45-degree cut at the bottom edge.

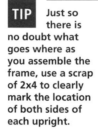 

TIP Just so there is no doubt what goes where as you assemble the frame, use a scrap of 2x4 to clearly mark the location of both sides of each upright.

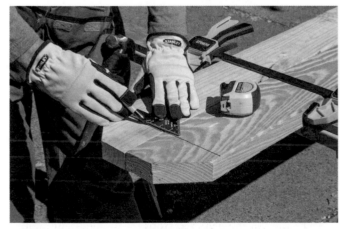

2 **MARK FOR THE UPRIGHTS.** Clamp the skids together upper edge to upper edge and mark for the location of each upright as shown in the drawing on p. 129.

3 **ROUGH-CUT THE UPRIGHTS AND ASSEMBLE THEM TO THE SKIDS.** "What You'll Need" gives the final lengths of the four uprights for each side, but you'll initially leave them at least an inch longer than their final lengths so that after you assemble them to the skids you can scribe them for cuts that follow the roof angle. Place the uprights along their layout lines, square them, and secure them to the skids with two 2½-in. deck screws at each connection.

4 MARK THE ROOF ANGLE ON ONE SET OF UPRIGHTS. With each upright squared up and fastened in its location, temporarily attach a 2x4 guide board to mark for the angled cuts along the roofline. Position the top of the guide board at 77½ in. on the longest upright and at 61 in. on the shortest upright. Mark a cutline on each upright.

5 CUT THE ANGLES. With the angles marked, detach the 2x4 guide board and slip it under the uprights to raise them so you can trim along each cutline with a circular saw.

TIP Unless you happen to have pieces of 2x4 around that will work for some of the uprights, use full-length 8-ft. 2x4s for the four longer (up-slope) uprights and make the four shorter (down-slope) uprights by cutting 12-ft. 2x4s in half.

6 TRANSFER THE CUTLINES. To be sure the frame members match up, lay the wall with the angle cuts atop the untrimmed wall frame. Trace along the angled ends and make the cuts.

7 ATTACH THE RAKE BOARDS. Corrugated metal roofing comes in 10-ft.-long sections, a limit on the length of the roof. To set the overhang, make a mark 5 in. from the end of each 10-ft. 1x4 rake. Fasten the rake boards flush to the angled ends of the frame using two 1⅝-in. deck screws at each connection.

8 **ATTACH THE FRAMES TO THE COOP.** Set the coop upright and clamp a board to the inside short side as shown to prevent tipping. Put the frames in place and temporarily tack them to the coop with a few 2½-in. screws. To avoid protruding fasteners, reach inside the coop to install 1⅝-in. exterior screws every foot or so through the plywood and into each upright. When done, remove the 2½-in. screws.

9 **ADD CROSSPIECES.** Cut the 2x4 crosspieces to length according to "What You'll Need." Using two 1⅝-in. deck screws per connection, attach the roof crosspieces through the 1x4 rake boards, drilling pilot holes when near the end of the board. Also drive in two 2½-in. screws where crosspieces meet uprights as shown. Install the two bottom crosspieces using 2½-in. screws fastened through each skid. The midway crosspiece is installed between the #4 uprights 34 in. up from the bottom of each skid.

Install the Door and Windows

The heavy lifting is done. Now it's time to assemble the door by screwing together rails and stiles and adding a plywood crosspiece that will stiffen the door. Next, you will install the doorstop—a piece of 2x4 that spans the uprights that flank the door so the top of the door will stop against it. Then you'll install the door and the acrylic windows in the fixed wall and cleanout door.

TIP The 29¾-in. door rail length given in "What You'll Need" assumes that the distance between the uprights flanking the door is 33 in. (Subtract 3 in. for the width of both stiles and ¼ in. for clearance.) Measure between the uprights in case you need to adjust your rail lengths.

1 **ASSEMBLE THE DOOR.** The perimeter of the door consists of two 2x4 rails between two 2x2 stiles. Attach the stiles to the rails with glue and two 1⅝-in. screws in predrilled holes at each connection.

2 **ADD THE DOOR BRACE.** This horizontal piece stiffens the door. Cut a piece of ½-in. plywood to 6 in. by the width of your door. Fasten it to the inside of the door 30 in. from the bottom with glue and 1¼-in. wood screws.

Get the Warp Out

If you find that one of your plywood doors or hatches has a warp to it, add a flat piece of plywood. Attach it to the worst area of warp a few inches away from the edges using exterior glue and six or eight ¾-in. wood screws. As the fasteners go in, they will draw up the warp.

3 INSTALL THE DOOR. Using staggered 2½-in. screws, attach the 2x4 doorstop to the back of the uprights that flank the door. Position the doorstop 57 in. above the skid. Leaving a ⅛-in. gap on each side of the door, clamp the door to the doorstop so their top edges align and install a pair of 3-in. hinges. Note that the door is set 2 in. above grade so it will clear the ground when it swings. If the uprights prove to be less than parallel, back out a few screws and realign them. Install the barrel bolt.

4 CUT THE ACRYLIC PANES. Cut two acrylic pieces to 14 in. x 14 in. to cover the portholes in the fixed wall and the cleanout door. For a neat cut, score the sheet several times with a utility knife guided by a metal straightedge. Position the cutline directly over the edge of your worktable and, holding a straightedge firmly over the cutline, crack the acrylic downward.

5 INSTALL THE ACRYLIC PANES. Predrill ⅛-in.-dia. holes in each acrylic pane. Make three holes on each side, about 1 in. from the edges, with one near each corner and one centered. Remove the cleanout door and fasten a pane inside with ¾-in. #10 pan-head screws. Attach a pane inside the fixed wall in the same way. Make the screws snug, not tight, so you won't crack the acrylic and to allow the panes to expand and contract with temperature changes. Reinstall the cleanout door.

Disassemble to Paint

Okay, it's only a chicken coop, but if you want a *really* neat paint job, begin by removing the hardware and detaching the coop from the run. This approach makes painting less fussy, a time-saver in the long run. Should you paint the interior? Chickens don't pick at wood much and it is fine to leave the interior walls of the coop bare, but a coat of paint will make cleaning easier down the road.

Install Screening and Roofing

Now you are closing in on the final details. You'll use roofing screws to install the screening on the door and all the open areas, being careful to seal up every place a wily predator might sneak in. Then you will add the corrugated roofing.

TIP If you choose plastic corrugated roofing, be aware that it expands and contracts. To avoid future cracking, drill screw holes with a carbide-tipped drill bit that is slightly larger than the size of the fastener.

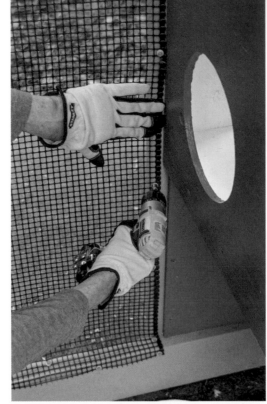

1 **INSTALL THE SCREENING.** Use #9 x 1-in. roofing screws spaced about every 6 in. to attach the screening to the inside of the run openings.

TIP Fencing staples have long been the default fastener for screening. They hold wonderfully but are challenging to install, especially on bouncy framing. A better choice is #9 x 1-in. roofing screws. Installed with a hex-head bit, they are self-tapping and nicely grab the screening with their flexible washers. Best of all, if you need to tighten up your screening, they are easy to back out and reinstall.

2 **SEAL IT UP.** Take care to cover all the areas where a predator might get in. Cover the large areas with screening first, then use cutoffs to fill in smaller areas.

3 **ATTACH SCREENING TO THE DOOR.** Attach the screening to the door stiles with roofing screws, stretching the screening over the crosspiece. The screw heads would prevent the rails from closing against the stop and the skid, so use 1-in. roofing nails instead about every 6 in. along the top and bottom edges.

4 **ADD THE ROOFING.** Corrugated roofing is available in 26-in. × 10-ft. panels. Overlap the panels 2 in. to yield a 4-ft. × 10-ft. roof. Position the roofing so it overhangs the downslope side by about ¼ in. to act as a drip edge. Attach the panels to the frame members using #9 × 1-in. roofing screws every 8 in. or so. A small block of wood will keep the panel from curling up as you attach it.

Make the Nesting Boxes

Hens relish privacy as they get down to work. Without a quiet, clean spot to lay her egg, a hen will leave it most anywhere where it can get dirty or damaged. This nesting box has four 9-in. x 12-in. x 12-in. compartments—plenty for up to eight hens because they lay at different times of the day. It is made a bit short for the coop space so you can easily lift it out for an occasional hosing down. The lip on both sides helps contain the bedding straw and keeps the eggs from rolling off.

Making the plywood nesting box is as easy as one-two-three. You'll cut and lay out the top and bottom, cut and attach the partitions, and then add 1x4 lips that will contain the straw that gives the hens a comfy place to lay.

NESTING BOX

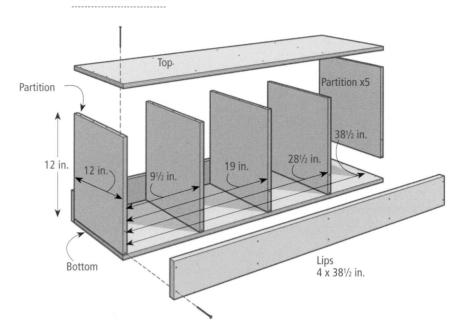

1 **PREPARE THE TOP AND BOTTOM OF THE NESTING BOX.** Cut the nesting box top and bottom to the dimensions listed in "What You'll Need." Clamp the pieces side by side and mark them together for the five partitions as shown in the "Nesting Box" drawing.

2 **CUT THE PARTITIONS AND ASSEMBLE ONE SIDE.** Cut the five 12-in. x 12-in. partitions. Drill four 1/8-in. pilot holes through the top and bottom pieces for 4d galvanized nails on each side of the partitions. Assemble the sides to the partitions with glue and 4d galvanized finish nails.

3 **ADD THE LIPS.** Cut the two 1x4 lips to fit across the length of the nesting box (one at the front and one at the back). Drill two pilot holes at each partition and attach with 4d nails.

TIP When making pilot holes through the partitions, drill from the inside so you can be sure to get the holes between the layout lines. This will guarantee that the nails won't miss the partitions when you nail through the top and bottom.

Add Final Details

Hens reveal their jungle origins by preferring to sleep while perched on a roost, so you will start by installing one inside and one outside. Then you'll drill holes in a ramp to give the girls traction when they climb up. Next, you will add 2x2 bars across the door side, a decorative touch that also affords the hens extra privacy. You'll make and install handles and install hooks and eyes to hold up the vent and access hatches. Hang the feeder and waterer, and you are ready to welcome your new tenants to their coop.

1 **MAKE THE ROOSTS.** A 2- to 3-in.-thick tree limb, bark and all, makes an ideal roost. Drill pilot holes in the frame and coop for 2½-in. deck screws to hold the limb. Add a temporary support (shown) to make installation easy. Hens like an outdoor *and* an indoor roost, so install both.

2 **MAKE THE RAMP.** Use a 5/4 x 6-in. cedar deck board to make a 74-in. ramp from the run to the coop. Slats placed every 6 in. or so work fine, but for something different, bore 1¼-in. holes with a hole saw. The holes offer plenty of traction while letting much of the poop fall through. Freehand the location of the holes about 3 in. apart in a zigzag fashion, making sure the holes are at least 1 in. from the edge.

3 **ADD THE BARS.** For a decorative touch that also affords the hens extra privacy, add the 71-in. 1x2s to the door side of the hen house. (If you prefer, leave the bars off.) Prefinish them with an exterior-grade finish such as tung oil before installing. Using a scrap of 1x2 as a spacer so each bar extends ¾ in. beyond the outside edge of the #4 upright, run them straight across the closed door. Use scraps of 1x2s as spacers between the bars, as shown. Attach them with a 1¼-in. exterior screw at every point the bar intersects with the framing. Be careful not to let the bars run beyond the right edge of the door.

TIP This handy countersink bit drills a pilot hole and then carves out an indentation for the screw head—a quick way to neatly sink screws flush to the surface.

4 **CUT THE BARS IN PLACE.** Once you've installed the bars, mark for cutting between the door and the frame. Use a scrap of 1x2 to set the cutting depth on a circular saw. Then cut along the line.

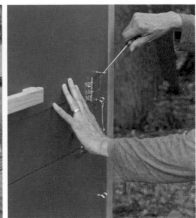

5 **MAKE THE HANDLES.** To make the three hatch handles, cut 1x2 into six 1½-in.-square blocks. Cut three pieces of 1x2 to 8 in. long. Glue two blocks to each handle and then clamp them all together as shown until the glue cures.

6 **ATTACH THE HANDLES.** The position of the handles on the vent and nesting box hatches and the cleanout door is shown in the drawing "Opening Layouts" on p. 133. To conceal the fasteners, clamp the handles in place as shown, and measure for a pilot hole for each handle block. Attach each block with 1⅝-in. deck screws from inside the hatch or door.

7 **INSTALL HOOKS AND EYES.** Locations for the hooks and eyes are given in the "Opening Layouts" drawing. Drill pilot holes and install hooks and eyes for holding open the ventilation hatch and the access door to the nesting box.

TIP Plastic-coated ³/₁₆-in. wire rope, ⅛-in. wire rope clamps, and a cheap carabiner, all available from a home center or hardware store, make a neat combo for supporting your feeder and waterer.

8 **HANG THE FEEDER AND WATERER.** Bore a ¾-in. hole in the roof crosspiece at the low end of the run. Position the hole 12 in. in from the corner. Bore a corresponding hole in the coop 8 in. down from the coop top and 9¾ in. from the inside edge of the upright. Push in an 84-in. piece of ½-in. rigid electrical conduit for hanging the feeder and waterer. The extra length allows for a bit of conduit in the coop in case you want to hang a light, feeder, or waterer for wintertime use.

THE CLEANOUT DOOR SIDE.

THE VENT AND NESTING BOX HATCH SIDE.

Furnishing the Coop

Once everything is assembled, you can go out and buy a waterer (get one with a built-in heating element if your winters are fierce). You'll want a feeder too, as well as straw for litter, feed, and crushed oyster shell—the stuff eggshells are made of. Make sure everything is ready before you introduce your hens to their new home—neither you nor your chickens will appreciate coping with a punch list of unfinished tasks when the chicken house is occupied. You can find the Little Giant® 30# feeder with 14-in. pan and the 3-gal. heated plastic poultry fountain used in this coop at fleetfarm.com.

TIP To avoid manure fouling the water, locate the waterer at the low end of the ramp. Also keep it well away from the outdoor roost.

PART TWO

PROJECTS FOR OUTDOOR LIVING

STANLEY

THE PROJECTS in this second part of the book are designed to make your outdoor living space a more inviting and beautiful place in which to relax and entertain. Often as not, enjoying our yards involves dining al fresco—the herb planter, barbecue cart, and picnic table and benches are all aimed at the pleasures of cooking and eating outdoors. And whether dining or just hanging out on your patio or deck, you want a pleasant view—the handsome planter will let you display a generous planting of flowers, while the trash and recycling corral will take those containers off display. The pergola is the perfect solution when you want to add a bit of shade without completely blocking the sun. Meanwhile, the storage bench provides extra seating, and when it's time to reluctantly head indoors, you can just open the lid and stash outdoor cushions out of the weather.

Herb
Planter

WOULDN'T IT BE GREAT to step just outside the kitchen to snip fresh herbs for tonight's dinner recipe? This handsome and generously sized planter will provide all the herbs any home kitchen could need and you won't even have to bend down to harvest them. It has two tiers. Most herbs such as oregano, chives, tarragon, and thyme are happy in shallow soil and will thrive on the lower tier. The upper tier is optional. It provides deeper soil for herbs like basil and rosemary that like to sink their roots deeper. Or you could fill the upper tier with flowering plants.

The planter is straightforward to build thanks to simple biscuit joinery. The legs are made from nominal 4x4 cedar posts that actually measure 3½ in. x 3½ in. The rest of the planter is built with nominal 5/4 x 6 cedar decking boards that actually measure 1 in. x 5½ in. These decking boards come with rounded edges that will save you some sanding. The posts and decking boards are readily available at home centers and lumberyards.

151

WHAT YOU'LL NEED

- 4 legs
  3½ in. x 3½ in. x 32 in., cedar
- 4 aprons
  1 in. x 7¾ in. x 29 in., cedar
- 4 cleats
  ¾ in. x 1 in. x 29 in., cedar
- 5 bottom boards
  1 in. x 5½ in. x 33 in., cedar
- 1 bottom board
  1 in. x 4¼ in., cedar

- 2 shelf supports
  1 in. x 2 in. x 34 in., cedar
- 5 shelf boards
  1 in. x 5½ in. x 35 in., cedar
- 2 end shelf boards
  1 in. x 3 in. x 29 in., cedar
- 4 apron caps
  1 in. x 4 in. x 37 in., cedar
- 8 center-box pieces (optional)
  1 in. x 5½ in. x 12 in., cedar

HARDWARE AND SUPPLIES

- 3d galvanized finish nails
- 4d galvanized finish nails
- 2-in. deck screws
- Exterior wood glue
- #20 joinery biscuits
- Furniture glides

HERB PLANTER

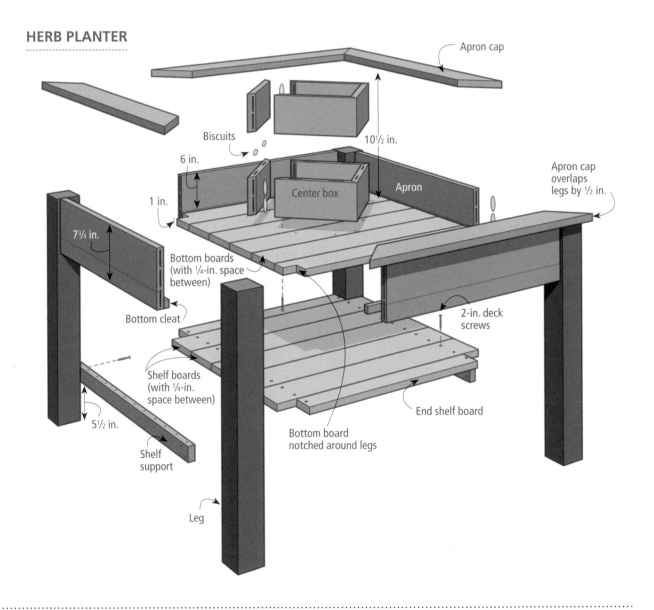

Apron cap

Biscuits

6 in.

1 in.

7¾ in.

Bottom boards (with ¼-in. space between)

Bottom cleat

Center box

10½ in.

Apron

Apron cap overlaps legs by ½ in.

2-in. deck screws

Shelf boards (with ¼-in. space between)

5½ in.

Shelf support

Bottom board notched around legs

End shelf board

Leg

Our cedar posts are a rich chocolaty brown that contrasts nicely with the lighter 5/4 boards, so we didn't want to stain our planter. We chose instead to finish it with four coats of pure tung oil mixed with an equal amount of mineral spirits. Tung oil deepens the wood's natural color without adding any gloss. It repels water, making it a great finish for outdoor furniture. And it is easily renewed by adding more coats.

> **TIP** If a 12-ft. 4x4 is too long to fit in your vehicle, ask the lumberyard or home center to cut it in half for you. They'll be happy to help you.

Make the Legs and Aprons

As mentioned, the legs are cut from nominal 4x4 cedar posts. You can make the four legs from one 12-ft. post. You'll cut the legs to length using a miter saw with a stop block to ensure that they all are exactly the same length. Then you'll mark the shelf support heights on the legs—it's easiest to mark them all at once before assembly.

Most lumberyards and home centers don't carry cedar stock wide enough to make the 7¾-in.-wide aprons, so make them by edge-joining nominal 5/4 x 6-in. deck boards. You'll start by cutting the boards to length. Then you will rip one rounded edge off each board before joining pairs of boards along the ripped edges using glue and joinery biscuits. Finally, you'll rip the aprons to final width.

> **TIP** For the cleanest cut with a power miter saw, lower the blade slowly through the workpiece.

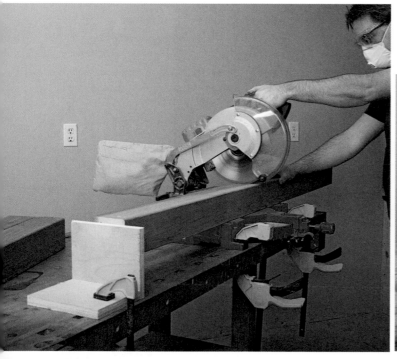

1 **CUT THE LEGS TO LENGTH.** Clamp your miter saw to the workbench so it can't shift position. Cut one end of the 4x4 stock square, then lay out a line and cut one leg to length. Place this leg against the sawblade, slide the stop fence up to the other end of the leg, and clamp a stop block to the bench (see "Making and Using a Stop Block," p. 171). Now you can just slide the stock up to the fence to cut the other three legs to length.

2 **MARK THE SHELF SUPPORT HEIGHTS ON THE LEGS.** Choose the two adjacent faces of each leg that you want to face out. Put one outside face of each leg down on the bench and clamp the legs together with the ends flush. Make a mark 7½ in. from the bottom of the legs and use a square to extend the mark across an inside face of all the legs.

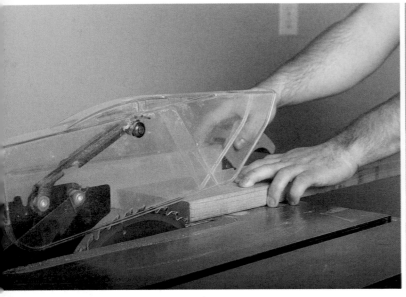

3 **CUT THE APRON BOARDS TO LENGTH AND RIP ONE EDGE OF EACH.** Cut the apron boards to 29 in. long. It is important that they all be exactly the same length. To achieve this, cut them with a miter saw and stop block as you did the legs. Now set the tablesaw fence to trim the roundover off one edge of the apron boards. Make those cuts.

4 **LAY OUT THE BISCUIT JOINTS ON THE APRON BOARDS.** Clamp a pair of boards together with the outside faces up and the trimmed edges flush. Draw layout lines across the joint for three biscuits—one centered and the others located about 1¾ in. from each end. Do this for the three remaining pairs of boards.

Pairing Boards

Before ripping edges for joinery, take a few minutes to choose visually pleasing pairs of boards. Cedar varies in color, so pairing boards that are most similar in color will help to hide the glue joints. Look for grain patterns that flow together. After glue-up, you'll be trimming 3¼ in. off the width of the aprons—you might be able to trim off the most unsightly knots by placing them on outside edges, perhaps ripping knots off one edge before ripping the other edge to final width.

5 **CUT THE BISCUIT SLOTS.** If your biscuit joiner has a removable fence, take it off. Set the cutting depth for #20 biscuits. Clamp a length of 2x4 to the bench, put an apron board against the 2x4, and press the board flat against the bench as you cut the biscuit slots. Do this for all the apron boards.

6 GLUE UP THE APRONS. Do a test fit: Put biscuits in the slots on one board. Clamp the boards together with two clamps near the ends. Make sure the ends are flush. Then flip the assembly over and add two more clamps. After the test fit, remove the clamps. Put glue in the slots and along the edge of one side of the joint and in only the slots on the other side. Clamp the joint together again. As you tighten the clamps, make sure the ends are perfectly flush—joinery biscuits are designed to allow some side-to-side adjustment.

7 RIP THE APRONS TO FINAL WIDTH. You'll rip both sides of the aprons to remove the rounded edges. As described in "Pairing Boards" on the facing page, you can strategically set the width of the first rip to remove unsightly knots as long as the rip is no narrower than about 8 in. Make the first rip on all the boards, then set the tablesaw fence to 7¾ in. from the blade and rip all the aprons to final width. Keep the offcuts—you'll use them later to make cleats.

Skimming Off Excess Glue

One way to remove glue squeeze-out is to just wipe the wet glue away with a wet sponge. The problem with doing this, especially with a porous wood like cedar, is that diluted glue can soak into the wood and show up as light spots when you apply finish. Instead, let the glue partially set for 20 to 30 minutes until the glue starts to change color around the edges—it will look a little like a sunny-side-up egg. Then skim the glue off with a chisel. (Squeeze-out doesn't matter for the inside faces of the herb planter aprons that will be covered by planting soil.)

Assemble the Aprons to the Legs and Add Cleats

This is when the planter really starts to take shape. You'll start by laying out and cutting slots for biscuits that will join the legs to the aprons. Then you will make two subassemblies, each consisting of two legs and an apron. When the glue sets, you'll attach the remaining aprons to the subassemblies.

TIP	Before assembly, sand the outside faces of the aprons with 80-grit, then 120-grit sandpaper. This is a lot easier than sanding into the corners that the leg reveals will create.

1 **MARK THE APRON-TO-LEG JOINTS.** Stand the legs upside down on the bench. Place the aprons upside down against the legs and mark an "A" on the end of one apron and on the face of the leg it will meet. Go around and mark all the apron-to-leg joints—the last one will be "H."

2 **LAY OUT BISCUIT SLOTS IN THE APRON ENDS.** The aprons are attached to the legs with three biscuits at each joint. Start by making three marks on the inside face of each end of all the aprons—one mark 1½ in. from each end and the third mark centered. (If you make the end marks farther in, there won't be room for three #20 biscuits.)

3 **TRANSFER SLOT LAYOUTS TO THE LEGS.** The legs have a ½-in. "reveal." In other words, the aprons will be recessed ½ in. from the outside of the legs. To accommodate this space, place scraps of ½-in. plywood on the bench and put an apron with its outside face down on the plywood. Place the correspondingly labeled leg face against the raised apron with the top of the leg flush to the top of the apron. Transfer the slot marks to the inside of the leg.

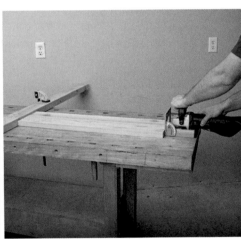

4 **CUT BISCUIT SLOTS IN THE APRONS.** Clamp a 2x4 across the bench. Place an apron on the bench with its outside face down. Put one end against the 2x4 as you cut #20 biscuit slots in the other end. Do this for both ends of all the aprons.

STANLEY

5 **CUT BISCUIT SLOTS IN THE LEGS.** Clamp a 2x4 along the bench. Place a leg against the 2x4 with an outside face down and a piece of ½-in. plywood against the leg to create the reveal. Put the biscuit joiner on the plywood and cut #20 biscuit slots.

6 **MAKE SUBASSEMBLIES.** Put glue in the slots and along one edge of an apron. Put glue in just the slots of the correspondingly labeled leg face. Insert the biscuits. Do the same on the other side of the apron. Make sure that the top of the apron is flush with the top of the legs. Apply two clamps across the legs as shown. Use just enough pressure to bring the joints completely together. Check that the apron is square to the legs. If it is not, loosen the clamps slightly and check for square again. Make another subassembly the same way, using the apron that will be attached solely to the other two legs.

Presquaring before Glue-up

Once glue is in place, you want to spend as little time as possible squaring the planter. To that end, you can "presquare" it during test assembly. Place the subassemblies vertically on the bench. Put biscuits in the slots and clamp the remaining aprons in place. Screw a length of scrap into the top of one leg and start a screw in the other end. Pull the assembly square and drive the other screw into the diagonal leg. Back the screws out of the legs, but leave them protruding slightly through the scrap. When you glue up the planter, screw one end of the scrap into the hole in the leg. When the other screw finds its hole, you'll know the planter is square.

7 **ADD THE REMAINING APRONS.** When the glue has set, remove the clamps from the subassemblies. Place the subassemblies vertically on the bench as shown. Put glue in the biscuit slots of the legs that are resting on the bench. Put glue in the slots and along both edges of the corresponding apron. Apply two clamps across the legs on the bench. Attach the fourth apron the same way with biscuits, glue, and clamps.

Add Cleats and Bottom Boards

The offcuts you saved when you made the aprons are already the right length for the cleats, so you just need to rip four pieces before installing them with glue and nails. Then you'll cut six bottom boards to length. You'll notch the first board to fit around two legs, then glue and nail it and four more boards in place with ¼-in. spacers between. Finally, you'll rip and notch the final filler bottom board to fit and install it.

1 **RIP AND INSTALL THE CLEATS.** Set your tablesaw fence ¾ in. from the blade and rip four cleats from the apron offcuts. For each cleat, put glue on a 1-in. face and clamp it in position flush to the bottom of an apron. Secure it with 3d finish nails using a hammer or a power finish nailer.

2 **CUT THE BOARDS TO LENGTH.** The bottom boards should be 33 in. long, but measure across aprons in case the dimensions of your planter vary a bit. Use a miter saw with stop block to cut six 5/4 x 6 boards to length.

3 **LAY OUT AND CUT THE FIRST NOTCHES.** The first board will need a 2-in. x 2-in. notch on each end to fit around the legs. Set a combination square by placing it against the leg and apron as shown at left. Clamp the board to the bench and use the square to lay out the notch (right). Cut the notches with a sabersaw or handsaw.

4 **INSTALL FULL-WIDTH BOTTOM BOARDS.** Make two spacers by ripping ¼ in. off a piece of scrap and cutting the rip into two pieces about 6 in. long. After checking that the notches fit, glue and nail the first bottom board to the cleats using 4d finish nails. Space the nails about 6 in. apart along the edge and use two nails into each end. Install the remaining four full-width bottom boards with glue and two nails into each end, putting spacers between the boards before nailing them.

5 **RIP, NOTCH, AND INSTALL THE FILLER BOTTOM BOARD.** Measure between the last full board and the apron. Subtract ¼ in. to get the width of the filler bottom board. Rip the board to width, notch it, and install against the apron with glue and nails.

Add the Shelf Support and Shelf

Besides providing storage, perhaps for a watering can, the shelf and its supports make the planter sturdier by tying the legs together. To make the shelf supports, you'll cut a piece of 5/4 stock to length and then rip the two supports from that piece. You'll screw the shelf supports across the inside of the legs.

Next, you'll cut five shelf boards to length to overhang the supports by 3 in. After installing those shelf pieces with ¼-in. drainage spaces between, you'll cut to length and rip end shelf pieces to fit between the faces of opposing legs. You'll install the end shelf pieces overhanging the ends of the supports by ½ in.

TIP If you find the distance between the legs at the shelf supports is slightly greater than at the top of the planter, you can put a clamp across them at the bottom to draw them together a bit before securing the supports.

1 **MAKE THE SHELF SUPPORTS.** You can rip both shelf supports from a piece of 5/4 x 6 stock—or if you happen to have a piece lying around, from 5/4 x 4 stock. But first, use a miter saw to crosscut the stock to the final length of 34 in. Then set the tablesaw fence 2 in. from the blade and rip the two shelf supports. Make both rips with the rounded end of the stock against the fence.

2 **ATTACH THE SUPPORTS.** With the planter on its side, place a support across two legs with the ripped edge aligned below the layout lines you made earlier. Center the support across the legs—it should end 1 in. short of the outside of the legs. Clamp the support in place and secure it with two 2-in. deck screws into each leg. Countersink the screw holes, offsetting them from each other. Flip the planter over and install the other support parallel to the first.

3 **MARK THE CENTER OF EACH SUPPORT BOARD.** Make a mark centered across the outside face of each shelf support—it should be at 17 in. from the legs, but measure to be sure.

4 **CUT SHELF BOARDS AND INSTALL THE CENTER ONE.** Use a miter saw to cut the five full-length shelf boards to 35 in. long. Make marks centered across the bottom face of both ends of a shelf board. Align the shelf marks to the support marks and use a combination square set to 3 in. to establish the overhang. Clamp the board in place and check for square before securing it with two 2-in. deck screws in countersunk holes.

5 **INSTALL THE REMAINING FOUR FULL BOARDS.** Put the ¼-in. spacers you made earlier between the center board and another shelf board. Check that the boards are flush on the end. Then clamp, predrill, countersink, and secure with deck screws as you did the center board. Install the remaining full boards the same way.

6 **CUT AND INSTALL THE END SHELF BOARDS.** On the miter saw, cut two 5/4 x 6 boards to 29 in. and then move to the tablesaw to rip them to 3 in. wide. Use the spacers to position each piece and attach to the support board with two screws on each end.

Breaking Edges

To make the end shelf boards match the full boards, round the ripped edge on one side of the end boards. You can accomplish this in a few minutes with a piece of 80-grit sandpaper, or, to make the job even quicker while making less dust, "break" the edge with a few strokes of a block plane before smoothing it quickly with sandpaper.

Make and Attach the Optional Center Box

The optional center box is set at a 45-degree angle to the apron. It's made from eight pieces of 5/4 x 6 stock cut to 12 in. long with bevel joints at both ends. You'll start by making 13-in.-long "blanks" on the miter saw and then you'll bevel both ends of the blanks on the tablesaw. After cutting the pieces, you'll use glue and biscuits to join the pieces into two four-sided boxes. Then you'll use glue and biscuits to attach one box atop the other before attaching them to the bottom boards with screws.

> **TIP** After setting your tablesaw blade to 45 degrees, make a test cut on a piece of scrap. Then use a square to check that the blade is at exactly the right angle before beveling the center box pieces.

Tablesaw Safety

Never make a cut on the tablesaw with the workpiece in contact with the fence and the miter gauge at the same time—the risk of the work binding and causing dangerous kickback is very high. The stop block used in steps 3 and 4 avoids this problem because the workpiece leaves contact with the block before it reaches the blade.

1 **MAKE THE BLANKS AND BEVEL ONE END. Start by** using a miter saw to cut eight pieces of 5/4 x 6 stock to about 13½ in. long. Tilt the blade on the tablesaw to 45 degrees and, with the outside face up, bevel one end of each blank.

2 **LAY OUT THE SECOND BEVEL ON ONE PIECE. Measure** across the outside of one piece (from the long side of the bevel) and make a mark at 12 in. Use a square to extend the mark into a 45-degree line across the edge of the piece that will be fed into the saw.

3 SET THE RIP FENCE AND BLOCK. With the blade still set to 45 degrees, align the bevel layout line on the edge of the first piece with the blade. Clamp a block of wood against the other end of the piece and lock the fence in position against the block as shown. Then unclamp the block and slide it toward the operator's side of the saw until it is at least 6 in. from the blade. Reclamp the block to the fence. Now the block will be the right distance from the blade to act as a stop, but the workpiece won't be in contact with the block when you slide the miter gauge forward to make the cut.

4 BEVEL THE SECOND END OF ALL THE PIECES. For each piece, put the already beveled end against the stop block with the long side of the bevel facing up. Use the miter gauge to make the cuts.

> **TIP** Don't be concerned if your center-box pieces come out a tad longer or shorter than 12 in. Thanks to the stop block, all the pieces will be exactly the same length, ensuring that the box will be square when you assemble it.

5 MARK FOR THE MITER BISCUITS. Set a combination square to 1½ in. and use it to mark the inside of each box side for two biscuit joint slots.

6 CUT THE BEVEL-JOINT BISCUIT SLOTS. If your biscuit joiner has a removable fence, take it off. Set the joiner to 45 degrees and to cut #20 slots. Clamp each center-box piece on the bench and cut a slot at each layout line.

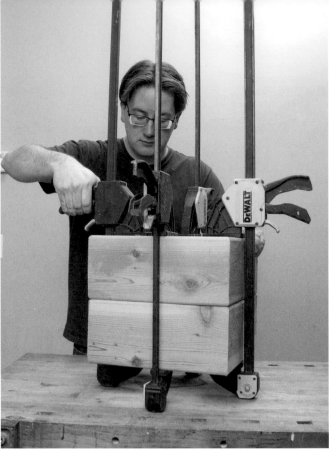

7 **GLUE UP THE BOX SECTIONS.** Test-assemble four of the box pieces with biscuits to make sure the box is square. Then put glue in all the slots and on one surface of each beveled joint. Insert the biscuits and apply four clamps—one at top and bottom in both directions as shown. Check for square and make sure the top surfaces are flush. Assemble the second box in the same way.

8 **JOIN THE BOXES.** Put glue on the top edge of one box, put the other box in place over it, and join the two boxes with four clamps—one centered over each side of the boxes.

9 **POSITION THE CENTER BOX.** Locate the center point of each apron—it should be at 14½ in. from the legs. Then draw centerlines across opposing aprons. Position the center box with the corners meeting the lines. Tack the box in place with two screws on opposite sides of the box. Drive the screws partway into the bottom.

10 **ATTACH THE CENTER BOX.** Turn the planter upside down on sawhorses. Secure the box with 2-in. decking screws driven through the bottom boards. (The spaces between the boards will let you see where the box is located.) Wherever possible, use two screws through each bottom board. Then remove the tack screws.

Make and Attach the Apron Cap

The apron cap adds an attractive detail but also has practical purposes: It covers the top of the legs, keeping water away from that end grain. It also extends 2 in. over the inside of the aprons, helping to keep soil contained in the planter.

You'll start by crosscutting four pieces to rough length and then ripping them to final width. You'll miter one end of each piece. Then you'll miter the other end of one piece and use it to set up a stop block to miter all the other ends. Next, you'll tack-nail all the pieces in position in case you need to reposition them to get the miter joints to line up. Then, one by one, you'll remove each cap piece, apply glue, and clamp it into place.

1 **MAKE BLANKS AND MITER ONE END.** The finished cap pieces will be 37 in. long—start by cutting 5/4 x 6 stock to about 38 in. Now rip these blanks to 4 in. wide on the tablesaw. Miter one end of each piece with the long side of the miter at the rounded edge that you didn't rip.

2 **MITER THE SECOND END OF ONE PIECE.** Lay out the second miter on one piece so that the long points of the miters will be 37 in. apart. After making a mark, use an angle square to lay out the 45-degree cutline. Cut the miter on the miter saw.

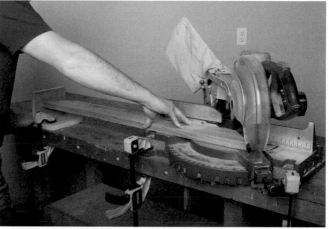

3 **CUT THE REMAINING MITERS.** Clamp the miter saw to the bench and lock the miter blade in the down position. Raise the guard and put the miter you just cut against the blade. Slide a stop against the tip of the miter on the other end (see "Making and Using a Stop Block," p. 171). Clamp the stop to the bench. Now, put each remaining piece against the stop to cut the remaining miters.

Sanding and Caulking

Use #80 grit and then #120 grit to sand all the areas that will not be hidden by dirt in the planter. Slightly round all the exposed edges to prevent splinters and improve adhesion of the finish.

When boards are planed to final thickness at the mill, the rotating cutters can compress the surface wood fibers; this causes the finish to adhere unevenly, revealing mill marks. And while the inside of the planter won't be seen, you will apply finish as a moisture barrier. For this reason, it's a good idea to sand the inside to #80 grit just to ensure optimal adhesion of the finish.

Cedar is a naturally rot-resistant wood, but it's a good idea to apply clear silicone caulk to seams and joints inside the planter where moisture would get trapped. Do this after sanding but before finishing. The caulk will adhere better to unfinished wood. The finish won't adhere to the clear silicone, but again, the inside won't be seen.

Apply the caulk inside the planter along the perimeter where the bottom boards meet the aprons and legs. Caulk where the aprons meet the legs and at the inside and outside of the bottom of the center box. Also caulk the inside of the center-box miter joints and the inside of the seam between the two box assemblies. Don't caulk the drainage spaces between boards. Smooth the caulk into the crevices with your finger or with a caulking tool as shown here.

Now you are ready to apply tung oil or another finish of your choice to the project. (See "Wood and Finishes for Outdoor Projects," p. 17.)

TIP If you don't have a lot of clamps, you can glue and clamp one cap piece at a time, letting the glue set between each glue-up.

4 **TACK-NAIL THE CAPS IN PLACE.** Put a cap piece in place so that the inside of both miters aligns to the inside corner of two legs. Tack the piece in place with one 4d finish nail driven into the top of each leg. Leave the nail heads protruding. Do this for all four caps.

TIP If a cap needs to be repositioned to close up the miters, pull its nails out of the apron but not out of the cap.

5 **GLUE AND CLAMP THE CAPS.** Pull off one cap piece, letting the nails protrude from the bottom. Put glue on the top of the apron and the exposed part of the top of the legs. Put the piece back in place, letting the nails find their original holes in the top of the legs. Secure the piece with three clamps. Now do the same for each cap piece. As you work your way around, put glue on the mitered face of the previous piece it will meet—you want glue on one face of each miter joint.

TIP It's a good idea to install furniture glides to raise the bottom of the legs a bit, preventing the end grain from wicking water (see step 4, "Install Furniture Glides," p. 183). Install the glides after applying the finish to seal the end grain.

Storage Bench

THIS SPACIOUS CEDAR storage
bench is designed to store outdoor
furniture cushions but could be used
to store anything from garden tools
to grilling accessories. Its simple lines
celebrate the beauty of the cedar
boards. The project is finished with
a translucent, cedar-tinted stain that
brings out cedar's natural multi-
toned color.

While the finish does add some
protection to the wood, be aware
that cedar will last for years with no
finish at all as long as it is kept clean
and in a place where it can dry quickly
after a rain or snow. Any applied finish will need to be renewed every
few years (see "Wood and Finishes
for Outdoor Projects," p. 17).

The cedar boards used for the lid
and the tongue-and-groove cedar
boards used for the box cladding

WHAT YOU'LL NEED

PINE

- 4 long rails
  ¾ in. x 3½ in. x 47¾ in.
- 4 short rails
  ¾ in. x 3½ in. x 23¾ in.
- 8 stiles
  ¾ in. x 3½ in. x 9 in.
- 2 long cleats
  ¾ in. x ¾ in. x 47¾ in.
- 2 short cleats
  ¾ in. x ¾ in. x 22¼ in.
- 13 bottom slats
  ¾ in. x 3½ in. x 23¾ in.
- 1 bottom filler slat
  ¾ in. x ½ in. x 23¾ in.

CEDAR

- 4 legs
  2½ in. x 2½ in. x 18 in.
- 24 cladding boards
  ¾ in. x 5 in. x 16⅛ in.,
  tongue and groove*
- 4 front and back cladding filler strips
  ¾ in. x 1⅜ in. x 16⅛ in.,
  tongue and groove
- 4 side cladding filler strips
  ¾ in. x 3⅝ in. x 16⅛ in.,
  tongue and groove
- 5 lid pieces
  ¾ in. x 5½ in. x 52⅞ in.
- 1 lid piece
  ¾ in. x 1⅛ in. x 52⅞ in.
- 2 long lid lips
  ¾ in. x 1½ in. x 54⅜ in.

- 2 short lid lips
  ¾ in. x 1½ in. x 30⅜ in.

*Note: Sold as nominal 1x6, these boards are 5⅜ in. wide but cover only 5 in. in width because the ⅜-in. tongue goes in the groove.

HARDWARE

- 96 coarse-thread pocket-hole screws, 1¼ in.
- 40 #20 joinery biscuits
- 4d finish nails
- Exterior wood glue
- 2 butt hinges, 1⅜ in. x 2 in.
- 1 lid support
- 4 furniture glides

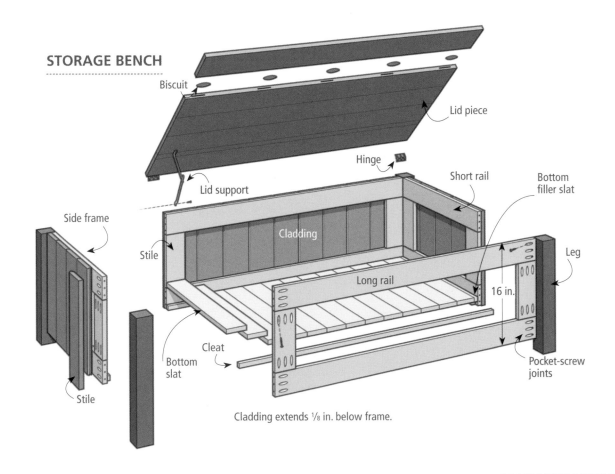

STORAGE BENCH

Biscuit

Lid piece

Hinge

Short rail

Bottom filler slat

Lid support

Side frame

Stile

Cladding

Long rail

Leg

16 in.

Stile

Bottom slat

Cleat

Bottom slat

Stile

Pocket-screw joints

Cladding extends ⅛ in. below frame.

come with one face planed smooth and the other face rough-sawn. We made the lid with the smooth side out because it will be sat upon and also to allow water to bead up and run off more readily. However, we chose to use the rough-sawn side for the box cladding to add some texture and to contrast with the legs and top. You can certainly use the smooth side out for the cladding if you prefer a less rustic look.

Make the Frames

The frame pieces are made of nominal 1x4 pine that is actually ¾ in. thick and 3½ in. wide, so you won't need to rip the stock to width. You'll start by cutting the pieces to length with a miter saw. The frames will be assembled with pocket-hole screws, so you'll use a jig to drill the pocket holes and then glue and screw the frames together.

> **TIP** Boards are usually square on the end when they come from the lumberyard, but sometimes they are not. So before you mark for a length cut, make it a habit to check the end for square, in case you have to square it with your miter saw.

1 **CUT THE FRAME PIECES TO LENGTH.** Use a miter saw with a stop block to quickly and accurately cut same-length pieces (see "What You'll Need" for lengths). The stiles are short, so you can clamp a stop block to the saw fence, as shown in the photo. For cutting the rails, see "Making and Using a Stop Block" below.

Making and Using a Stop Block

This stop block takes minutes to make, works equally well for a hand miter saw or power miter saw, and will let you quickly and accurately cut pieces to the same length. You need two scraps of ¾-in. plywood that are about 6 in. long. One piece will be the fence and needs to be wide enough so that when set upright, workpieces on the saw will bump into it. The other needs to be wide enough to clamp to the bench. Assemble the pieces with three 1¼-in. all-purpose screws through the face of the fence.

Clamp your saw to the bench so it can't shift position. To set the stop, measure and mark a cut on one workpiece and cut it to length. Place that piece against the sawblade, slide the stop fence up to other end of the piece, and clamp the stop to the bench. Now every piece of stock you butt into the fence will be cut to the same length as the first piece.

2 **CUT POCKET HOLES IN THE FRAME PIECES.** Each frame piece gets three pocket-screw holes in each end. These holes will be used to attach the stiles to the rails and to attach the rails to the legs. Center one hole across the width of each frame piece and locate the center of the other holes about ¾ in. from each side. Drill the holes with a pocket-hole jig.

TIP When putting glue on the rails, lay a stile next to it as a gauge for how long to make the glueline.

3 **ATTACH THE STILES TO THE RAILS.** Clamp a rail on edge in your bench vise as shown. Put glue on both ends of the rail where the stiles will join it and clamp it to the rail, making sure the side of the stile is flush to the end of the rail. Insert three pocket-hole screws. Attach a stile to the other side of the rail in the same way. Now clamp a same-length rail into the vise. Glue, clamp, and screw one stile to the rail, then do the same on the other end to complete the frame. Assemble the remaining three frames.

Make and Attach the Legs

The cedar legs are 2½ in. x 2½ in. wide and thick. Stock of those dimensions is not readily available, so you'll need to rip down 4x4s. You can make the four legs from a single 8-ft.-long 4x4 (actual dimensions 3½ in. x 3½ in.) that you will rip down on the tablesaw. You'll cut the pieces to length first because shorter pieces are easier to rip safely.

1 **CUT THE LEGS TO LENGTH.** Use a miter saw with a stop block to cut the legs to length. Because you are cutting only four legs, using the stop block won't save you much time over marking each piece. But it's still a great way to ensure that all four legs are exactly the same length—essential to making a bench that won't rock.

2 **MAKE THE FIRST PASS.** A 10-in. tablesaw blade won't cut all the way through a 3½-in.-thick piece, so you will need to make the first rip on each leg in two passes. Set the blade as high as it will go and set the fence 2½ in. from the blade. Run a leg through the saw. Be careful to keep your hand away from the blade as it emerges on the operator's side of the cut.

3 **COMPLETE THE FIRST RIP.** Flip the leg over and run it through the saw again to complete the first rip.

Sand the Legs and Round the Edges Now

Four-by-four lumber usually comes with rounded edges. After cutting the legs, one rounded edge will remain. You'll round all the edges to match and then sand the legs, tasks that are easier to do now than after the bench is assembled. Rounded edges look good, will be less painful if someone bumps into them, will prevent splinters, and will hold finish better.

PLANE THE EDGES. If you have a block plane, you can save a bit of time and sawdust by using it to make a few angled passes on the corners to approximate the existing roundover. If you don't have a block plane, you can skip this step.

SAND THE LEGS. Use 80-grit sandpaper to smooth the legs. An orbital sander like the one shown will speed the work, but you can use a piece of sandpaper wrapped around a block of wood.

SMOOTH THE CORNERS. Hand-sand the corners with 80-grit sandpaper to smooth the roundovers. Repeat steps 2 and 3 with 120-grit sandpaper.

4 **MAKE THE SECOND RIP.** Lower the tablesaw blade to about 2⅝ in. and leave the fence at 2½ in. from the blade. Place the surface you just ripped down on the saw and make another rip cut. Repeat steps 1 through 4 to make the remaining legs.

5 **ASSEMBLE THE LEGS TO THE SIDE FRAMES.** Put glue along a vertical edge of one side frame and lay the frame on the bench with the pocket holes facing up. Clamp a leg against the frame, making sure it is flush to the inside and top of the frame, then insert three pocket screws. Remove the clamp and attach a leg to the other side in the same way. Assemble legs to the other side frame.

TIP Place waxed paper under glue joints to prevent glue from getting on your bench. The glue won't bond to waxed paper.

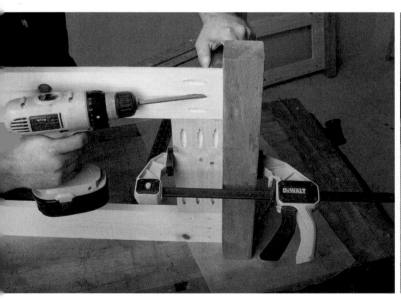

6 **ASSEMBLE THE FRONT AND BACK FRAMES TO THE LEGS.** Place a side-frame assembly on the bench with the bottom of the legs sticking up. Put glue on one end of a front frame and clamp it flush to the top and inside of a leg with the pocket holes facing out. Insert the pocket screws. Attach the back frame to the assembly in the same way, then attach the front and back frames to the legs of the other side-frame assembly.

7 **SQUARE THE BENCH.** Use a framing square to check that all the inside corners are square. Likely as not, the bench will be a bit out of square. If so, tack-screw a length of scrap to the bottom of one leg. Put the other end on the diagonally opposing leg and start a screw in it. Now push or pull on the scrap brace until the box is square. When the bench is square, drive the screw partway in until it holds in the leg. Leave the brace in place while the glue cures, preferably overnight.

Install the Cleats and Bottom Slats

Like the frames, the bottom slats are made of nominal 1x4 pine, so no ripping is necessary except for a filler piece. The slats will be supported by ¾-in. x ¾-in. pine cleats that will be glued and nailed along the bottom of the frames. Ripping stock for the cleats is a great chance to use up scrap you might have around the shop. Or you can make all the cleats from a single 8-ft. 1x4.

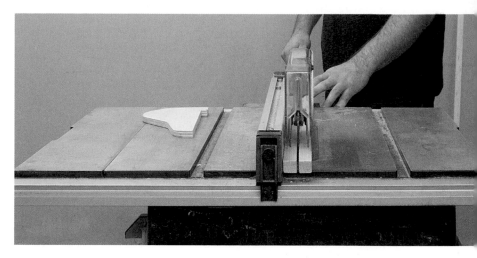

1 **RIP CLEAT STOCK.** Set the tablesaw fence to ¾ in. from the blade to rip ¾-in.-thick stock to width for the cleats. Set up a roller or outfeed table, or have a helper catch the rips as they come off the saw. Be sure to use a push stick to keep your hands away from the blade when making these narrow rips.

2 **CUT THE LONG CLEATS.** Cleat lengths are given in "What You'll Need," but it's easy and accurate to scribe the cleats in place to fit. Place one end of the cleat stock against the inside of one bottom side rail and use a utility knife to nick the stock where it meets the opposing rail. Put the stock on the bench and use a square and utility knife to extend the nick into a scribed cutline. Make the cut with a miter saw.

3 **INSTALL THE LONG CLEATS.** Put glue on the long cleats and set them in place flush to the bottom of the frames. Use two or three clamps to hold each cleat in position while you secure it with 4d finish nails spaced about 6 in. apart. You can use a hammer or a power finish nailer.

TIP Power nailers automatically set nails below the surface. If you are installing finish nails with a hammer, set all the nails with a nailset.

4 CUT AND INSTALL THE SHORT CLEATS. Scribe between the long cleats on each end to mark the length of the short cleats. Cut them on a miter saw and install with glue and nails.

> **TIP** If you have a piece of 1x6 long enough to make a slat, you can rip it to fit the space of the last full slat plus the filler strip, eliminating the need for a filler.

5 CUT THE SLATS. As listed in "What You'll Need," the bottom slats should be 23¾ in. long, but as always, it's a good idea to measure between the front and back bottom rails in case your dimensions vary. Make the cuts with a miter saw and stop block as you did the frame pieces.

6 INSTALL THE SLATS. Put glue on the top of the cleats and install the first bottom slat against one side frame, securing it with two 4d finish nails on each end. The bottom slats are installed with a little space between them for ventilation. To create the space, place two 8d common nails against the first slat as spacers and place the second slat against the first, letting the nails hang by their heads. Nail the second slat in place, remove the nails, and install the rest of the full slats the same way.

7 RIP AND INSTALL THE FILLER SLAT. Measure between the last full slat and the side bottom rail. Subtract ⅛ in. for the ventilation space, then rip a filler slat to width on the tablesaw. Nailing might split such a narrow slat, so put glue on the cleats and clamp the slat in place. Your clamps probably won't fit over the bottom rail, so use a piece of scrap as shown between the clamps and the slat.

Cut and Install the Cladding

The cladding is made from cedar tongue-and-groove boards that will be installed vertically flush to the top of the frames. These boards usually come rough-sawn on one side and planed smooth on the other—as mentioned, we chose to use the rough-sawn side face out.

The front and back each have nine full-width cladding boards and a narrow filler strip on each end to meet the legs while each side has three full boards and slightly narrower boards on each end.

You'll start by cutting the boards to 16⅛ in., which is ⅛ in. longer than the distance from the top to the bottom of the frame. The boards will be installed flush to the top of the frames. The extra ⅛ in. at the bottom will act as a drip edge, helping to keep water away from the bottom of the frames and cleats.

For each of the four sides, you'll first install one board centered between the legs and then install all but the last full board on each side of the center board. Then you'll test-fit the last full boards and measure for cladding filler strips or boards on each end. If you were to try to install the end strips or boards after installing the last full boards, you would run the risk of splitting the last grooves. Instead, you'll install the last full boards together with their mating end strip or board.

1 **CUT THE CLADDING BOARDS AND MARK FOR GLUE AREAS.** Use a miter saw with stop block to cut all the cladding to length. Then, working in batches, put the boards on your bench with the outside face down and strike lines 3½ in. from the top and bottom of each.

2 **LOCATE THE CENTER BOARD.** The first board will be centered across the front. Measure across the top of the front rail and make a mark halfway along the rail's length—the mark should be at 23⅞ in. Measure across the top of the first cladding board and make a mark halfway across its width, excluding the tongue.

3 **INSTALL THE CENTER BOARD.** Put glue on both ends of the first cladding board and align the mark on the board with the mark on the top rail. Clamp the board to the top rail and use a square to make sure the board is perpendicular to the rail. Then clamp the bottom of the board in place. Check again for square and secure the first board with two 4d finish nails at top and two at bottom.

4 INSTALL SIX FULL-WIDTH FRONT CLADDING BOARDS. Put glue on another cladding board, put it in place on one side of the first board, check for square, and secure it with four nails. Repeat this process until you have installed three boards to each side of the center board.

5 MEASURE FOR THE FILLER STRIPS. Dry-fit a full-width board in place on each end of the front, and measure for the width of the filler strips. When measuring, include the depth of the groove on one side and exclude the tongue on the other side.

To Fill or Not to Fill?

If you chose to install the cladding boards with the smooth side out, you can fill the nail holes with exterior wood filler and then sand the boards before applying finish. However, since we decided to expose the rough-sawn sides of the cladding, we chose not to fill the nail holes. That's because it's difficult to fill the holes neatly without sanding them and sanding would just make the spots more obvious. For the rough-sawn look, neat rows of small nail holes look just fine.

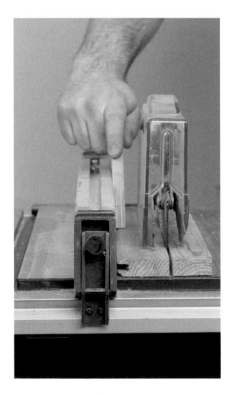

6 RIP THE FRONT FILLERS TO WIDTH. One filler strip will retain the tongue and the other will retain the groove. On the tablesaw, rip one strip to width with the tongue against the fence. Then adjust the fence if necessary, and rip the other piece with the groove against the fence.

7 **INSTALL THE REMAINING BOARDS AND FILLER STRIPS.** Test-fit each last full board with its strip. Then put glue on the top and bottom rails rather than the cladding. Put tongues in grooves, and press the two pieces into place as shown. Now use the same procedure to clad the back and sides of the bench.

Make the Lid

The lid is made of cedar boards assembled with glue and joinery biscuits. The back edge of the lid will be hinged flush to the outside of the back legs. The lid's side edges will overhang the legs by about 1/16 in. The front edge will overhang the front legs by about 1/8 in. Because the legs are 1 in. proud of the outside of the cladding, the lid overlaps the cladding by about 1 in., which gives the cladding some protection from rainwater, provides some room for your heels while sitting on the bench, and also makes it easy to grasp the front of the lid to open it.

1 **CUT THE BOARDS TO LENGTH.** The lid will be made from five full-width nominal 1x6 boards that are actually 5½ in. wide, plus a narrow piece that you will rip to width in the next step. For now, measure from the outside of one front leg to the outside of the other, and from the outside of one back leg to the outside of the other. The measurements should be the same, but if they vary slightly, use the larger measurement. Add ⅛ in. to your measurement and use a miter saw with a stop block to cut six boards to length.

TIP Part of the beauty of cedar is that boards often display a variety of colors and grain patterns. Take a few moments to juggle the boards around until you find the most pleasing blend of patterns and colors for the top of the lid. Put the narrow strip wherever it will be least conspicuous.

2 **MEASURE FOR AND RIP THE FILLER PIECE.** To find the exact width for the filler piece, clamp the five full boards together atop the storage bench and align the assembly flush to the back legs. Next, measure from the front of the assembly to the outside of the front legs. Again, if the measurements are not exactly the same, use the larger one. Add ⅛ in. to your measurement and rip the sixth lid board to this width. Keep the offcut handy—you will use it later.

3 **MARK FOR THE BISCUIT SLOTS.** Clamp the lid boards together on your work surface with the ends flush with the outside faces up. Tighten the clamps enough to keep the boards from moving. Then make marks across one joint about 2 in. from each end and about 12 in. apart. Using a framing square, extend marks across all the joints (no need to be precise in the spacing).

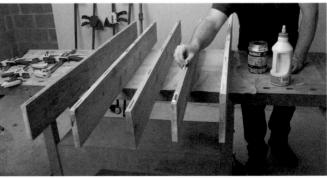

4 **CUT THE BISCUIT SLOTS.** Remove the fence from the biscuit joiner and set it to cut for #20 biscuits. Clamp a piece of 1x or 2x stock to your bench as a stop. Place each lid board against the stop and press down to make sure it is flat on the bench while you cut the slots.

5 **GLUE UP THE LID.** Put biscuits in the joints and clamp the boards together in a test assembly just to make sure the boards fit together properly. Leave your clamps open and on hand so you can glue up quickly. Put glue along the edge and in the slots of one side of the first joint and in just the slots on the other side of the joint. Insert #20 biscuits in the slots on one side of the joint, then assemble the joint, making sure the boards are flush on the end. Repeat this procedure for all the joints.

6 **CLAMP THE LID PIECES.** Check again that the edges are flush, then put five long clamps across the assembly. To ensure that the lid remains flat while the glue sets, clamp the lid to the workbench at four points. Leave the clamps on overnight, then remove them and sand the top with 80-grit and then 120-grit sandpaper. Round over the top edges of the lid with sandpaper and slightly round the bottom edges, too—just to make sure there will be no splinters when the lid is grabbed to open it.

TIP Because of their football shape, biscuits allow side-to-side adjustment that makes it easy to get the edges of the lid flush. However, as soon as the biscuits come in contact with glue, they start to swell and it quickly becomes more difficult to adjust the joint. That's why it's a good strategy to get glue on both sides of a joint before inserting biscuits and then check that edges are flush as soon as a joint is assembled.

No Biscuit Joiner? No Clamps? No Worries

If you don't have a biscuit joiner, you can join the top boards with glue alone. The biscuits are not needed for strength; they just make glue-up easier by automatically aligning the boards into the same plane. If you align the boards without biscuits, you'll probably need to sand the top a bit more to get the boards perfectly flush.

And if you don't have clamps to do the glue-up, you can assemble the boards with glue and opposing pocket screws. Stagger opposing screws and space the pairs about 12¾ in. apart as shown in the drawing.

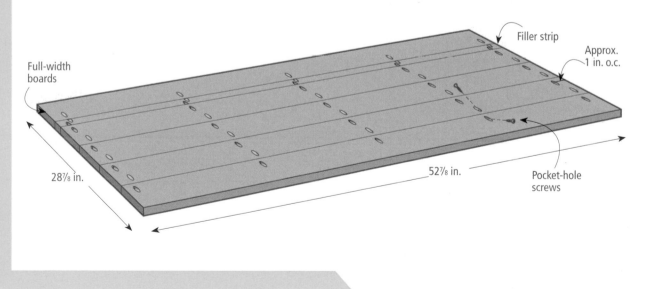

Full-width boards

Filler strip

Approx. 1 in. o.c.

28⅞ in.

52⅞ in.

Pocket-hole screws

Install the Hardware

The lid is fastened to the bench with two butt hinges that you'll screw to the back of the lid and the back legs. The lid support locks to keep the lid open. It also prevents the lid from falling away from the box, which could yank out the hinge screws. The nylon furniture glides are simply nailed to the bottom of the legs. The glides prevent rot at the bottom of the legs by raising them slightly off the deck or patio so the end grain won't wick water.

1 **INSTALL THE HINGES.** Position the lid on the box flush to the back of the legs and with equal slight overhangs on each side. Hold the lid in position with two long clamps—one from the top of the lid to the bottom of each back leg. Use just enough clamping pressure to prevent the lid from sliding while you screw in the hinges—clamping down hard might cause the hinges to bind. Next, align the hinge barrel between the leg and top, and center it across the leg—you can eyeball this. Predrill and insert the center hinge screw in the lid. Check that the hinge barrel is aligned, then predrill and install the remaining screws. Do the same for the other hinge.

2 **MARK FOR THE LID SUPPORT.** Place the bench on your work surface with the back down and the lid open. Place a 1x scrap under the back legs so the lid will be opened 90 degrees. Next, to locate the lid support screw inside the box, make a mark on the top rail 6⅞ in. from the center of the hinge barrel. Then use a combination square to extend the mark ⅜ in. in from the top of the rail. Check the instructions that came with your lid support in case the screw position varies from the support used here.

3 **INSTALL THE LID SUPPORT.** Predrill a hole at the mark on the top rail and screw the lid support to the rail. Then lock the support in the open position and predrill and insert the two screws that fasten the support to the lid.

4 **INSTALL FURNITURE GLIDES. Draw** diagonal lines to locate the center on the bottom of each leg. Use a hammer to tap in the furniture glides.

Adding Cleats to the Lid

One day, after our storage bench had sat in the sun for a few weeks, we noticed that the lid had developed a slight upward curve. A few days later, after a rain, the lid was flat again. We realized that the top and bottom surfaces of the lid were being subjected to different levels of humidity. The sun sucked moisture out of the top surface, causing it to contract more than the bottom. So the lid was forced to curve up. Rain replaced the moisture, causing the lid to flatten again.

To keep the lid flat, we added a couple of cleats to the inside of the lid. They're made from 2½-in.-wide rips of 5/4 cedar—you can use pine if that is what you have handy. We made the cleats 22 in. long and, just for show, we added a ½-in. chamfer on the ends. To clear the lid support and the inside of the front and back, we positioned the cleats 3½ in. from the back of the lid, 3 in. from the front, and 4 in. from the sides. The cleats are attached with 1½ in. deck screws staggered as shown in the photo on pp. 168–169.

Finishing the Box

You can apply finish, or even paint, to the inside of the box, but the inside doesn't need protection from the elements and we thought it looked just fine the way it is. Also, the aroma of the unsealed cedar might help to repel moths and other insects, a consideration if you'll be storing furniture cushions inside. If you decide to leave the interior unfinished, do brush stain on the tops and bottoms of the legs and cladding boards to seal up the end grain. Whether or not you intend to finish the interior, lightly sand the edges of the frames to eliminate any splinters.

It's a good idea to install the hinges and lid support before finishing the storage bench, just in case you need to sand legs or lid edges a bit for a perfect fit. Then remove the lid hardware (you can leave the lid support attached to the box if you won't be finishing the inside). It will take just a few minutes to reinstall the hardware after finishing.

If the interior will not be finished, use a perimeter of painter's tape to prevent finish from getting on the bottom of the lid when you apply finish to the edges of the lid.

Barbecue Cart

FORGET SIX TRIPS to the kitchen to bring out everything you need for your next outdoor barbecue. And then once you get the food, drink, condiments, and utensils outside, where do you put all that stuff? Solve the problem with this lightweight, sturdy, and mobile cart. Just load up the three generous shelves in the kitchen and roll it all out to the grill. (You might even find yourself using this eye-catching piece to move food from the kitchen to the dining room.)

The rustic and warm look of cedar boards offsets the sleek legs made of painted aluminum angle. Cedar won't rot and aluminum won't rust, making for a cart that will stand up to many years of outdoor use. Plus, both materials are easy to cut and drill and they are readily available at home centers. We finished the cedar with four coats of tung oil.

There's no complicated joinery here—everything is simply screwed together. There are, it should be noted, plenty of screws. You'll swap out the battery in your drill/driver a few times during this project.

The cart gets its mobility from solid skate-wheel casters that come in many colors. We used red wheels to match the red spray paint we used on the legs.

WHAT YOU'LL NEED

CEDAR

- 2 top frame long aprons
  ¾ in. x 3½ in. x 40 in.

- 4 middle and bottom frame
  long aprons
  ¾ in. x 1½ in. x 40 in.

- 2 top frame short aprons
  ¾ in. x 3½ in. x 20½ in.

- 4 middle and bottom frame
  short aprons
  ¾ in. x 1½ in. x 20½ in.

- 4 top and middle long cleats
  ¾ in. x ¾ in. x 38½ in.

- 4 top and middle short cleats
  ¾ in. x ¾ in. x 19 in.

- 4 caster blocks
  1½ in. x 3½ in. x 3½ in.

- 2 bottom long cleats
  ¾ in. x ¾ in. x 30 in.

- 2 bottom short cleats
  ¾ in. x ¾ in. x 12 in.

- 3 top shelf boards
  1 in. x 5½ in. x 42¼ in.

- 2 top end boards
  1 in. x 3¼ in. x 42¼ in.

- 18 middle and bottom shelf boards
  ¾ in. x 3½ in. x 22 in.

- 4 middle and bottom end shelf boards
  ¾ in. x 3½ in. x 22 in.

HARDWARE AND SUPPLIES

- 4 pieces 2-in. x 2-in. x 36-in.
  aluminum angle

- 56 #10 x ¾-in. stainless-steel
  pan-head wood screws

- 1¼-in. deck screws

- 2-in. deck screws

- Exterior wood glue

- 4 solid skate-wheel casters,
  two locking, available from
  Coolcasters.com

- 1 can exterior spray paint

BARBECUE CART

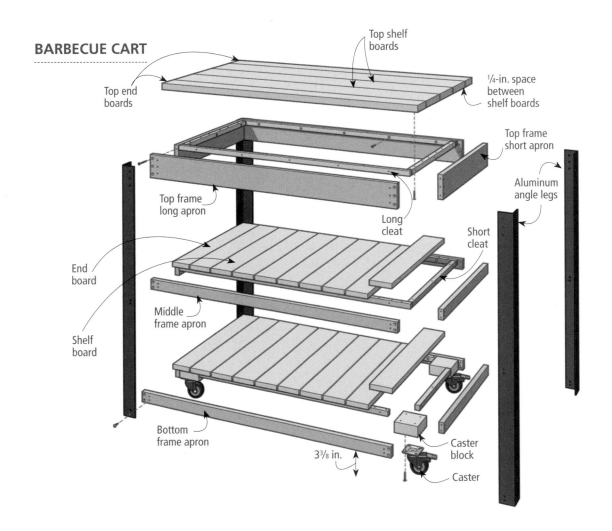

Top shelf boards

Top end boards

¼-in. space between shelf boards

Top frame short apron

Aluminum angle legs

Top frame long apron

Long cleat

Short cleat

End board

Middle frame apron

Shelf board

Bottom frame apron

3⅜ in.

Caster block

Caster

Make the Shelf Frames

The cart has three shelf frames. The top frame and middle shelf frame are made in exactly the same way with pieces of the same length. The only difference is that the top shelf aprons are 3½ in. wide, whereas the middle shelf aprons are 1½ in. wide. All the frames have cleats that will be used to attach the shelf boards. The bottom shelf frame is constructed a bit differently to fit cleats around blocks for attaching the casters.

If you make the top aprons from nominal 1x4 cedar (actual dimensions ¾ in. x 3½ in.), you won't need to rip stock to make them. The middle and bottom aprons are ripped from 1x4s, as are all the cleats.

> **TIP** Typically, cedar 1x stock has one rough side and one smooth side. You'll want to use the smooth side up for the shelves. You can do the same for the aprons, but we decided to add a little texture by putting the rough side out on our aprons. This eliminated the need to sand the aprons.

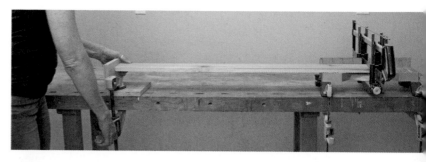

1 CUT THE APRONS TO LENGTH. Clamp a hand or power miter saw to the bench. Measure and lay out a line and use the miter saw to cut one piece of 1×4 to 40 in. long. If you are using a power saw, lock the blade in the down position. Put the piece you just cut against the blade. Place a stop block against the other end of the board and clamp it in place (see "Making and Using a Stop Block," p. 171). Use the block to cut three more pieces of 1×4 to 40 in. Two of the pieces will be top long aprons and two will be ripped to make the four middle and bottom long aprons. Use the same procedure to cut four pieces of 1×4 to 20½ in. for all the short aprons.

2 RIP THE MIDDLE AND BOTTOM APRONS TO WIDTH. Set your tablesaw fence 1½ in. from the blade and rip two of the 40-in.-long pieces and two of the 20½-in. pieces to make all the middle and bottom aprons.

> **TIP** If you don't have a miter saw, you can make all the cuts for this project using the miter gauge on the tablesaw. Extend your layout line across the top of the board and down one side as shown. Position the board so that the blade is to the waste side of the line. Be sure to put the saw's guard down before making the cut.

3 PREASSEMBLE THE TOP FRAME. You'll start by assembling the frame with screws alone, then you'll remove the screws and reassemble the frame with glue and screws. This way, you won't have to fuss with predrilling and squaring during glue-up. Start by butting the end of one short apron into a long apron. Clamp the pieces to the bench and make sure the outsides of the pieces are flush. Use a framing square to check that the pieces are perpendicular, then predrill and countersink for three 1¼-in. exterior deck screws. Insert the screws. Repeat this process for all the corners.

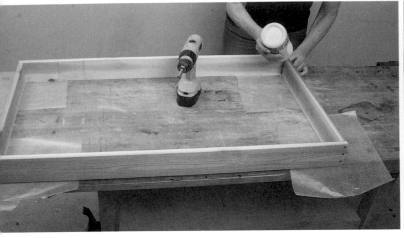

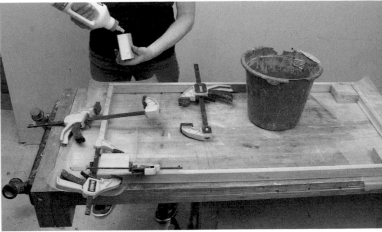

4 **GLUE UP THE FRAME.** Remove the screws from one corner. Pull the joint apart and put glue on the end of the short apron, then reinsert the screws. Do this for each corner. Next, preassemble and glue up the middle and bottom frames using two screws at each joint. Check again for square before the glue sets.

5 **CUT AND INSTALL THE CASTER BLOCKS.** Use a miter saw, or the miter gauge on the tablesaw, to cut four 3½-in.-long pieces of nominal 2x4 (actual dimensions 1½ in. x 3½ in.). Put glue on two adjacent edges of each block and clamp in place in a corner, flush to the top and bottom of the bottom frame. As always, have a bucket of water and a sponge handy to clean up glue squeeze-out.

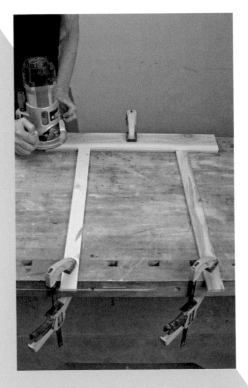

Rounding the Edges

You'll want to slightly round the bottom edges of the aprons as well as the top edges of the middle and bottom shelf boards. (Usually the 5/4 x 6 boards used for the top shelf already have rounded long edges; you'll just need to round the top edges of their ends.) Rounding gives a nice finished look and also prevents splinters and helps hold finish or paint. You can do this slight rounding, often called "breaking the edges," easily enough with sandpaper, but it's quicker to use a ⅛-in. roundover bit in a router. Do the rounding before assembling parts.

Mounting the router in a table is the most efficient method, but if you don't have a router table, you can still make quick work of rounding the edges by clamping two pieces of scrap across your bench as shown. This lets you use just one clamp on the workpiece: First, clamp down the right side of the workpiece, rout from left to right until you meet the clamp, then move the clamp to the left to complete the pass. If you are routing an apron, turn the board over and rout the other side of the bottom edge. If you are routing a shelf board as shown here, continue routing to the right end, then flip the board around and repeat the process on the other top edge.

BOTTOM SHELF FRAME (UNDERSIDE)

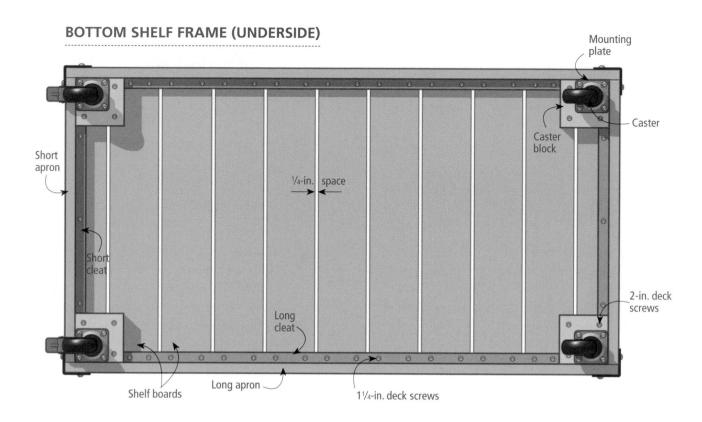

Mounting plate

Caster

Caster block

Short apron

Short cleat

¼-in. space

2-in. deck screws

Long cleat

Shelf boards

Long apron

1¼-in. deck screws

Squaring the Frames

Sometimes, even if you squared all the corners, a frame may turn out slightly trapezoidal. This is easy to fix: Turn the frame topside up. Put a piece of scrap diagonally across as shown and screw one end into the top of the frame—no need to drive the screw home. Pull on the scrap until the frame is square, then drive a screw through the other end of the scrap to pin the frame in position. Leave the scrap in place until the glue cures.

6 **RIP AND CROSSCUT THE CLEAT BLANKS.** You'll scribe the cleats for a nice, snug fit. For now, use the tablesaw to rip 1x stock to ¾ in. wide for all the cleats, then cut pieces that are about ½ in. longer than the lengths listed in "What You'll Need."

TIP If you are working with a hand miter saw, you can skip drawing the layout line on the cleats. Just place the sawblade right into the nick you made and carefully make the first stroke.

7 **MARK AND CUT THE CLEATS.** All the cleats will be installed flush to the top of the frames. On the top and middle aprons, start with the long cleats. Butt one end of a long blank against a short apron and then use a utility knife to nick where it meets the opposing short apron. Use a pencil and square to extend the mark across one face of the cleat, then cut it to length with a miter saw or with the miter gauge on a tablesaw.

8 **ATTACH THE CLEATS.** Put glue on a long cleat and clamp it in place flush to the top of the frame. Predrill through the cleat and into the apron for five evenly spaced 1¼-in. screws. Insert the screws and remove the clamps. Now install the other top and middle long cleats, then scribe and cut the short cleats to fit between them. Attach the short cleats with glue and three screws. Finally, scribe and cut the bottom shelf cleats to fit between the caster blocks. Install those cleats with glue and four screws each.

Cut and Install the Shelf Boards

The top shelf boards are made of nominal 5/4 x 6 cedar. They run lengthwise along the top and overhang the aprons by 1 in. on all sides. The middle and bottom shelf boards are made of 1x4s. Because 1x4s are not as strong as thicker 5/4 boards, the middle and bottom shelf boards run across the width of the cart. These boards end flush to the aprons on all sides. You'll start by cutting all the boards to length.

There are three full-width top boards. You'll install one centered across the short aprons, add the other full boards, and then rip the end boards to fit. You'll use the same strategy to install the nine full boards and two end boards on the middle frame and on the bottom frames.

> **TIP** As mentioned previously, you'll want to round over the edges of the shelf boards before installing them (see "Rounding the Edges," p. 188). It's also most convenient to sand them now. You only need to thoroughly sand the faces that will be up. Hit the bottom edges quickly with 80-grit sandpaper just to knock off any splinters. Sand the tops with #80 grit, then #120 grit.

1 **CUT THE SHELF BOARDS TO LENGTH.** Cut one top shelf board to 42¼ in. long and then, as you did for the aprons, use it to set up a stop block to cut the remaining four top boards to length. You'll do the same for all the middle and bottom shelf boards, but because the boards must be exactly flush to the outside of the long aprons, use a pencil to scribe the length of the first board, just in case the width of your frames varies slightly from the dimensions in "What You'll Need." Scribe in a corner in case an apron is bowed a bit in the middle.

2 **LAY OUT THE POSITION OF THE TOP CENTER BOARD.** Find the center point along the length of one short apron and use a square to strike a light pencil line on the apron face. Then find the center point across the width of one end of a full-width top board and strike a short line on the bottom of the board.

3 **INSTALL THE TOP CENTER BOARD.** Place all three full-width top boards upside down on the bench. Put the frame on top and position the lines on the center board and frame. Check that the ends of the center board are equidistant to the outside faces of the short aprons, and then clamp the apron and center board to the bench. Check that the center board is square to the aprons. Predrill and countersink two holes through each short cleat into the board and insert 1¼-in. exterior screws.

4 **INSTALL THE REMAINING FULL-WIDTH TOP BOARDS.** The boards will be spaced about ¼ in. apart. Make two spacers from scrap plywood or any other ¼-in.-wide material. Put the spacers between the center board and one of the other full-width boards. Make sure the boards are flush on the ends. Then clamp, predrill, and install the board with two screws into each cleat. Do the same for the other full-width board.

5 INSTALL THE TOP END BOARDS. Put one of the end boards in position with spacers between it and a full board. Mark the edge of the board 1 in. from the outside of the apron. Extend this line over one edge of the board and set the tablesaw fence to this line. Make the rip. Install the board as you did the full boards, placing the ripped edge to the outside. Do the same for the other end board. Install the end boards with two screws at each end and five screws along the long cleats.

TIP Lay the boards for each shelf on your bench and take a few minutes to arrange the boards in a pleasing way. For example, three of the boards for our middle shelf were lighter than the others, so we decided to put them in the middle to add a touch of symmetry.

6 INSTALL FULL MIDDLE AND BOTTOM SHELF BOARDS AND SCRIBE THE END BOARD RIPS. This procedure is the same as for the top boards except, of course, these boards run across the width of the frames and there are nine full-width boards and two end boards on each frame. Install all the full boards with screws through the cleats, but don't drive any screws through the caster blocks yet. Put the end boards in position with spacers and scribe a line where they meet the top of the short aprons.

Adjusting Spacing to Fit

The actual width of your nominal 1x4 boards might be slightly different than 3½ in. So it's a good idea to make 10 spacers so you can put all the boards in position on a frame to make sure the end boards will be wide enough. The width of our boards, for example, turned out to be about 1/16 in. shy of 3½ in. wide. As a result, when we laid out the 11 boards with a 1-in. overhang on one side and ¼-in. spacers, the 1/16-in. multiplied by 10 spaces meant that the end board of the other side came approximately flush to the opposing apron instead of overhanging an inch.

Scrounging around the shop, we found some nominal ⅜-in. plywood that was actually 5/16 in. wide and made new spacers. You, too, may need to find or rip spacers that are slightly more than ¼ in.

7 **RIP THE END BOARDS.** Extend the line you scribed on one end board over one end and use that line to set the tablesaw rip fence. Rip the board to width and then do the same for all the end boards, resetting the fence as necessary. Be sure to put the saw's guard down before making the cut.

8 **MARK FOR THE CASTER SCREW HOLES.** You want to do this now so you can be sure the screws you use to attach the shelf boards to the caster blocks won't be in the way when you install the casters. Align a caster's mounting plate to the inside corners of the aprons and mark the holes with a pencil.

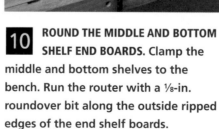

9 **ATTACH THE MIDDLE AND BOTTOM END BOARDS.** For the middle shelf, attach the end boards with two 1¼-in. screws at each end and three screws into the short aprons. For the bottom shelf, also use three 1¼-in. screws into the short aprons. Where screws will need to go through a caster block, predrill and countersink for four 2-in. screws positioned as shown. Install these screws.

10 **ROUND THE MIDDLE AND BOTTOM SHELF END BOARDS.** Clamp the middle and bottom shelves to the bench. Run the router with a ⅛-in. roundover bit along the outside ripped edges of the end shelf boards.

11 **ROUND THE CORNERS OF THE TOP SHELF.** Use a piece of 80-grit sandpaper to round the corners of the top shelf. Then smooth the corner with 120 grit. There's no need to do this for the middle and bottom shelves because the legs will cover their corners.

TIP Unless you plan to paint the shelves the same color as the aluminum legs, apply paint or finish to the shelves and frames now before the legs are attached.

Attach the Legs

The legs are made of ⅛-in.-thick aluminum angle. Each side is 2 in. wide. We purchased four pieces of 36-in.-long angle iron so we didn't have to cut it. If you can't find 36-in. lengths, aluminum is easily cut with a hacksaw. Otherwise, all you need to do is drill holes for the pan-head screws that will attach the legs to the frames and then spray-paint the legs.

TIP Aluminum is easy to drill, but be sure to wear safety glasses and gloves. The shards are very sharp and they can fly off the drill bit.

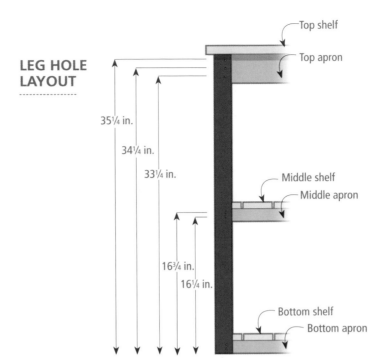

LEG HOLE LAYOUT

- Top shelf
- Top aprON
- 35¼ in.
- 34¼ in.
- 33¼ in.
- Middle shelf
- Middle apron
- 16¾ in.
- 16¼ in.
- Bottom shelf
- Bottom apron

1 **LAY OUT THE SCREW HOLES.** The hole positions are shown in the drawing "Leg Hole Layout." The holes are located 1¼ in. from the corner of the aluminum angle to keep the leg screws away from the screws that hold the aprons together. Set a combination square to 1¼ in. and use it to guide a marker as you draw a line down the length of each side of each angle. Then use a tape measure to mark screw positions along the line.

2 **CENTER-PUNCH THE HOLES.** You need to center-punch a dimple at each screw position to prevent the drill bit from skittering across the metal surface. Place an aluminum leg on a length of 2x4 and clamp them along the side of the bench with one aluminum leg overhanging as shown. Hit a center punch with a hammer to make a dimple at each screw-hole position. If you don't have a center punch, a nailset will do the trick, too.

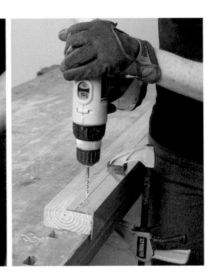

3 **DRILL THE HOLES.** With the leg still clamped in place, use a ³⁄₁₆-in. bit in the drill to make each hole. Drill slowly with moderate pressure. Now clamp, punch, and drill holes on each side of all the legs.

4 **ATTACH THE TOP AND MIDDLE FRAMES TO THE LEGS.** Mark one edge of two legs 18 in. from the bottom. Place the top shelf at one end of the bench with a short apron down and the 1-in. shelf overhang against the side of the bench as shown. Slide the marked legs underneath the short apron, butted against the bottom of the shelf. Use a framing square to make sure the top shelf is square to the legs, then predrill and install three ¾-in.-long #10 stainless-steel pan-head screws into the top holes on each side. Align the middle shelf to the 18-in. marks, square it, predrill, and insert screws. Now put the other legs in place, square them, and attach them.

TIP Spray-paint the aluminum angle before assembling the legs to the aprons. To paint all sides of ours at once, we suspended the legs on a piece of wire threaded through the top screw holes and then tied the wire to nails driven into two trees.

5 **ATTACH THE BOTTOM SHELF.** Clamp the bottom shelf to the bench with the bottom of the aprons down. Stand the legs up and fit them over the bottom shelf. Predrill holes and drive in the screws.

6 **INSTALL THE CASTERS.** Predrill holes in the caster blocks at the locations you marked earlier. Put each caster in place and install it with the screws provided.

Picnic Table & Benches

HERE'S A REFINED TAKE on the traditional picnic table and benches. Rather than the typical bolted-together cross-legged design, these pieces feature sleeker splayed legs with a lower rail between them. There are no bolts, and all the screws are hidden (unless you crawl under the table or benches).

Though refined, the legs are actually quite easy to build using biscuit joinery. Of course, you could build just the table and pull up half a dozen chairs. Or you might just want to build a shorter version of the bench to place in a nice corner of the garden. (If the bench is 4 ft. or shorter, you can skip the center seat cleat.)

We were thinking of building this project from cedar, a wood that naturally resists rot and weather. But once we priced all those cedar 2x6s, we chose to build our table with inexpensive spruce construction lumber and paint it an eye-catching red. With a couple of coats of exterior paint, the table will weather many years of use.

SPRUCE

- 10 tabletop and bench seat boards
  1½ in. x 5½ in. x 70 in.
- 2 bench seat boards
  1½ in. x 2½ in. x 70 in.
- 2 table braces
  1½ in. x 2½ in. x 18⁷⁄₁₆ in.
- 4 bench braces
  1½ in. x 2½ in. x 15⅝ in.
- 4 table legs
  1½ in. x 2½ in. x 26⁹⁄₁₆ in.
- 2 table upper rails
  1½ in. x 2½ in. x 30¼ in.

- 2 tabletop cleats
  1½ in. x 2½ in. x 30¼ in.
- 2 table leg cleats
  1½ in. x 1½ in. x 30¼ in.
- 2 table lower rails
  1½ in. x 2½ in. x 20 in.
- 4 bench upper rails
  1½ in. x 2½ in. x 12 in.
- 6 bench seat cleats
  1½ in. x 2½ in. x 12 in.
- 4 bench leg cleats
  1½ in. x 1½ in. x 12 in.

- 8 bench legs
  1½ in. x 2½ in. x 13⁵⁄₁₆ in.
- 4 bench lower rails
  1½ in. x 2½ in. x 7⅝ in.

HARDWARE AND SUPPLIES

- #10 joinery biscuits
- Exterior wood glue
- 2½-in. deck screws
- 2-in. deck screws

PICNIC TABLE

Prepare the Lumber

With the exception of the leg cleats, all of the parts for the table and benches are made from 8-ft. lengths of nominal 2x6 lumber that is actually 1½ in. thick and 5½ in. wide. You'll use full-width boards to make the tabletop and two of the three seat boards on each bench. You'll make all of the 2½-in.-wide pieces listed in "What You'll Need" by ripping 2x6s. To make the leg cleats for the table and benches, you'll rip a single 8-ft. 2x4 whose actual dimensions are 1½ in. x 3½ in.

A dozen parts comprising the tabletop boards and seat boards will be cut to 70 in. long, so you'll save time by setting up a stop and cutting them with a power miter saw (see "Making and Using a Stop Block," p. 171).

TIP Select your straightest stock for the full-width tabletop and seat boards. You don't want to use twisted or badly bowed stock at all for this project, but if a board has a slight bow over its full length, save it to make shorter pieces—the bow will become negligible over shorter lengths.

TIP When cutting long pieces on the miter saw, your work will be easier and safer if you make a support like the one shown clamped to the bench in step 1. Make the support in the same way as the stop block, except cut the upright piece to the same height as the miter-saw table.

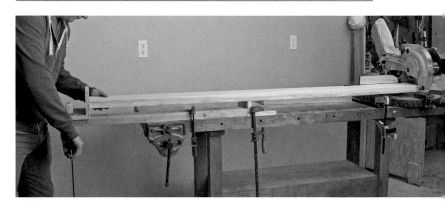

1 **CUT FULL-WIDTH PARTS TO LENGTH.** With the miter saw clamped to the workbench, start by marking and cutting one 2x6 table board to length. Then lock the sawblade down and put the piece against the blade. Slide the stop against the blade and clamp it to the workbench. If your bench isn't long enough, as shown here, clamp a 2x4 extension to the bench and then clamp the stop to the extension. Use the saw and stop to cut all the tabletop boards and the single 2x4 to 70 in.

Crosscutting with a Circular Saw

A power miter saw is the quickest way to make accurate cuts, but you can accomplish all the crosscuts in this project with a circular saw guided by an angle square with an adjustable arm. Leave the arm set to 0 degrees (actually 0 degrees from 90 degrees) to make the square cuts in step 1. Later, you'll set the arm to 12 degrees (12 degrees from 90 degrees) to lay out and make the 78-degree cuts on the ends of all the legs and rails. First, set the arm and use the square to lay out a cutline. Then clamp the workpiece to the workbench, align the sawblade to the cutline, and slide the square against the saw base to guide the cut.

2 CUT BLANKS FOR THE BRACES, LEG ASSEMBLY PARTS, AND CLEATS. All of the remaining parts will have angled cuts on their ends, except for the braces, which will be notched to meet cleats and rails at 45 degrees. So start by using a power miter saw or circular saw to make square-cut blanks. Make the brace blanks about 2 in. longer than the lengths listed in "What You'll Need." Make all the other blanks about 1 in. longer than listed. Remember, you'll rip two 2½-in.-wide parts from each 2x6 blank and two leg cleats from each 2x4 blank.

3 RIP THE BLANKS TO WIDTH. Set the tablesaw fence 2½ in. from the blade and rip the blanks for the table and bench rails, legs, tabletop cleats, seat cleats, and braces to width. Reset the fence to 1½ in. from the blade and rip all six leg cleats to width.

> **TIP** Because you will be preparing a lot of parts at once, be sure to label each blank and then each part as you rip the blanks. Being able to quickly identify the parts will save you lots of time later.

Cut Angles and Notches

The legs on the table and the benches are splayed at 78 degrees. To achieve this angle, you'll cut parallel 78-degree angles on both ends of all the legs and opposing 78-degree angles on the lower rails. This same angle is used to make decorative cuts at the ends of all the upper rails and cleats.

The 45-degree braces on the table and benches are notched to fit around cleats and lower rails. You'll notch one end of each table and bench brace, measure for length, and then notch the other end.

BRACE NOTCHES LAYOUT

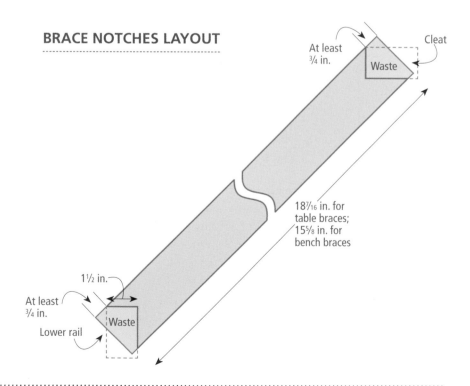

Cleat

At least ¾ in.

Waste

18⁷⁄₁₆ in. for table braces; 15⁵⁄₈ in. for bench braces

1½ in.

At least ¾ in.

Waste

Lower rail

1 CUT ONE END AT A 78-DEGREE ANGLE. Set the power miter saw to cut a 78-degree angle—the mark on the saw table at 12 degrees from the 90-degree square cut. (If you don't have a power miter saw, see "Crosscutting with a Circular Saw," p. 199.) With the 2½-in. face against the saw table as shown at top, cut one end of all the upper and lower rails and all of the legs. Then, with the 1½-in. face on the table as shown above, cut one end of all the cleats.

> **TIP** When you make the angled cuts, keep two of the offcuts—you'll use them as clamping cauls when you assemble the legs to the rails.

2 MAKE THE REMAINING 78-DEGREE CUTS. On one table leg, use one of the angled ends you just cut as a template to lay out a 78-degree cut 26⁹⁄₁₆ in. from the first cut. Make sure the layout line is parallel to the cut on the other end. Make the cut on the power miter saw. Then, just as you did for the 70-in. pieces, set up a stop to cut the other three table legs to length. Repeat steps 1 and 2 to make the 13⁵⁄₁₆-in.-long bench legs. Use the same process to cut all the other 78-degree angles but with one difference: On all the other parts, the angled end cuts will oppose each other—they won't be parallel like the leg cuts.

3 LAY OUT A NOTCH. Lay out a notch on one end of all six table and bench braces as shown in the drawing "Brace Notches Layout." To allow room for both ends of the notch to come to a point, start by making a mark ¾ in. from one end of the blank and draw a 45-degree line from that point across the board. Make a mark at 1½ in. along that line and draw another 45-degree line intersecting the first at that point. Completing the layout lines across the board will help you guide the circular saw when you make the cut.

4 CUT THE NOTCHES ON ONE END OF EACH BRACE. It is important for the notch to be square to the faces of the brace. Making the cuts with a circular saw will ensure this—check that the blade is square to the base. Clamp each brace to the bench and use the circular saw to carefully cut to the intersection of the two layout lines. Use the lever to raise the guard so it doesn't force your cut off course.

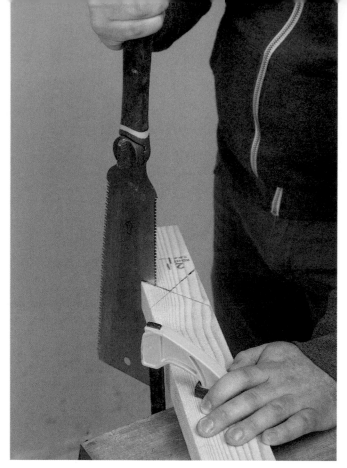

5 **COMPLETE THE NOTCHES.** Finish the notch cuts with a few strokes of a handsaw held perpendicular to the faces of the brace. Handsaw blades are thinner than circular-saw blades. So when you complete the notch cuts, guide the handsaw against the outside of the circular-saw cut so the faces of the notch will be flat. It helps to twist the handle slightly toward the outside of the cut.

TIP If all your notch cuts came out completely flat, congratulations on your skill with the handsaw! More likely, some notch faces won't be absolutely flat. That's easy to fix. Just clamp the brace to your bench as shown, put the flat of a chisel against the notch face, and tap with a mallet to chop out the excess.

Make the Leg Assemblies

Here we will lead you through the steps for one table leg assembly—the leg assemblies for the table and the benches are built in exactly the same way using biscuit joinery to attach the upper and lower rails to the legs. To make them extra strong, each joint will include two biscuits placed side-by-side across the width of the joint.

For each assembly, you'll start by clamping the parts together to mark for biscuit slot locations. Then you'll cut all the slots before gluing up the assembly. After making all the leg assemblies, you'll round the edges of all the parts.

1 **POSITION THE LOWER RAIL.** In assembling the legs, the distance between the top rail and the lower rail must be correct so that the braces will fit properly. That distance must be 10 in. for the table leg assemblies and 8 in. for the bench leg assemblies. Put the legs and rails in position on your work surface with the bottom rail at the correct distance from the top rail. Clamp the lower rail to the legs using the offcuts you saved as cauls to provide parallel surfaces for the clamp jaws. Check the distance between rails after clamping.

TIP Usually biscuit-slot locations need not be exact, but in this case you'll be using biscuits that are only slightly shorter than the width of the rails and legs, so it's important to measure to get them centered across the joints.

2 **MARK FOR THE BISCUIT SLOTS.** Draw a line centered across the width of the top rail. Use the line to center the top rail over the legs. Mark where the inside of the legs meet the top rail, then clamp the legs to the rail. Now mark for biscuit slots centered across all the joints.

3 **EXTEND THE SLOT LAYOUTS ACROSS THE JOINTS.** Extend the biscuit layout marks across the faces of each side of all the joints. This is necessary because each joint will have two biscuits.

Sanding the Parts

After gluing up the leg assemblies, it's time to sand all the parts. If you'll be painting the project, all you need is 80-grit sandpaper to remove mill marks and create the perfect surface for primer. If you'll be using stain or a clear finish, start with 80 grit, then sand again with 120 grit. An orbital sander is the perfect tool for sanding the legs, cleats, and braces. A belt sander is ideal for the tabletop and bench boards.

4 **CUT THE BISCUIT SLOTS.** If your biscuit joiner has an auxiliary fence, remove it. Set the cutting depth for #10 biscuits. Clamp the workpiece to your workbench. (The clamps will remove any slight bow that might misalign the slots.) With the base of the joiner firmly on the bench, cut slots along the layout lines. Now flip the piece over and cut another slot at each layout line.

5 **GLUE UP THE LEG ASSEMBLIES.** As always, do a dry run to make sure all the biscuits are properly aligned. Put glue in the slots and on one face of each joint. Insert the biscuits and clamp the assembly together again.

Rounding Inside Corners

You don't want edges to be rounded over where they meet at joints. That's why you glued up the leg assemblies before routing the edges. The router bit won't reach all the way into corners, but a few strokes with a piece of sandpaper will complete the job. You'll also need to use sandpaper to round the narrow edges of angled cuts.

6 **ROUND OVER ALL EDGES.** You want all the edges of all the parts to be slightly rounded, not only to provide a more finished look but also to prevent splinters and so that paint or finish will adhere well. You can do this easily enough with a piece of sandpaper, but since there are a lot of linear feet of edge, you'll save time by using a ⅛-in. roundover bit in the router. Clamp the parts to your work surface and always rout in a clockwise direction so the cutter will scoop into the wood rather than trying to climb out of the cut. Don't round edges that will be against the bottom of the tabletop or the edges of the brace notches.

7 **ATTACH THE LEG CLEATS.** If neither the top rail or leg cleat have any bow across their tops, you can simply put glue on one face of the leg cleat, align the cleat flush to the ends and top of the upper rail, and clamp it in place. In the case shown here, the top rail was slightly bowed, so we straightened it by clamping it down on the workbench and then clamping the cleat to it.

Assemble the Legs and Braces to the Tabletop and Bench Seats

This part is easy but the sequence is important: On paper, where dimensions are precise, if the table legs are 8 in. from the ends of the tabletop and the tabletop cleats are 20½ in. from the ends, the braces should fit perfectly between them.

But, of course, lumber dimensions are not usually precise. To ensure tight joints with the braces, you'll start by installing a tabletop or bench leg. Then you'll put the brace in position against the lower rail and clamp the tabletop cleat or bench seat cleat firmly against the brace's bottom notch before screwing the cleat to the tabletop boards. Finally, you'll glue and screw the brace in place. If the distance between the cleats and the ends of the table or bench winds up being a fraction of an inch different than shown in the drawings, it matters not at all.

> **TIP** If you are working on sawhorses, drive finish nails through the spacers between the tabletop boards so the spacers won't slip through.

1 **LAY OUT THE LEG POSITIONS.** You'll need ¼-in.-thick spacers—they can be scraps of plywood or any other material such as the scraps of medium-density fiberboard used here. Lay the six tabletop boards on sawhorses with their better faces down. Use the spacers at both ends to form gaps between the boards. Clamp the boards lightly together with their ends flush. Don't clamp tightly, just enough to bring the spacers into contact with the boards—you want to be able to pull the spacers out when you are done with them. Now draw layout lines across the width of the table, 8 in. from each end.

2 **ATTACH THE TABLE LEG ASSEMBLIES.** Place a table leg assembly top rail along the line, center it across the table, and clamp it in place. Secure the leg cleat to the tabletop with 2½-in. deck screws in predrilled and countersunk holes. Use two screws in each tabletop board.

3 **MARK CENTERS ON THE BOTTOM RAIL, TABLETOP CLEAT, AND BRACE.** Draw centerlines across the inside face of the lower rail and along the exposed wide face of the tabletop cleat. Use a combination square set to ¾ in. to mark the center point at the tip of the long side of each brace notch as shown.

4 **POSITION AND ATTACH THE TABLETOP CLEAT.** Put the brace in position against the lower rail and the tabletop cleat in position against the brace. Align the center points on the brace to the centerlines on the rail and cleat. Center and square the cleat across the table and clamp it in place. Secure the cleat to the tabletop with 2½-in. deck screws in predrilled and countersunk holes. Use two screws in each tabletop board, staggering the screws as shown. With cleats secured, you can remove the end clamp and spacers from that side.

5 **SECURE THE BRACE.** The braces are attached with glue and one screw in each end. Use a 2½-in. screw to attach the brace to the tabletop cleat. Use a 2-in. screw to attach the brace to the lower rail to ensure that the screw won't come through the other side of the rail. Predrill and countersink holes perpendicular to the rail and cleat. Put glue in the notches and attach the brace with the screws.

TIP When predrilling holes at 45 degrees to the surface as you will be doing for the braces, you may find that the bit skips across the surface instead of boring into the wood. To solve this, drill perpendicular to the surface for ⅛ in. or so. Pull the drill out and then reenter the hole at 45 degrees.

Clamping Boards into the Same Plane

We assembled our picnic table on sawhorses because the tabletop is wider than our bench. This means there was no flat surface under the tabletop boards to keep them in the same plane as we screwed down cleats. Usually this is no problem—the screws pull the cleats tight to the boards. But occasionally we found ourselves with a gap between a cleat and one or more tabletop boards. If this happens, back the screws out of the problem boards. Then clamp a length of 2x4 under the tabletop boards, just to the side of the cleat. Reinsert the screws and remove the clamps.

Assembling the Benches

The sequence for assembling the legs to the benches is exactly the same as for the tabletop. The bench seats are composed of two 5½-in.-wide boards with a 2½-in.-wide board between, and the legs will be 4 in. from the ends of the benches. Use just one screw to secure each bench leg cleat to the narrow center board. Trace the footprint of the braces onto the bench seat cleats. When you secure that cleat to the narrow center board, use two screws offset inside the footprint so they are out of the path of the screw that fastens the brace.

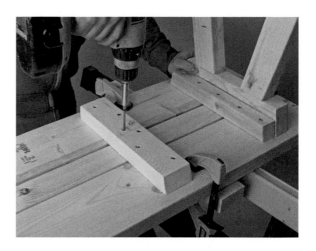

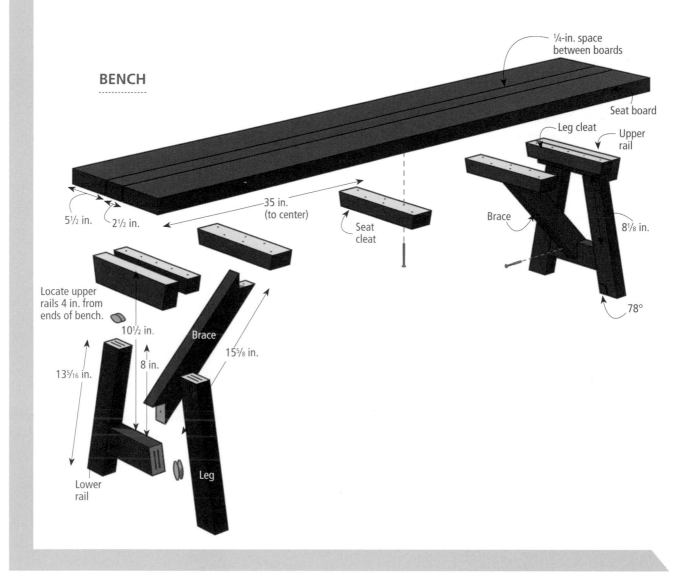

BENCH

¼-in. space between boards

Seat board

Leg cleat

Upper rail

Brace

35 in. (to center)

Seat cleat

5½ in.

2½ in.

8⅛ in.

78°

Locate upper rails 4 in. from ends of bench.

10½ in.

Brace

15⅝ in.

13⁵⁄₁₆ in.

8 in.

Lower rail

Leg

Planter

FILL THIS HANDSOME PLANTER
with flowering plants of your choice to
enhance the beauty of your deck or
patio. At 30 in. x 30 in. and 12 in. deep,
it has plenty of room.

The outside features warm, multi-
toned cedar tongue-and groove boards
and legs made of cedar posts. This
planter will serve you for decades
because the inside is constructed of half
a sheet of pressure-treated plywood
that won't rot. The plywood panels are
attached to the legs with pocket-hole
screws. Holes are drilled in the bottom
to provide drainage.

We finished our planter with four
coats of pure tung oil mixed with an
equal amount of mineral spirits. This
emphasized and enhanced the various tones of the boards and legs. The
tung oil also seals the surface from the
weather and can be renewed by adding
additional coats.

WHAT YOU'LL NEED

CEDAR

- 4 legs
  2½ in. x 2½ in. x 18 in.
- 12 cladding boards
  ¾ in. x 5 in. x 14⅛ in. tongue
  and groove*
- 8 cladding boards
  ¾ in. x 4½ in. x 14⅛ in. tongue
  and groove
- 4 cap pieces
  1 in. x 3 in. x 30 in.

* Note: Sold as nominal 1x6, these
boards are 5⅜ in. wide but cover
only 5 in. in width because the ⅜-in.
tongue goes in the groove.

PRESSURE-TREATED WOOD

- 4 box sides
  ¾ in. x 14 in. x 24 in.
- 4 cleats
  ¾ in. x 1 in. x 24 in.
- 1 bottom
  ¾ in. x 23⅞ in. x 24 in.

HARDWARE AND SUPPLIES

- 40 pocket-hole screws, 1¼ in.
- Ceramic-coated deck screws, 1¼ in.
- Exterior wood glue
- Construction adhesive
- 1 tube clear silicone caulk

PLANTER

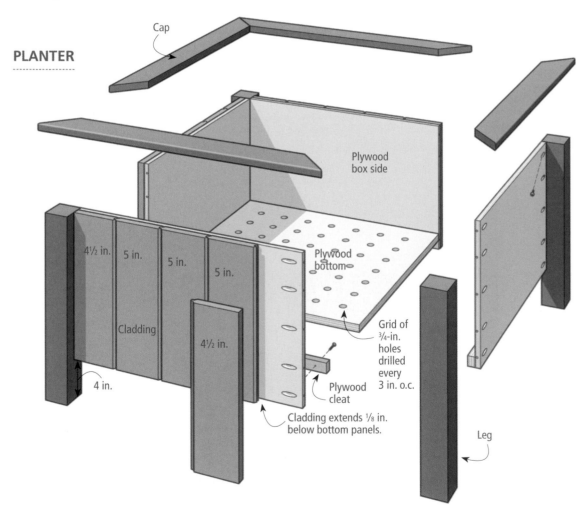

Cap

Plywood box side

Plywood bottom

4½ in.

5 in.

5 in.

5 in.

Cladding

4½ in.

4 in.

Grid of ¾-in. holes drilled every 3 in. o.c.

Plywood cleat

Cladding extends ⅛ in. below bottom panels.

Leg

Cut the Legs and Plywood Pieces

You'll make the legs from a single 8-ft. 4x4 cedar post. These legs are the same dimensions as the legs used in the storage bench project and they are made in exactly the same way. See steps 1 through 4 of "Make and Attach the Legs" on p. 172 and "Sand the Legs and Round the Edges Now" on p. 173 in that project. You'll need a stop block for your miter saw, so also see "Making and Using a Stop Block" on p. 171.

When you purchase a 4x8 sheet of plywood, have the lumberyard or home center rip it at 24 in. along its length. This will make it easy to cross-cut the sides and bottoms and will make the sheet easier to transport. Once the parts are cut, you'll drill drainage holes in the bottom piece.

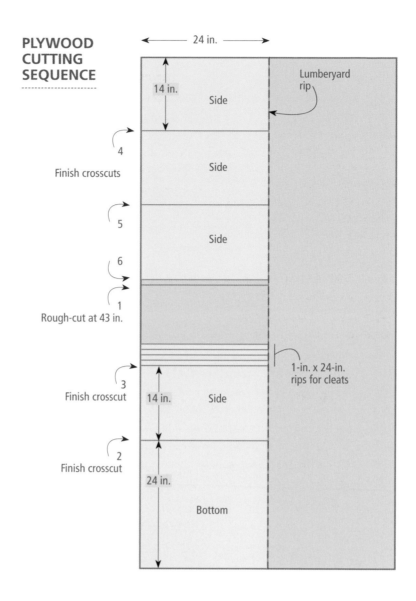

PLYWOOD CUTTING SEQUENCE

24 in.

Lumberyard rip

14 in. — Side

4 — Finish crosscuts — Side

5 — Side

6

1 — Rough-cut at 43 in.

1-in. x 24-in. rips for cleats

3 — Finish crosscut — 14 in. — Side

2 — Finish crosscut — 24 in. — Bottom

1 **MAKE A ROUGH CROSSCUT.** As shown in "Plywood Cutting Sequence," making a rough crosscut near the middle of the 24-in. × 96-in. piece of plywood will give you two pieces that won't be unwieldy when you make final crosscuts on the tablesaw. Place the plywood on the bench or sawhorses with two 8-ft. 2×4s underneath to support both sides of the cut. Set the saw-cutting depth to about ⅞ in. Lay out a line at 43 in. and make the cut (1) with a circular saw.

2 **CUT THE BOTTOM AND SIDES.** Set the tablesaw fence to 24 in. and crosscut the longer piece at 24 in. (2). Run the factory edge, not the rough cut, against the fence and use rollers, a table, or a helper to support the workpiece where it extends past the side of the saw. Reset the fence to 14 in. Place the edge you just cut against the fence and crosscut one side (3). Now crosscut three sides from the 43-in.-long piece. Do these in the sequence (4, 5, 6) shown so that the rough cut is never against the saw fence.

3 **LAY OUT AND DRILL DRAINAGE HOLES.** Use a T-square or framing square to lay out a grid of 3-in. squares on the bottom piece as shown in the drawing on p. 210. Raise the piece on 2×4s to protect your bench and use a spade bit to drill a ¾-in.-dia. hole at each line intersection.

Assemble the Box to the Legs

You'll use pocket-hole screws to attach the box sides to the legs. The inside faces of the sides will meet at the inside corner of the legs. You'll drill pocket holes in the sides, then make up two subassemblies, each consisting of a side glued and screwed to two legs. Then you will glue and screw the remaining sides to the subassemblies.

1 **DRILL POCKET HOLES.** Lay out five pocket holes in each 14-in.-long end of all four side pieces. Position the holes at 1 in., 3½ in., 7 in., 10½ in., and 13 in. Drill pockets for 1¼-in. pocket-hole screws.

2 **MAKE SUBASSEMBLIES.** Place the least attractive side of a leg down on the bench so it will be on the inside of the box. Clamp the leg to the bench. Put glue along the mating edge of a side piece, make sure it is flush to the top of the leg, and then assemble with 1¼-in. pocket screws. Attach another leg to the other side in the same way, and repeat the process to make the other subassembly.

3 **ADD THE THIRD SIDE.** Stand a subassembly upside down with its top edge on the bench. Apply glue to the edge of a third side piece and clamp it to one leg of the subassembly. Insert pocket screws. Now remove the clamp, put glue on the other end of the side piece, and clamp between subassembly legs as shown. Temporarily clamp the fourth side piece between subassemblies as shown to keep the box square while you screw the third side piece to the second subassembly.

4 **ADD THE FOURTH SIDE.** Put glue on both ends of the fourth side piece and clamp it in place between the subassemblies. You can use a hammer to tap it into exact position before installing screws on both ends.

TIP When you are done assembling the box sides to the legs, drop the bottom piece inside, letting it rest on the workbench. This will ensure that the box is square as the glue dries.

Quick Pocket-Hole Layout

Here's a time–saving way to lay out all 40 pocket-hole positions on the box side pieces: Stack the four sides with edges flush. Mark the hole spacing along the edge of one piece, then use a square to strike lines down the edge of all four sides. Now use a T-square or framing square to strike lines along the length of each side.

Install the Cleats and Bottom

As shown in "Plywood Cutting Sequence" (p. 211), the cleats that support the bottom of the box are ripped from the plywood offcut left when you made the sides and bottom. The rips will already be at the right length to make two of the cleats. The other two cleats will be crosscut to fit. After gluing and screwing the cleats in place, you'll install the bottom with glue and screws.

(p. 211)

TIP Deck screws are designed to drive without predrilling. However, drilling narrow pieces of solid wood or drilling near the end of a solid board can cause splitting along the grain. If, for example, the 1-in.-wide cleats were made of solid wood, you would predrill them. There's no need to predrill the plywood cleats, however. They are not prone to splitting because plywood is made of veneer layers that alternate in grain direction.

1 **RIP THE CLEATS TO WIDTH.** Set the tablesaw fence 1 in. from the blade. Rip four cleats from the 24-in.-long plywood offcut.

2 **INSTALL THE LONGER CLEATS.** Turn the box upside down, put glue on a 1-in.-wide face of a cleat, and set it in place flush to the bottom of the box. Secure the cleat with five 1¼-in. deck screws. Do the same to install a cleat on the opposing side.

3 **INSTALL THE SHORTER CLEATS.** Butt a cleat into one of the cleats you just installed and use a utility knife to make a notch where it meets the opposing cleat. Extend the notch into a layout line and cut the cleat to that length. Do the same for the remaining cleat, then install them both with glue and screws.

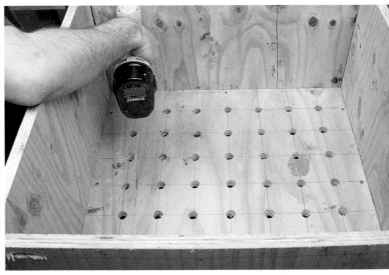

4 **INSTALL THE BOTTOM.** Turn the box right side up, put glue on the top of the cleats, set the bottom in place, and secure it with three 1¼-in. deck screws into each cleat.

Cut and Install the Cladding

Each side is clad with three full-width cladding boards flanked on each side with a board that you'll rip to width to fit. You'll start by cutting the boards to 14⅛ in. long, which is ⅛ in. longer than the width of the plywood sides. The boards will be installed flush to the top of the box. The extra ⅛ in. at the bottom will act as a drip edge, helping to keep water away from the bottom of the sides and the cleats.

For each side, you'll first install one board centered between the legs. Then you'll test-fit one board to each side of the center board and measure for the width of the boards that will butt into the legs. If you were to try to install the end boards after installing all three full boards, you would run the risk of splitting the last grooves. Instead, you'll install the end boards together with their mating full boards.

> **TIP** It's a good idea to make a support to hold longer boards level to the miter-saw table as shown in step 2 below. Make the support in the same way as the stop block. However, instead of making the upright leg of the block high enough for stock to butt into it, cut it to the same height as the miter-saw table. Clamp it to the bench to support the stock.

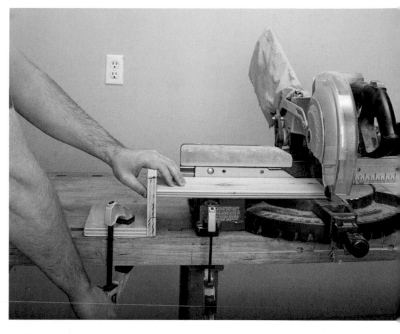

1 **CUT THE FIRST BOARD AND SET THE STOP.** Clamp the miter saw to the bench and use it to cut one board to 14⅛ in. Lock the blade in the down position. Slide that first piece up against the blade and then slide the stop against the piece. Clamp the stop to the bench.

2 **CUT THE CLADDING TO LENGTH.** Check that the end of a piece of tongue-and-groove stock is square. If it isn't, cut it square. Then butt that end into the stop to cut the next piece of cladding. Cut all the cladding pieces in the same way.

3 **LOCATE THE CENTER BOARD.** Measuring from the inside of a leg, mark the top of a side at 12 in. Then measure across the top of the first cladding board and make a mark halfway across its width, excluding the tongue. Extend the line across the top edge of the board.

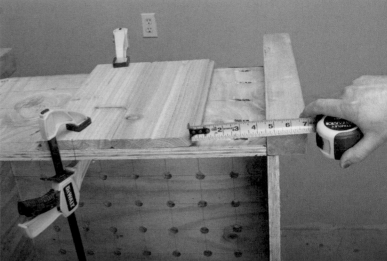

4 INSTALL THE FIRST BOARD. Put construction adhesive on the back of the center board. Align the mark on the top of the board with the mark on the top of the box side. Check that the board is square to the top and bottom of the box, then clamp it in place. Don't clamp it down hard as you would for wood glue—use just enough pressure to keep the board in place.

5 MEASURE AND CUT THE FIRST END BOARD TO WIDTH. Put a cladding board in place with its groove over the center board's tongue. Measure the distance from that board to the leg, *excluding* the tongue—the measurement should be about 4½ in. Cut a board to that width with its groove along the tablesaw fence so you are removing the tongue.

6 MEASURE AND CUT THE SECOND END BOARD TO WIDTH. Put a cladding board in place on the other side of the center board—this time you will be putting a tongue in the center board groove. Now measure the distance to the leg, *including* the groove—the measurement should be about 5 in. Cut a board to that length with its tongue against the tablesaw fence so you are removing the groove.

7 PUT ADHESIVE ON THE BOX SIDE. Put adhesive on the plywood to one side of the center board. Use a bead of adhesive around the perimeter of the area and dabs in the middle; it's not necessary to cover the whole surface.

8 **INSTALL THE BOARDS.** Fit the pair of boards together and push them into place to one side of the center board. Repeat for the other side of the center board. Use a rubber mallet to tap the boards to get them flush to the top of the sides. Install cladding boards on all four sides of the box.

Construction Adhesive vs. Wood Glue: Pros and Cons

If you are building this planter to complement the storage bench project on p. 168, you may be wondering why we used exterior wood glue to attach the cladding on the bench but construction adhesive to attach it to the planter. Here's why:

Wood glue requires clamping pressure to bond wood fibers together. When joining two bare, smooth pieces of wood such as the cladding to the storage bench's pine frame, this creates a strong bond. And, because the glue soaks into the fibers, it leaves no visible gap or glue seam between parts. But wood glue won't bond across gaps.

Construction adhesive, like exterior wood glue, is waterproof. It doesn't require clamping pressure to bond, and it can fill and bond across rough material such as the planter's construction-grade plywood sides. However, because it doesn't soak into the wood fibers, construction adhesive creates a visible seam between parts.

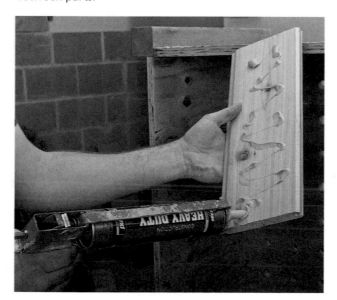

When you open the storage bench, you see where the top of the cladding meets the top rails of the frame. An unsightly seam of construction adhesive would have been visible.

In the case of the planter, a cap covers the top edge, so the construction adhesive seam is hidden. While construction adhesive isn't strong enough for joinery that will be stressed, it's plenty strong enough to bond cladding to plywood panels.

Finally, we used finish nails to provide clamping pressure when we glued the cladding to the storage bench. Using construction adhesive lets us forgo that step on the planter. It's quick and easy to use a cartridge gun to squirt dabs of adhesive on one of the surfaces to be bonded.

Make and Attach the Cap

The cap adds an attractive detail and covers the top of the legs, keeping water away from that end grain. It's made from nominal 5/4 x 6 cedar decking boards that actually measure 1 in. x 5½ in. These boards have rounded edges. You'll rip one of these edges off and use the other rounded edge to form the outside perimeter of the cap.

You'll start by crosscutting the four cap pieces to rough length and then ripping them to final width. You'll miter one end of each piece. Then you'll miter the other end of one piece and use it to set up a stop to miter all the other ends. Next, you'll tack-nail all the pieces in position in case you need to reposition them to get the miter joints to line up. Then, one by one, you'll remove each cap piece, apply glue, and clamp it into place.

1 **MAKE BLANKS AND MITER ONE END.** The finished cap pieces will be 30 in. long. Use the miter saw to make blanks that are about 31 in. long. Then rip the blanks to 3 in. wide. Miter one end of each piece, making the cut with the long side of the miter at the rounded edge that you didn't rip.

2 **MITER THE SECOND END OF ONE PIECE.** Lay out the second miter on one piece so that the long points of the miters will be 30 in. apart. After making a mark, use an angle square to lay out the 45-degree cutline. Cut the miter on the miter saw.

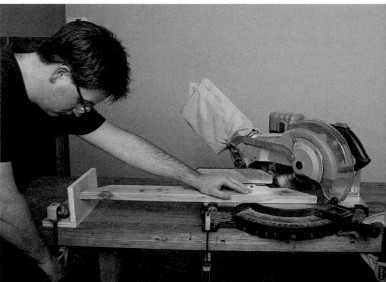

3 **CUT THE REMAINING MITERS.** Lock the miter blade in the down position. Raise the guard and put the miter you just cut against the blade. With the miter saw clamped to the bench, slide a stop against the tip of the miter on the other end. Clamp the stop to the bench, then put each remaining piece against the stop to cut the remaining miters.

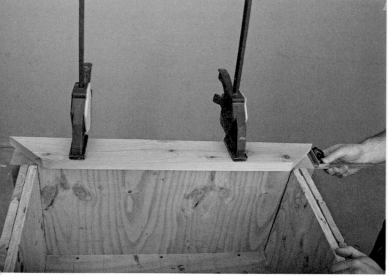

4 **POSITION THE FIRST CAP.** Put a cap piece in place so that the miter crosses an inside and outside corner of each leg. Use a combination square to check that the cap piece overlaps the outside faces of both legs by ½ in. Clamp the piece in position.

5 **TACK-NAIL THE FIRST CAP PIECE IN POSITION.** Tack the piece in place with one 4d finish nail driven into the top of each leg. Leave the nail heads protruding. Position and tack-nail all the caps in place. If a cap needs to be repositioned to close up the miters, pull its nails and do so.

TIP It's a good idea to install furniture glides to raise the bottom of the legs a bit, preventing the end grain from wicking water (see step 4, "Install Furniture Glides," p. 183). Install the glides after applying finish to seal the end grain.

6 **GLUE AND CLAMP THE CAPS.** Pull off one cap piece, letting the nails protrude from the bottom. Apply glue to the top of the box, the cladding, and the exposed part of the top of the legs. Put the piece back in place, letting the nails find their original holes in the top of the legs. Secure the piece with three clamps. Now do the same for each cap piece, letting the glue set between pieces if you are short on clamps. As you work your way around, put glue on the mitered face of the previous piece it will meet—you want glue on one face of each miter joint. Finally, set all the finish nails.

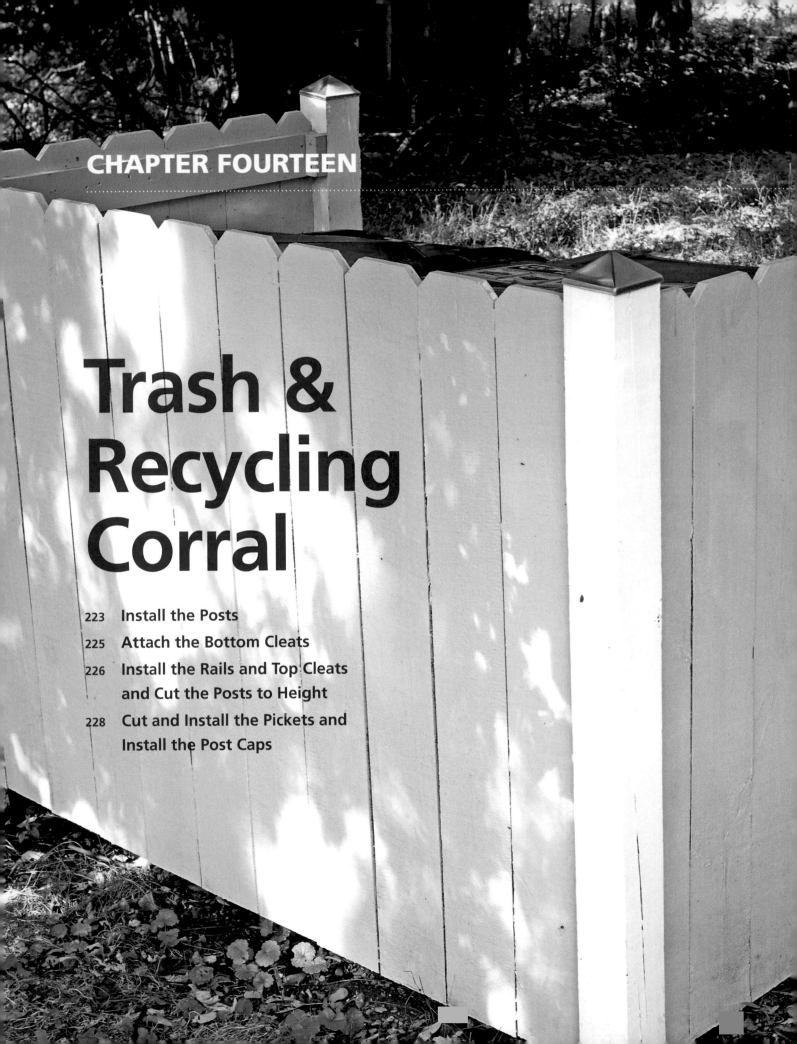

Trash & Recycling Corral

HERE'S A SIMPLE PROJECT that'll get those unsightly trash and recycling containers out of sight this weekend. Although you can build this three-sided corral to hide any type of refuse receptacle, it's designed specifically to screen two wheeled bins with hinged lids that flip up from the side opposite the wheels. This type of bin is used with automated collection trucks that have become common nationwide.

The corral is just a few inches higher than the bins so you can reach over the front to open the lids. The back of the corral is open to provide access to the handles on the wheeled side so you can easily pull the bins out. It's built with pressure-treated fence pickets that come with the top corners decoratively clipped at 45 degrees.

We painted the pickets of our corral to match the clapboards of the house and the posts to match the white house trim. You might choose to stain it, or just allow the wood to weather to gray.

WHAT YOU'LL NEED

- 4 posts
  3½ in. x 3½ in. x 60 in.,
  pressure-treated pine
- 2 top and bottom front rails
  ¾ in. x 3½ in. x 62 in., pine
- 4 top and bottom side rails
  ¾ in. x 3 in. x 36 in., pine
- 19 pickets
  ⅝ in. x 5 in. x 46 in.,
  pressure treated

- 2 front end pickets
  ⅝ in. x 5⅛ in. x 46 in.,
  pressure treated
- 4 side end pickets
  ⅝ in. x 3⅝ in. x 46 in.,
  pressure treated
- 12 top and bottom cleats
  1¼ in. x 1¼ in. x 3½ in.,
  pressure treated

HARDWARE

- Mason's twine
- Construction adhesive
- 2½-in. deck screws
- 1¼-in. deck screws
- 4 copper 3½-in. x 3-in. post caps

TRASH AND RECYCLING CORRAL

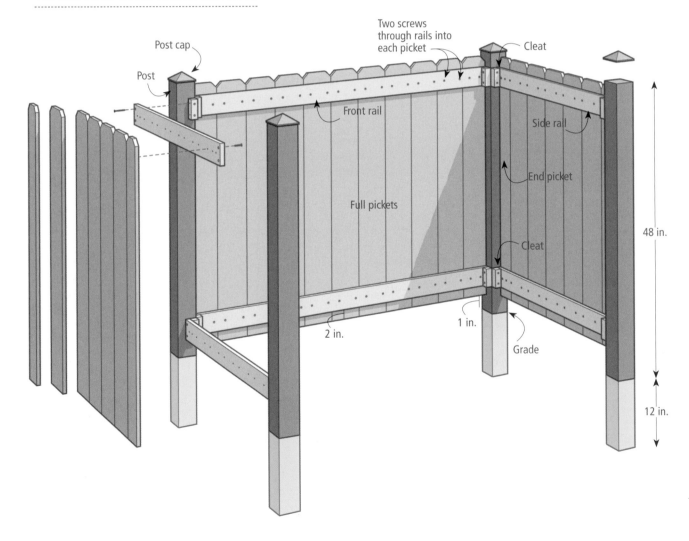

Install the Posts

To make it easy to maneuver the bins, you'll need at least 2 in. of space between the bins themselves and the inside of the posts. So start by measuring your bins to determine the footprint of your corral. Our corral is built to screen a trash container and a recycling container, both measuring about 28 in. wide and 35 in. deep. The drawing "Sizing the Corral" shows how these bins fit into our corral. Once you decide on the footprint, you'll begin work by laying out the centers of your four posts. As shown in the drawing, our posts are centered at 65½ in. at front and back and 39½ in. at the sides.

You'll use string and nails to lay out the post centers, then you'll dig the post holes.

| TIP | To make layout easier, use a garden rake to remove large stones and to make the work area flat. |

SIZING THE CORRAL

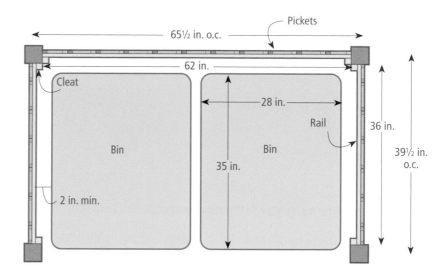

Pickets

65½ in. o.c.

62 in.

Cleat

28 in.

Rail

36 in.

Bin

Bin

39½ in. o.c.

35 in.

2 in. min.

1 **LAY OUT THE FRONT AND ONE SIDE.** Hammer a nail in the ground to indicate the center of one front post. Measure across, in our case 65½ in., to find the center of the other front post. Tie mason's twine between the two nails. Turn a corner with the string and use a framing square to run the string roughly perpendicular to the front. Tie it to another nail to indicate the length of one side, in our case 39½ in.

2 **COMPLETE THE LAYOUT.** Now use the 3-4-5 method (see p. 56) to make the two legs of string perfectly perpendicular. Use a felt-tip marker to mark the side leg of the string at 3 ft. Place a nail along the front leg of the string 4 ft. from the corner nail and hook a tape measure on that nail. Check the measurement where the tape meets the mark. If necessary, adjust the position of the nail closest to the mark until the mark aligns with a measurement of 5 ft., indicating that the corner is square. Continue the string to complete the perimeter and use the 3-4-5 method to square the opposing corner.

3 **DIG THE POST HOLES.** Remove the string but leave the corner nails until you start the holes. Use a post-hole digger to dig holes centered over the four corner nails. Dig down about 12 in.

4 **INSERT THE POSTS.** Set three posts in their holes and pack in enough dirt to hold them upright. Put a pair of 2x4s against the posts to form a corner as shown. Drive a screw into one of the 2x4s located 3 ft. from the inside corner formed by the 2x4s. Make a mark at 4 ft. along the other 2x4. Run your tape measure between the screw and mark and use the 3-4-5 method to get the boards perpendicular, then align the posts against the boards. Pack dirt tightly around the posts. Insert the fourth post with enough dirt to hold it up, move one of the 2x4s to form a new corner, and use the 3-4-5 method to align the fourth post before packing dirt around it.

Check the Slope

Your site doesn't have to be level, but if it slopes too much across the front of your corral, you'll either have to add soil to level it or choose a new site. You want the top of your bins to be no less than about 2 in. below the top of the pickets to hide them and no more than about 8 in. below the pickets so you can easily reach in to open the bins. Once you have laid out positions for the front of your corral, place a straight 2x4 along the string with one end at the upslope nail. Put a 4-ft. level on the 2x4 and raise it to level. Measure the vertical distance from the downslope nail to the bottom of the board. The slope is gentle enough if that distance is no more than 6 in.

Attach the Bottom Cleats

The cleats will be attached to the posts and the rails will be attached to the cleats. As shown in the drawing on p. 222, top and bottom cleats are attached to two sides of each front post and to one side of each back post.

You'll start by attaching just the bottom cleats and the three bottom rails. This will prevent the posts from wobbling while you cut the posts to length. You'll add the top cleats and rails after you cut the posts to height so they won't get in the way of the circular saw.

1 **MAKE AND PREDRILL THE CLEATS.** Use a power miter saw or the miter gauge on a tablesaw to cut a piece of 1¼-in. by 1¼-in. deck baluster to twelve 3½-in.-long pieces. Or you can set a tablesaw blade 1¼ in. from the fence and make two rips on a piece of 2x4. To prevent the cleats from splitting when you install them, predrill and countersink two holes for 2½-in. deck screws in each hole.

2 **FIND THE HIGHEST GRADE.** In most cases, the ground won't be level, so you need to find which post is at the highest point. The bottom of all the pickets will be 1 in. above this level. To find the highest grade, place a 2x4 with a level atop it against posts on each side around the perimeter.

3 **MARK THE HEIGHT OF THE FIRST BOTTOM CLEAT.** Draw a line 6½ in. from the ground across the post that's at the highest grade. Make this line on one of the faces that will support a cleat.

4 INSTALL THE FIRST CLEAT. Clamp a cleat to the high post with its top aligned to the line you just drew. Make the cleat flush to the inside corner of the post. Attach the cleat with two 2½-in. deck screws into the predrilled holes.

5 MARK AND INSTALL THE REMAINING BOTTOM CLEATS. Rest one end of a level on the first cleat and extend it across to its nearest neighbor. Center the level bubble and mark a line when the bottom of the level meets the second post. Mark the farther post by resting the level on a straight 2x4 as shown. Mark all the bottom cleat positions.

Install the Rails and Top Cleats and Cut the Posts to Height

Planting posts isn't an exact science, so it's unlikely that each post is placed exactly on the center points you marked. Fortunately, it doesn't matter if rail lengths are an inch or less different than you planned. As long as each top rail is the same length as the bottom rail below it and the posts are plumb, the pickets will fit fine and it won't matter if the footprint is slightly out of square.

To help ensure the posts will be plumb, you'll cut each bottom rail to fit between posts and you'll cut a top rail to the same length. Then you'll install the bottom rails, which will keep the posts from wobbling while you cut them to proper height. You'll install the top cleats and rails after cutting the posts so the cleats and rails won't get in the way of the saw.

1 MEASURE FOR THE RAILS. Measure between posts at the top of opposing bottom cleats to determine the length of each pair of bottom and top rails.

2 **CUT THE RAILS.** Use an angle square to lay out the length of the front bottom rail on a piece of 1x4. Place the blade on the cutline and slide the square up against the base to guide a straight and square cut. Cut a top rail to the same length. Do the same for both pairs of side rails.

3 **INSTALL THE BOTTOM RAILS.** Start a 1¼-in. screw into each end of a bottom rail. Put the rail in place against the outside faces of the cleats as shown and drive in the screws. Check that the posts are plumb, then add another screw to each side. Do this for all three bottom rails.

4 **CUT OFF THE POSTS.** Mark the cut-off height of each post as described in "Determining Post Height." Use a square to extend the mark into lines on all sides of the post. Set your circular saw to the deepest setting and make sure the blade is square to the base. Cut along the lines on three sides, holding the saw firmly with both hands.

Determining Post Height

The tops of the bottom rails are all at the same level, so you'll measure up from them to mark the posts for cutting. To get the measurement, measure the height of your bins and subtract 3½ in. Our bins are about 45 in. tall, so we marked the posts for cutting at 41½ in. above the bottom rails.

5 **INSTALL THE TOP CLEATS AND RAILS.** Install the top cleats in the same way as the bottom cleats. Locate them 3 in. from the top of the posts. As you did for the bottom rails, start two screws in each top rail, put it in place, and drive in the screws. If the ends of the rails aren't butting squarely into posts, check the posts for plumb. You may need to shove on them a bit to plumb them. When you are sure the posts are plumb, add another screw to each end of each top rail.

Cut and Install the Pickets and Install the Post Caps

First, you'll find the length of your pickets by measuring the distance from the bottom of the bottom rails to the top of the top rails and adding 4 in. Next, you'll cut the pickets to length before attaching them to the rails. You'll start by installing a center picket, then full pickets to each side of it, and finally you'll rip end pickets to fit and install those.

To give the project a finished look and to protect the end grain at the top of the posts, you'll add post caps. The caps come in various styles and prices—ranging from very inexpensive plastic to simple or more elaborate wood versions. Top-end caps combine wood and copper. We chose simple, relatively inexpensive solid copper caps.

1 **CUT AND MARK THE PICKETS. If you have a power miter saw, you can save time by using it with a stop block to quickly cut all the pickets to length (see "Making and Using a Stop Block," p. 171). Otherwise, it's easy enough to cut them with a circular saw guided by an angle square as you did the rails. Once the pickets are cut to length, lay them out in batches of four or five as shown here and use a framing square to strike lines 2 in. from the top of each one.**

2 **MARK THE CENTER PICKET. On one picket, measure across the 2-in. line to find the center, then draw a line from that point to the top of the picket. Measure across the top of the top rail to make a center mark there.**

3 **POSITION THE CENTER PICKET. Align the 2-in. line you made on the center picket to the top of the front rail and align the centerline on the picket to the center mark on the rail. Clamp the picket to the top rail. Use an angle square to check that the picket is square to the top rail and bottom rail, then clamp the picket to the bottom rail.**

4 **INSTALL THE FULL PICKETS. Attach the center picket by screwing through the rails into the picket. Use two 1¼-in. deck screws through the top rail and two through the bottom rail. Install the remaining full-width pickets in the same way, aligning the 2-in. line with the top of the rail, clamping them in place, and checking for square before driving the screws.**

5 INSTALL THE END PICKETS. The pickets can vary slightly in width, so don't rely on math to determine the width of the end pickets. Instead, measure the space between picket and post. Take measurements at top and bottom and if there is a slight difference, use the smaller measurement to rip the pickets to width on a tablesaw. Screw the end pickets in place. Repeat steps 2 through 5 to lay out and install pickets on the sides.

6 INSTALL THE POST CAPS. Some wooden post caps have a hole in the top so you can attach them with a screw. Most, including the copper caps shown here, are best installed by simply squirting a little exterior construction adhesive around the inside perimeter and sticking them in place.

Clip the End Pickets

When ripping the end pickets to width, you'll remove one of the angled top corners. If you want to be fussy about detail, you can replace the angled cut. Just put the end picket in place with the ripped side against the post as shown below left. Put the offcut against the post and flush to the top of the end picket. Then use a pencil to scribe the angle cut onto the end picket. Clamp the picket to sawhorses or a bench and make the cut with a circular saw as shown below right.

> **TIP** If you'll be painting your corral and you'll be using copper post caps, install the caps after painting. That way, you won't have to worry about getting paint on the caps.

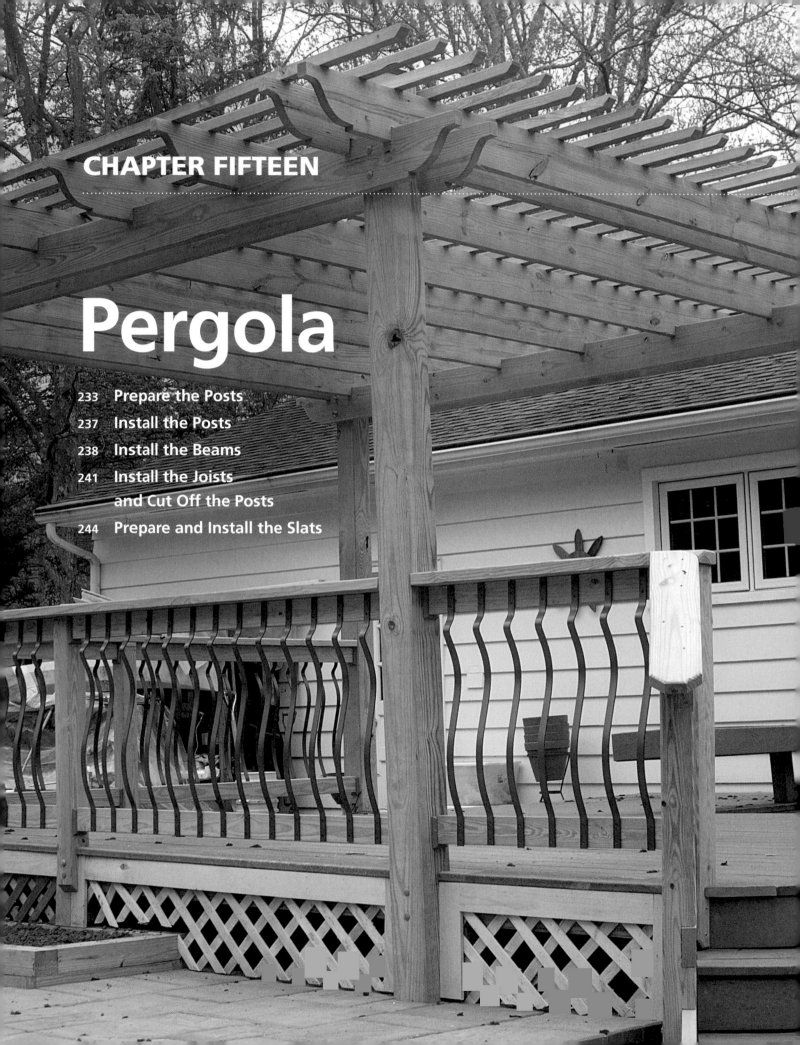

CHAPTER FIFTEEN

Pergola

THIS PERGOLA will add character, beauty, and versatility to your landscape. You can use it to add just the right amount of shade to a patio or you can integrate it into a deck as shown here. Or you can make this same design freestanding to define and shade a particularly nice spot in your yard.

The dimensions given in "What You'll Need" are for a pergola with posts set 12 ft. on center from each other. You can use those dimensions if you are building a freestanding pergola. If you are incorporating your pergola into an existing deck or patio, you'll need to adapt the dimensions, something that is very easy to do—we'll show you how as the project progresses. The pergola shown here, for example, was built around an existing deck. Its posts are close to, but not exactly, 12 ft. on center.

The roof of the pergola consists of 2x8 beams crossed by notched 2x8 joists. The joists are topped with slats made by ripping 2x4s in half. The shape on the ends of the beams and joists was drawn freehand by the owner of this pergola. You can follow the pattern provided, or you can get creative

WHAT YOU'LL NEED

- 4 posts
  5½ in. x 5½ in. x 14 ft., pressure-treated for ground contact pine

- 4 beams
  1½ in. x 7¼ in. x 173½ in., pressure-treated pine

- 9 joists
  1½ in. x 7½ in. x 182½ in., pressure-treated pine

- 24 slats
  1½ in. x 1¾ in. x 182½ in., pressure-treated pine

- 2 slats
  1½ in. x 1¾ in. x 138½ in., pressure-treated pine

- 4 overhang pieces
  1½ in. x 1¾ in. x 22 in., pressure treated-pine

HARDWARE AND SUPPLIES

- Gravel
- Concrete
- 4-in. deck screws
- 2-in. deck screws
- ⅝-in.-dia. x 6-in. galvanized carriage bolts*
- ⅝-in.-dia. x 8-in. galvanized carriage bolts**
- ½-in.-dia. x 10-in. carriage bolts
- 5½-in. x 5½-in. copper post caps, optional
- Guide string

*As needed for notched posts
**As needed for posts without notches

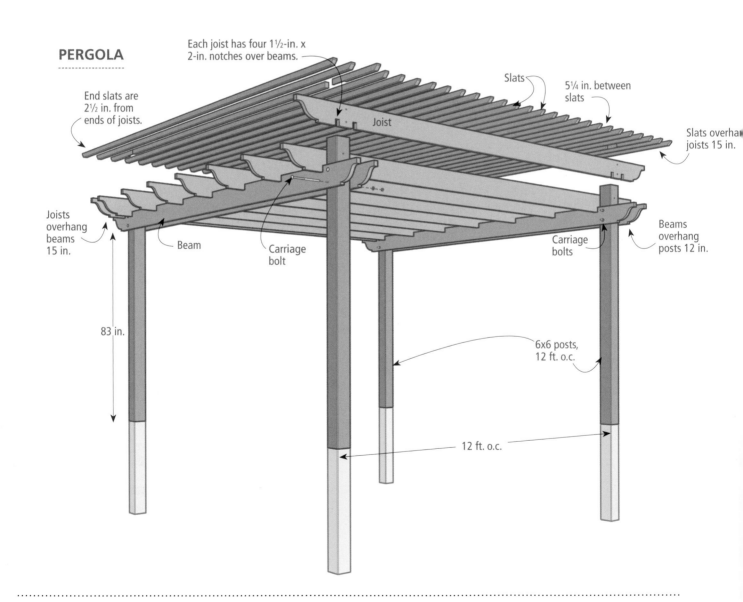

PERGOLA

Each joist has four 1½-in. x 2-in. notches over beams.

End slats are 2½ in. from ends of joists.

Slats

5¼ in. between slats

Joist

Slats overhang joists 15 in.

Joists overhang beams 15 in.

Beam

Carriage bolt

Carriage bolts

Beams overhang posts 12 in.

83 in.

6x6 posts, 12 ft. o.c.

12 ft. o.c.

and come up with your own design. But keep it simple; there are a lot of 'em to cut!

Overall, there is nothing complex about building a pergola. However, you'll be moving around some big pieces of lumber, so you will get a workout and you'll definitely need a helper.

Prepare the Posts

For this pergola, three of the posts have 1½-in.-deep notches to fit over the deck rim joists. The notches are to accommodate the design of a deck railing that will be added later, so you can skip the notches if you don't need them. If you are notching the posts, you'll tamp down the gravel, then use a length of 2x4 as a "story pole" to mark the location of the notch on each post. If you won't be notching the posts, skip to "Install the Posts" (p. 237).

Dressing Up the Posts

To dress up the posts a little, we routed a chamfer along the four edges. Put a piloted chamfering bit in your router. We set ours to make a chamfer of about ¼ in., but you can make your chamfer any width that pleases you. Be sure to rout from left to right so the bit will scoop the wood out cleanly.

1 MARK A STORY POLE. Put a length of 2x4 in the hole and use a 4-ft. level to plumb it. Mark where the 2x4 meets the top and bottom of the rim joist.

2 LAY OUT THE NOTCH ON A POST. On sawhorses, place the story pole along a post with the ends flush as shown. Transfer the top and bottom of the notch layout to the post and use a square to extend the layout across the face of the post.

Laying Out and Digging Post Holes

The sequence illustrated here is for a square pergola with four posts that are 12 ft. on center. The pergola covers only part of a preexisting deck, which predetermines the location of two of its posts. One is located at an outside corner, while the other is diagonally across at an inside corner of an opening for the basement door. If your pergola will be attached to four corners, all of your post locations are predetermined. If your pergola is freestanding, use the method described in "Lay Out the Garden Posts" on p. 27. This method will work for any square layout.

A. From the outside corner of the deck, measure 12 ft. toward the house and make a mark. Then measure from the same corner along the front of the deck and make another mark at 12 ft.

B. Drive a nail or screw partway in at the marks and at the basement entrance post location. Run strings between the basement entrance post location and the two marks you made at the deck perimeter.

C. The 3-4-5 method is an easy way to check if something is square: If one side of a right triangle is 3 ft. long and another side is 4 ft. long, the diagonal hypotenuse will be 5 ft. long. Of course, you can use any multiple—here we used 6 ft., 8 ft., and 10 ft. Use this method to check if the right front corner and the left rear corner are square. Adjust the position of the marks if necessary to form square corners.

LAYING OUT THE POSTS

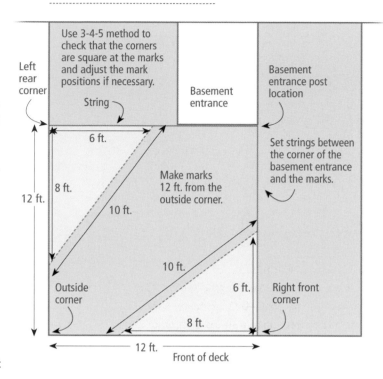

Use 3-4-5 method to check that the corners are square at the marks and adjust the mark positions if necessary.

Left rear corner

String

Basement entrance

Basement entrance post location

Set strings between the corner of the basement entrance and the marks.

6 ft.

8 ft.

12 ft.

10 ft.

Make marks 12 ft. from the outside corner.

Outside corner

10 ft.

6 ft.

Right front corner

8 ft.

12 ft.

Front of deck

DIG THE POST HOLES

Holes for posts that will be set in concrete should be approximately three times the width of the posts, so you'll want the holes for the nominal 6x6 posts used here to be about 18 in. in diameter. Make the holes about 42 in. deep to provide plenty of lateral support. Since the post holes are oversized, they need not be perfectly centered across the post-center layout marks, so you can eyeball their locations.

You can use a post-hole digger as shown here, or, if your ground is hard or rocky, you might want to rent a power post-hole auger. Add a few inches of gravel to the hole and tamp it down with a length of 2x4 or 4x4.

TIP On this pergola, two of the posts are not located at corners. These two posts will be notched 1½ in. deep all the way across one face. The post at the inside corner by the basement door is not notched at all, while the post at the outside corner gets the corner notch described in steps 7 and 8. If your pergola will be notched over all four corners of a deck, skip to step 7.

3 **KERF THE FULL NOTCHES.** Set the circular saw to cut 1½ in. deep. Make cuts along the layout lines on the face of the post—be sure to cut to the inside of the lines. Then make a series of cuts, or kerfs, through the face of the notch, spacing the kerfs about ½ in. apart.

4 **CHOP OUT THE FULL NOTCHES.** Use a hammer and chisel to chop the waste out of the notch. Then use the chisel to clean out the bottom of the notch. Use the saw marks at the bottom of the notch as a guide to get a flat notch of the right depth.

5 **DRILL BOLT HOLES THROUGH THE FULL NOTCHES.** Use a square to extend the notch layout to the opposing face of the post. Then use a ⅝-in. spade bit to drill two holes that are centered across the post and about 1 in. from the top and bottom of the notch.

6 **LAY OUT THE CORNER NOTCH.** Set a combination square to 1½ in. and use it to scribe a line across the top and bottom notch layout lines.

7 **KERF THE CORNER NOTCH.** With the circular saw still set to cut 1½ in deep, cut the top and bottom of the notch and a series of kerfs, stopping when the cut meets the line you made with the combination square.

8 **CHOP OUT THE CORNER NOTCH.** Use a chisel and hammer to knock out as much of the corner-notch waste material as you can. Then, working from both sides of the notch, chop straight down to clean out the two faces of the notch. Outside corner posts won't be bolted to the deck, so there is no need to drill bolt holes.

Sanding the Pergola Parts

If you want to give your project a more refined look, take the time to sand the posts, beams, and joists with #80 grit. You can do the entire job with a random-orbit sander, or you can speed the job by using a belt sander on the wide surfaces.

You'll make the top slats by ripping 2x4s down the middle. There is no need to sand the surfaces of the slat. After each rip, just use the random-orbit sander as shown here to quickly round the newly cut edges to match the factory edges. To avoid moving pieces around more than necessary, sand each piece after you cut it.

Install the Posts

If you are attaching your pergola to a deck, you'll start by bolting into place any posts that are not at outside corners. Outside corner posts won't be bolted, so you'll need to brace those when you place them. If you are building a freestanding pergola, brace the posts as described in step 3 "Install and plumb the corner posts" and step 4 "Stake the braces" on pp. 30–31. Once the posts are bolted or braced, you'll fill the holes with concrete. Because your post-hole locations are likely to be at different elevations, the posts' heights will vary. You'll cut them all off to the same height after the beams and joists are installed.

TIP If your drill bit isn't long enough to go through the post notch and all the way through the rim joist, drill as deep as you can, and then move the post to one side so you can drill the joist hole through.

1 **INSTALL BOLTED POSTS. Strike a line down the side of the rim joist. Locate the line 2¾ in. from the post's on-center point. Fit the post notch over the joist and align the post to the line you just drew. Plumb the post and drill through the holes in the post into the joist.**

2 **BRACE THE CORNER POST. Use 2x4s to brace the corner post or posts against the deck rim joists.** Because of the notch, the corner post or posts will protrude 4 in. from the joists at each side of the corner. To bring the bottoms of the 2x4 braces into approximately the same plane as the outside of the post, make a "packout" by clamping a piece of 4x4 and a piece of 5/4 scrap to the joists about 3 ft. from the posts. Attach two 2x4 braces near the top of the outside faces of the post using one screw in each brace. Put the post in place with the notch overlapping the corner. Plumb one side of the post and drive a screw through the brace into the packout. Then plumb the other side and fix the post in place with a screw in the other packout.

TIP If you want to avoid mixing concrete, you can use quick-setting concrete. Just pour water and the dry concrete directly into the hole as described on the package.

3 **MIX CONCRETE AND FILL HOLES.** Pour a bag of concrete into a mixing bin or wheelbarrow and gradually add water while you mix it with a hoe. You want the mix to be wet but not soupy. Then use a shovel to fill the holes to the top with concrete. Let the concrete cure overnight before removing the braces.

Install the Beams

For this design, there are four parallel beams, two attached to opposing sides of two posts. You'll start by cutting a 2x8 to length for the beams, and then, if you choose to, you'll add a decorative cut to the ends. You'll raise and level this beam and then tack it in place with screws. Then you'll cut a second beam and raise, level, and tack it on the other side of the same two posts. You'll secure these beams with carriage bolts running through them and the post between.

The next step is to strike a line on one of the remaining posts that's at the same level as the top of the first two beams. To do this, you'll use a level and one of the 2x4s you bought that later will be ripped into slats. Then you'll cut and install the remaining two beams.

1 **CUT DECORATIVE ENDS ON THE FIRST BEAMS.** Place a 2x8 across sawhorses and use a circular saw to cut it to 173½ in. long. If you will be cutting decorative ends, make a template as described in "Creating a Template for Decorative Ends" on the facing page. Trace the shape onto the ends of the boards (top). Before you cut the decorative ends, draw a line across the bottom of the beam 12 in. from one end. You'll use the line to center the beam across the post. Cut the shape on both ends with a sabersaw (bottom).

TIP If the ground under your posts slopes at all, find the post that is at the lowest elevation. You can do this by placing one of the 16-ft. 2x4s you purchased for the slats against pairs of posts and putting a level on the 2x4. Strike a line across the lowest post 83 in. from the ground.

2 **MARK THE HEIGHT OF THE FIRST BEAM.** Strike a line on a post 83 in. from the deck surface or ground. Drive an 8d or 10d nail into this line, leaving it protruding about 1¾ in.

Creating a Template for Decorative Ends

DECORATIVE END PATTERN

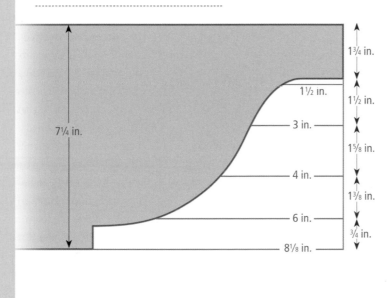

7¼ in.

1½ in.
3 in.
4 in.
6 in.
8⅛ in.

1¾ in.
1½ in.
1⅝ in.
1⅜ in.
¾ in.

If you want, you can simply leave the ends of your beams and joists square, but most pergolas feature some kind of embellishment on the ends of these members. You can duplicate the shape used on the pergola shown here or create any shape that pleases you. Either way, draw your shape on a piece of cardboard or stiff paper—we used a manila folder—and cut it out to use as a template.

To duplicate the pattern shown here, plot out the reference points shown in the drawing. Use the reference points to draw the curves—don't worry about duplicating our pattern exactly as long as the final result is pleasing to your eye.

3 **RAISE THE FIRST BEAM.** With a helper, raise the beam against the post with one end resting on the nail. Align the 12-in. line on the bottom of the beam to the outside of a post. Level the beam with a 4-ft. level, and then clamp the beam to the posts. Drive a couple of 2½-in. screws into each end of the beam to fix it in place temporarily.

4 **RAISE THE SECOND BEAM AND INSTALL BOLTS.** Use a square to extend the bottom level of the first beam to the opposing sides of the same two posts and drive a supporting nail in at each line. Raise the second beam, check it for level, and fix it in place with two screws on each end. At both posts, drill two ½-in.-dia. holes through the beams and post. Center the holes across the beam, about 2 in. from the top and bottom of the beams. Use a hammer to tap ½-in.-dia. bolts through the beams and posts, put washers and nuts on the ends, and tighten with a wrench.

Customizing the Size of your Pergola

The lengths for beams, joists, and slats given in "What You'll Need" (p. 232) are for a square pergola with posts that are 12 ft. on center. The beams extend 12 in. from the outside of the posts, the joists extend 15 in. past the outside of the beams, and the slats extend 15 in. over the outside of the end joists. To keep these same overhangs for a different post spacing, simply add or subtract from the post on-center spacing. For example, if your pergola has posts that are 11 ft. (132 in.) on center, your beams would be 161½ in. long instead of 173½ in. long, while your joists and slats would be 170½ in. long.

5 **LEVEL AND INSTALL THE REMAINING BEAMS.** To find the level for the top of the parallel beams, rest one end of a long 2x4 across the installed beams, level the 2x4 with a 4-ft. level, and mark where the bottom of the 2x4 meets the post. Install the remaining beams as you did the first two.

Install the Joists and Cut Off the Posts

As with the beams, you'll prepare one joist at a time and put it in position before moving on to the next one. The joists have the same end decoration as the beams, so as with the beams, you'll start by cutting a joist to length and then cutting the decorative ends.

Each joist has four notches that fit over the beams. Cutting the notches is easy, but getting them in exactly the right spots to fit over both pairs of beams is tricky if you try to do it by measuring between posts. To ensure success, you'll measure and cut the two notches at one end of each joist, put those notches in place on the beams, and mark the positions of the other two notches at the other end of the joist. This means you need to lift each joist into place twice, but the extra work is worth it.

Once the joists are installed, you'll cut all the posts off at the same height.

JOIST NOTCH LAYOUT

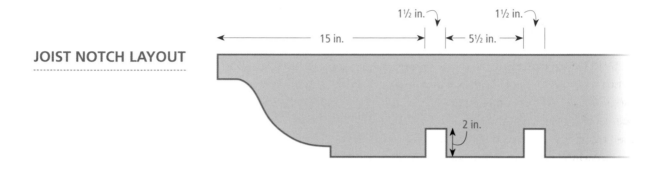

15 in.   1½ in.   5½ in.   1½ in.   2 in.

1 **CUT THE END DECORATION AND LAY OUT THE NOTCHES.** Cut a joist to 182½ in. long. Then strike a line across the joist located 15 in. from each end. Lay out and cut the end decorations as you did for the beams. Now lay out the two notches on one end as shown in the drawing "Joist Notch Layout." To quickly lay out the correct notch widths, use a scrap of the 2x8 stock as a template. Place one side of the scrap squarely against the 15-in. layout line and scribe the width of the other side of the notch. Measure 5½ in. from the first notch and use the scrap to scribe the width of the second notch.

2 **KERF THE JOIST NOTCHES.** Use a square to transfer a notch layout to the bottom of the joist. Set the circular saw to cut 2 in. deep. Clamp the joist to sawhorses with the bottom facing up. Now make cuts to define the sides of a notch and then cut several kerfs across the bottom between the side cuts. Repeat for the second notch.

Calculating Joist Spacing

If posts are set exactly 12 ft. on center, there will be 135½ in. between them, and the seven joists between the posts will be spaced 22⁵⁄₁₆ in. o.c. But in the real world, posts rarely get set exactly where you want them, and besides, you may be building a pergola with a post spacing other than 12 ft. o.c. Here's how to calculate and lay out your joist spacing.

To determine how many joists you need, start with the assumption that you want your joists to be spaced no farther apart than 24 in. o.c. Dividing the space between posts (135.5 in.) by 24 gives you 5.6. Round down to five joists. Then add in the four joists that will be attached to the posts to find that you need nine joists for posts 12 ft. o.c.

The next step is to subtract 1½ in. from the space between the posts. This is because you want to calculate your on-center spacing from the center of each of the two joists that are attached to the inside of the posts. The result in our example is 134 in.

Now divide 134 in. by the number of spaces between the joists. There will be six spaces between the seven between-post joists. That gives you joists that are 22⁵⁄₁₆ in. o.c.

Lay out the joist spacing after you install the four joists that flank the posts. Working from your left side, place your tape measure against an inside flanking joist and mark the on-center intervals across the top of one of the beams. Do the same on one of the opposing beams. The interval measurements for a pergola with posts 12 ft. on center are given in the drawing below. Notice on that drawing that if you start measuring from the left, the joists are placed to the left side of the lines.

JOIST SPACING

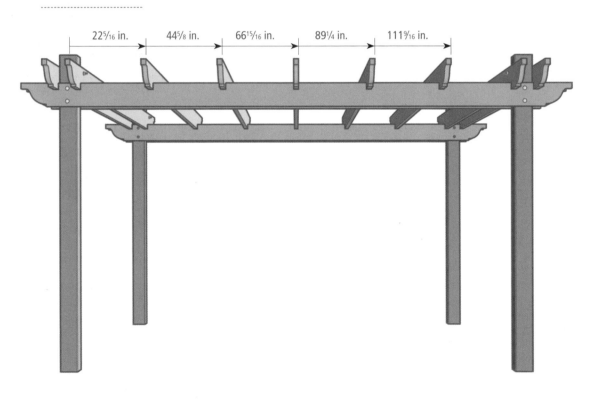

22⁵⁄₁₆ in. 44⁵⁄₈ in. 66¹⁵⁄₁₆ in. 89¼ in. 111⁹⁄₁₆ in.

3 **CLEAN OUT THE NOTCHES.** Lay the joist wide side down. Place the flat of a chisel at the bottom of the kerfs and hit it with a hammer to chop out the waste.

4 **SCRIBE AND CUT OPPOSING NOTCHES.** Put the joist in place along the layout lines on the opposing beams (see "Calculating Joist Spacing" on the facing page) with the notches resting over the beams—no need to push the notches down. Then mark the positions for the remaining notches by placing a square against each side of the beam and scribing lines. Take the joist down and cut the notches.

> **TIP** You know you made the space between notches 5½ in. wide to match the post width, but somehow the notches are not aligning over the beam. Not to worry—one or both of the beams is bowed a bit. If the space between the notches is too wide, just use a clamp to pull the beams together until the notches fit over them. You can reverse the pads on some clamps to use as a spreader if the space is too narrow. Otherwise, cut a scrap to 5½ in. as a temporary spacer and use a hammer to tap the scrap between the beams. Once the joist notches are fitted over the beams, knock the scraps out.

5 **INSTALL THE JOIST.** Put the joist in place along the layout line and push it down onto the notches. If the beam is against a post, attach it to the post with two staggered 4-in. deck screws. If the joist is not against a post, secure it with 4-in. deck screws, driving one screw at an angle into each beam. At each end, drive one screw through one side of the joist into one beam and the other screw into the other side of the joist into the neighboring beam.

6 **CUT OFF THE POSTS.** You'll cut the posts off so that they'll protrude 2 in. above the 1½-in. slats. Measure up 3½ in. from the top of the joists and use a square to lay out the cut on three sides of the post. Make the cut with a 7-in. blade in a reciprocating saw. To give the posts a finished look, you can add copper post caps. Just put the caps on with construction adhesive as shown in step 6 "Install the post caps" on p. 229.

Prepare and Install the Slats

You'll make the 26 slats that provide the shade for this pergola by ripping 16-ft. 2x4s in half along their length. Before you rip them, you'll cut the 2x4s to length and add a simple decorative chamfer to both ends of 24 slats. That way, you'll make each crosscut 12 times instead of 24 times. Two slats will be cut to length to fit between posts.

Once all the slats are made, you'll install one slat on each end of the pergola and run a string between them so you won't need to measure the overhang for each slat. You'll cut a couple of spacers so you can gauge the spaces between slats without measuring. You'll install each slat with one 2-in. screw into each joist. You'll measure and cut the two slats that butt into the inside of the posts, then you'll finish up by making four separate overhang pieces to butt into the outside of the posts.

> **TIP** If you are using lightweight sawhorses like the ones shown here, put some weight on them so they won't tip as you make the rip cuts. Here, we borrowed a couple of pavers from a patio that was being installed along with the pergola.

1 **LAY OUT THE END CHAMFER.** Use a miter saw to cut one end of a 2x4 square. Then stand the 2x4 on edge and make a mark 1 in. from the end. Use a square to draw a 45-degree line from the mark to the end of the board.

2 **CUT THE CHAMFERS.** Set the miter saw to 45 degrees and cut the chamfer along the layout line as shown. Put the other end of the board on the saw table and make a square cut 182½ in. from the long end of the first chamfer. Then lay out and cut the second chamfer, making sure the long ends of both chamfers are on the same face of the board. Repeat steps 1 and 2 for 12 of the 13 boards.

3 **RIP THE SLATS TO WIDTH.** At the end of one slat, make a mark at 1¾ in. across its width. Put a rip guide on the circular saw and position it so the blade will cut through the mark. Set the saw to cut about 2 in. deep. Clamp a scrap of 2x4 atop each horse so the saw will cut into the scrap instead of the top of your horses. Place the 2x4 slat stock atop the scrap with a few feet overhanging the side of each horse. Clamp one end of the stock to the scrap and start ripping from the other end. When you reach the clamp, reposition the board with the cut past the clamp and complete the cut. Rip all 13 of the 2x4s.

> **TIP** Tiny spacing variations can accumulate over the course of 26 slats. So when you put the 14th slat in place, check if it is the same distance from the post you are working toward as the 13th slat is from the post you are working from. If the distances vary more than ½ in. or so, recalculate the spacing you have left and recut spacers accordingly.

4 **INSTALL THE END SLATS AND GUIDE STRING.** As mentioned, the slats will overhang the joists by 15 in., so make a mark on the bottom of two end slats, 15 in. from one end. Then mark the top of both end joists 2½ in. from both ends. Align the marks and attach the end slats with a 2-in. deck screw into each joist, checking as you go that the slats are 2½ in. from the end of each joist. Tack a finish nail to one end of each slat and tie a string between the nails as shown.

5 **MAKE THE SPACERS AND INSTALL THE SLATS.** Cut two pieces of scrap to 5¼ in. to use as spacers as you install the slats starting from one end. (See "Calculating Slat Spacing" below if your joists are not 182½ in. long.) Use one 2-in. deck screw into each joist. Depending on the length of your joists, the third slat in from each end of the joists is likely to intersect two posts. Cut these slats to butt between the posts—you'll cut separate overhang pieces later. "What You'll Need" gives the theoretical length of these slats, but the distances between your posts will probably vary from that, so measure between posts for a snug fit.

6 **CUT THE OVERHANG PIECES TO LENGTH.** If the full width of a slat butts into a post, just measure between the string and the outside of the post and cut two overhang pieces, including end chamfer, to that length. If, as shown here, only part of the slat's width overhangs, you'll need to notch the overhang pieces to fit around the post. In that case, start by making an overhang piece that's about 24 in. long. Align the piece to the string and mark where it meets the slat that butts into the post. Cut two pieces to that length.

Calculating Slat Spacing

Let's say, for example, you are making a pergola with posts 10 ft. on center with joists that are 134½ in. long. If you want the end slats to be 2½ in. in from the end of the joists like the pergola shown here, subtract 5 in. to get 129½ in. You want about 5 in. of space between each slat. One slat at 1¾ in. wide plus one 5 in. of space equals 6¾ in. Dividing 129.5 by 6.75 tells you that you'll need 19 slats. At 1¾ in. wide, those 19 slats will take up 33¼ in., leaving you with 96¼ in. There will be 18 spaces between the slats, so 96¼ in. divided by 18 means the slats will be spaced 5⅜ in. apart.

7 **MARK THE NOTCH DEPTH.** With the overhang pieces cut to length, put a spacer in place, put the overhang piece in place against the post, and mark the depth of the notch on the end of the piece. Do the same for the overhang piece for the opposing post.

8 **KERF THE NOTCHES.** Use a square to extend the notch length mark into a line. Set your circular saw to cut to the depth of the notch. If the notch is deep as shown here, make lots of kerfs to ensure you won't break the piece when you knock out the waste with a chisel.

9 **REMOVE THE NOTCH WASTE.** Working from the end of the overhang piece, use a hammer and chisel to remove the waste from the notch. Next, notch the opposing overhang piece. Make a notch on two overhang pieces for the remaining posts (if necessary).

10 **INSTALL THE OVERHANG PIECES.** Put each overhang piece in place and install it with one 2-in. screw into the post and one into the joist.

RESOURCES

FOR THE CRITTER-PROOF
FENCE (P. 24)

Hex-web fencing:
Available from Deer
Busters, 888-422-3337,
deerbusters.com

EasyGate®: Available
from Homax® Products,
Inc., 888-890-9029,
homaxproducts.com

Carpentry for the critter-
proof fence and the
garden shed by Bowie
Construction, LLC,
973-903-0540

FOR THE GARDEN SHED
(P. 52)

Window and door
hardware: Available
from Shed Windows and
More, 843-293-1820,
shedwindowsandmore
.com

FOR THE CHICKEN COOP
(P. 126)

Little Giant 30# feeder
with 14-in. pan and 3-gal.
heated plastic poultry
fountain: Available from
Mills Fleet Farm, 877-633-
7456, fleetfarm.com

CREDITS

All photos by David Schiff,
except:

Steve Cory (p. 6, right)

Courtesy Stanley (p. 9, bottom
left; p. 11, top right; p. 12,
top left, bottom left; p. 13,
top right, bottom)

Scott Phillips (p. 22, top left;
p. 23, left; pp. 100–101;
pp.116–117; p. 148, top left;
p. 149, right; pp. 168–169;
pp. 184–185; pp. 220–221)

Rebecca Anderson/Dave Toht
(p. 22, bottom left;
pp. 126–147)

METRIC EQUIVALENTS

INCHES	CENTIMETERS	MILLIMETERS	INCHES	CENTIMETERS	MILLIMETERS
1/8	0.3	3	13	33.0	330
1/4	0.6	6	14	35.6	356
3/8	1.0	10	15	38.1	381
1/2	1.3	13	16	40.6	406
5/8	1.6	16	17	43.2	432
3/4	1.9	19	18	45.7	457
7/8	2.2	22	19	48.3	483
1	2.5	25	20	50.8	508
1 1/4	3.2	32	21	53.3	533
1 1/2	3.8	38	22	55.9	559
1 3/4	4.4	44	23	58.4	584
2	5.1	51	24	61	610
2 1/2	6.4	64	25	63.5	635
3	7.6	76	26	66.0	660
3 1/2	8.9	89	27	68.6	686
4	10.2	102	28	71.7	717
4 1/2	11.4	114	29	73.7	737
5	12.7	127	30	76.2	762
6	15.2	152	31	78.7	787
7	17.8	178	32	81.3	813
8	20.3	203	33	83.8	838
9	22.9	229	34	86.4	864
10	25.4	254	35	88.9	889
11	27.9	279	36	91.4	914
12	30.5	305			

INDEX